Online Newsgathering

Online Newsgathering

Research and Reporting for Journalism

Stephen Quinn
and
Stephen Lamble

AMSTERDAM • BOSTON • HEIDELBERG • LONDON
NEW YORK • OXFORD • PARIS • SAN DIEGO
SAN FRANCISCO • SINGAPORE • SYDNEY • TOKYO
Focal Press is an imprint of Elsevier

Acquisitions Editor: Cara Anderson
Publishing Services Manager: George Morrison
Senior Project Manager: Brandy Lilly
Assistant Editor: Robin Weston
Marketing Manager: Marcel Koppes
Cover Design: Alisa Andreola
Interior Design: Alisa Andreola

Focal Press is an imprint of Elsevier
30 Corporate Drive, Suite 400, Burlington, MA 01803, USA
Linacre House, Jordan Hill, Oxford OX2 8DP, UK

∞ Recognizing the importance of preserving what has been written, Elsevier prints its books on acid-free paper whenever possible.

Library of Congress Cataloging-in-Publication Data
Quinn, Stephen, 1953-
   Online newsgathering : research and reporting for journalism / Stephen Quinn and Stephen Lamble.
     p. cm.
   Includes bibliographical references and index.
   ISBN-13: 978-0-240-80851-2 (pbk. : alk. paper)   1. Journalism—Computer network resources.
2. Reporters and reporting—Computer network resources.   I. Lamble, Stephen.   II. Title.
   PN4729.3Q56 2008
   070.4'30285—dc22   2007020305

British Library Cataloguing-in-Publication Data
A catalogue record for this book is available from the British Library.

ISBN: 978-0-240-80851-2

For information on all Focal Press publications
visit our website at www.books.elsevier.com

07 08 09 10 11   5 4 3 2 1

Printed in the United States of America

Contents

Introduction

Journalism is changing around the globe. The change seems to have accelerated in the past decade. Indeed, since the start of the new millennium we have seen the spread of media convergence (which has influenced newsroom practices around the world), the arrival of citizen or participatory journalism, a boom in the number of blogs and related publishing forms such as moblogs, podcasts and wikis, and the spread of multimedia forms of reporting.

The premise of this book is simple. As the changes listed above develop and as reporters move from working in one medium to working in several, they will need to change the way they gather information. Hence the subtitle of this book: Research and Reporting for Journalism. In times of rapid and large-scale change, two constant stars seem to make a difference: quality and trust. The only long-term way to provide quality content and ensure or consolidate trust is through education and training, and through a commitment to excellence. To paraphrase Aristotle, excellence is not gained overnight but earned over an extended period. This book exists to help mono-media journalists and students in journalism programs around the world move into the realms of multimedia reporting.

Each of the changes mentioned here requires new ways of doing journalism. Granted, the basics of journalism do not change: We still need to collect good information, write succinctly, clearly and for a specific audience, and conduct ourselves ethically. We still need to acknowledge the importance of accuracy within a context of an awareness of legal constraints. But to these basics we need to add new skills and, perhaps more importantly, we need to develop new mindsets. With media convergence for example, where reporters provide content in more than one medium, reporters need to work to new deadlines. Working with citizen or participatory journalism means listening to our audiences and learning from them. Blogging and related forms such as moblogging, podcasting, and video blogs mean that journalists must find new ways to work with their audiences. And multimedia reporting requires new ways of gathering information. Mainstream media needs to learn to work with these new media forms, and share the best of what is available.

One of the big changes is a new relationship with breaking news. The early years of the twenty-first century have seen the arrival of a new news cycle, via the Internet. It is debatable when audiences first started turning to the Internet for breaking news. But we would argue that big news stories in 2005 and 2006 such as the London and Mumbai transport bombings, the disasters in New Orleans, and Saddam Hussein's execution have seen audiences turning to the Internet first for news. In countries where broadband is not widely available, breaking news is more likely to be delivered via a third generation mobile phone or portable data assistant such as a Treo or Blackberry. Increasingly, video of news events becomes available on the Internet and the mobile phone at about the same time, such as the video of Saddam Hussein's death in January 2007. The news cycle has evolved over the past century. Until the arrival of radio in the 1920s, newspapers and news agencies had a monopoly on the spread of news, with word of mouth their sole competitor. News broke primarily on the radio until the 1950s. Television later embraced the live broadcast and broadcasters dominated breaking news when they introduced 24-hour news channels. But by the early years of the twenty-first century, the Internet and the mobile phone are the places audiences go when they want the latest news. Certainly the Internet and the mobile phone offer two places where innovation and journalism meet.

As an interesting aside, on January 18, 2007, *The New York Times* published a video obituary of humor columnist Art Buchwald, who died that day. Buchwald recorded his own obituary. You can watch it at http://www.nytimes.com/packages/html/obituaries/BUCHWALD_FEATURE.

As the century evolves, we will see the Internet assume an even more significant role in publishing and delivery of news. Professor Bob Papper of Ball State University believes newspapers will become a boutique subset of online. "I've been saying that for years now and people look at me less strangely today [2004] than when I first started saying it five years ago [1999]." Newspapers would have multimedia aspects that will look more like an online publication (quoted in Quinn 2006: 141). Buzzmachine's Jeff Jarvis believes reporters and photographers should carry multimedia tools—a digital voice recorder, still camera, and a laptop—with them at all times. Reporters need to be encouraged to work in multimedia. "Then they should tell the story however it is best told" (Jarvis 2005). Newsrooms are changing around the world, and will continue to adapt. The prescient and erudite Kerry Northrup, Ifra's director of publishing, has been pointing out the multimedia future of journalism for almost a decade. Northrup talks about the four stages of news in chapter 6. Newsrooms need to change to adapt to, and adopt, these stages of news.

And newsrooms need to learn to become aggregators of news. This requires an acceptance of the idea that our audiences know as much, or often more, than the reporters in our newsrooms. Dan Gillmor refers to this concept as "news as conversation," which accepts that news becomes an exchange between audiences and journalists. Again, this requires a new mindset and a new approach to newsgathering. In future years the criterion of completeness, of a story being as good as we can manage by a given deadline, could be judged on the number of links to relevant sources as much as it is judged by the reporter's skill at gathering good information.

What, then, is the likely future of news? Certainly news and journalism have a future, because people continue to want to be informed. It will be accessible all the time: at any time and any place, through any device. News will need to be transparent—that is, audiences will want to know as much about news sources and the trustworthiness of those sources as they do the news event itself. Trust takes a long time to build, but can be destroyed through mistakes or ethical breaches. A key word is authentic: in the news environment of the twenty-first century, trust is the new mantra. News will be more participatory: a conversation rather than a lecture and involve many and varied communities. Because of the over abundance of information, news will be edited more tightly in some media. Journalists will put their energies into writing more tightly. Daily newspapers must learn to look forwards rather than backwards. That is, instead of reporting what happened yesterday they need to consider what will happen today, tomorrow and later in the week.

An Outline of this Book

Chapter 1 sets the scene for this book, looking in a broad-brush way at how the Internet and related technologies have changed journalism and media. It notes how audiences are fragmenting in an environment of excess information, and considers the boom in online advertising relative to mainstream media revenues. It also discusses the way that the Internet threatens traditional commercial media business models. All of the chapters that follow are more hands-on and specific. Chapter 2 shows how to use various parts of the Internet such as the UseNet and listservs to generate story ideas that are beyond the often PR-generated news agenda, and how to find experts to interview for those stories. Chapter 3 does the same with blogs and related new media such as moblogs and podcasts. Chapter 4 considers the issue of citizen or participatory journalism and discusses how this phenomenon, often called audience-generated content, relates to newsgathering and the future of journalism. Chapter 5 looks beyond the usual suspects such as Google and offers ways to use the Internet technologies to find background information for stories. Chapter 6 works from the premise that the multimedia reporter will need to adopt different information-gathering processes compared with the mono-media reporter, and shows how to do that.

Chapter 7 looks at how to assess the quality and veracity of information we find on the Internet. Technologies give us access to a vast amount of data, but how reliable and accurate are those data? Chapter 8 shows how to develop a beat using the Internet. It offers strategies for developing an area of expertise. Chapter 9 reflects the generosity of journalists on the Internet. It introduces the vast array of resources that reporters have made available for their colleagues around the world. Chapter 10 considers the legal implications of gathering information online and reporting news on the web. Chapter 11 shows how to do deeper forms of journalism using the Excel spread sheet and drawing on the wide range of statistics available on the Internet.

References

Jarvis, Jeff. (2005). http://www.buzzmachine.com/archives/2005_06_10.html

Quinn, Stephen. (2006). *Conversations on Convergence: Insiders' views of twenty-first century news production* New York: Peter Lang.

How the Internet Is Changing Journalism, and How It Affects You

All journalism today involves computers. Regardless of whether you write for a newspaper or magazine, an online site, or for a television or radio newscast, you almost certainly will write with a desktop computer or laptop and some form of word-processing package. Computers are also involved in most of the news production process after a story leaves a reporter's desk. You are also probably using the Internet as a newsgathering tool. But if you are not using it to its fullest capacity, you are ignoring a goldmine of information. Professor Steve Ross formerly of Columbia University's Graduate School of Journalism has been tracking the adoption of the Internet by journalists each year since 1996, and by 2002 he concluded Internet adoption was almost universal. By the early years of the new century, Ross said, journalists had embraced the Web and e-mail as reporting tools (Ross 2002: 22–23).

The phrase computer-assisted reporting (CAR) describes this combination of computers and reporting. Any journalist who uses the Internet is doing a form of CAR. Journalism is, after all, about working with information and the Internet is one of the world's single largest sources of information. The section Journalists and Technology: Some Context and History notes that when journalists first started using telephones, stories were labeled "telephone-assisted reporting." We face a similar situation with CAR. With time the phrase "computer-assisted" will atrophy, just as the phrase "telephone-assisted reporting" has become redundant. CAR is about using technology to help gather better quality information to produce better quality reporting. Any journalist younger than 30 probably takes computers for granted. They are the first generation to have been surrounded by computers during their high school years. The Internet is now as common and available to high school and university students as the encyclopedia and library were to earlier generations.

This book reserves the phrase deep CAR for a sophisticated form of reportage that involves analysis of spreadsheets, databases, and other high-end software packages. We believe that deep CAR is one of the most important new tools available to journalists, and we dedicate the last chapter to it. Figure 1.1 describes the levels of CAR as they are applied in this book. Perhaps it is because the authors started with manual typewriters and dial-up phones, and initially accessed the Internet via slow modems rather than broadband that we appear so pedantic.

This book is about learning skills to make you a better journalist, regardless of the terminology people have adopted. Professor Philip Meyer, a CAR pioneer who also coined the phrase "precision journalism," argues that CAR has become so broad that the phrase should be abandoned. He fears that online research, under the mantle of CAR, diverts attention from complex data analysis and other powerful uses of the computer. In the interests of keeping things simple, we will concentrate on the idea of using technology to produce better journalism.

At the turn of the last century, one of the authors wrote that the Internet would "prove to be the most significant human development since Gutenberg's

Figure 1.1

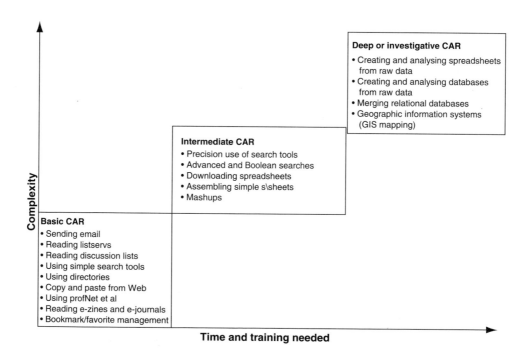

invention of moveable type in the middle of the fifteenth century" (Quinn 2001: ix). This book acknowledges the massive changes since then, and believes that the Internet will continue to produce more change as we move further into the new century. One of the biggest changes will be the trend toward a multimedia form of journalism, which necessitates a multimedia focus and mindset during the newsgathering process. That is the focus of this book: How to gather good information in the context of an evolving form of journalism that is interactive and incorporates multimedia.

This opening chapter deliberately takes a big picture overview. Those of you who like jigsaws will understand the process. When building a jigsaw the most efficient approach is to establish the outline first, then fill in the middle. That is the purpose of this chapter. It looks at how the Internet is influencing journalism and newsgathering and consider how audiences are fragmenting and how journalists need to change to accommodate those fragmented audiences. We also consider one of the major reactions to fragmenting audiences: the phenomenon known as media convergence. It is both a management and a journalistic change. At the editorial level, convergence represents a new form of journalism that requires new skills. As a business process, convergence is an attempt to reaggregate or regather splintered audiences. People get their news from a variety of sources, at different times of the day. The only way a news organization can reach as large an audience as possible is by offering news via different media at different times of the day. We need to consider the economic environment in which the worlds of media and journalism operate, so we need to consider the changing forms of media economics. This chapter concludes with a short outline of the tools the journalism profession has embraced in its relatively short history.

The Web and e-mail are becoming, as journalism researcher Steve Ross notes, the "soul of newsgathering." Increasingly the rhythm of the news business "keeps time with the Internet" (Ross 2002: 4). Nine out of ten people who responded to his national survey of American journalists said that the Internet had "fundamentally changed" the way they worked. Slightly more (92 percent) agreed that new technologies and the Internet had made their jobs easier and made journalists more productive (Ross 2002: 27). A study of media students in Australia showed they were more likely to obtain their news from the Web than from printed newspapers. They all used e-mail extensively, researched online rather than with books, and seemingly carried their mobile phones with them at all times (Quinn and Bethell 2006: 51).

This chapter needs to be read in the context of major change within journalism and the world of media. One of the biggest changes is the emergence of convergent forms of journalism. Convergence is also known as multi-platform publishing (in some parts of the world each medium is seen as a platform; thus we have the newspaper platform or the radio platform). Convergence comes in several forms. Editorial staff work together to produce multiple forms of journalism for multiple platforms to reach a mass audience. In many cases the one newsroom produces content for a daily newspaper, radio and television bulletins, online sites, and sometimes magazines and weekly newspapers. Some reporters only work for the newspaper; others only work to produce television news. But some reporters work across media, and others produce interactive content especially for the Web on a 24/7 basis. For the last group, convergence represents a new form of journalism. A converged newsroom has links with traditional media and draws from its history and traditions, but convergence als o requires reporters to produce original content in multimedia forms. This form of journalism is often expensive and time-consuming. For more on this international trend, see Stephen Quinn's 2005 books in the reading list. Media organizations around the world are merging their newsrooms. An international study in 2002 showed that two out of three media organizations in both print and broadcast have shared their newsrooms with the online team (Ross 2002: 20–21).

Mike Game, chief operating officer of Fairfax Digital, the online arm of what has become Australia's biggest newspaper publisher, noted how people were turning to the Internet for breaking news. The Internet's great strength, he said, was its ability to attract people during the day for short news grabs. "In many ways it is displacing more traditional media like radio news services" (quoted in MacLean 2005: 18). In a major research report released late in 2004, the Carnegie Foundation noted that 39 percent of men aged 18–34 got their news from the Internet compared with 5 percent who read newspapers. Women in the same age group preferred local television news (42 percent), compared with 7 percent who read newspapers (Brown 2005: 1–2). In a landmark speech to the American Society of Newspaper Editors in Washington on April 13, 2005, News Corporation chairman Rupert Murdoch cited the Carnegie figures:

> What is happening is ... a revolution in the way young people are accessing news. They don't want to rely on the morning paper for their up-to-date information. Instead, they want their news on demand, when it works for them. They want control over their media, instead of being controlled by it (Murdoch 2005).

In response, news has become a 24-hour continuous process, demanding major changes in the way journalists work. To provide unique content for their Web sites, major American newspapers such as *The Washington Post, The New York Times, The Chicago Tribune, USA Today*, and *The Los Angeles Times* introduced groups of rewrite journalists on "continuous" or "extended" news desks. The aim is to publish breaking news online as soon as possible after stories become available. These teams function like the rewrite desks that were common in afternoon newspapers until the 1960s. Groups of senior editorial staff at these major newspapers talk to reporters about stories they are working on, or rewrite reporters' early versions of stories in conjunction with wire copy while events are still unfolding.

The continuous news desk at *The Washington Post* is based in the newspaper's newsroom in Washington, DC. The Web site, WashingtonPost.com, is located across the Potomac River in Arlington, Virginia. Robert McCartney, assistant managing editor for continuous news, said a team of three editors and two writers solicited and edited breaking news from reporters in the field—"especially during peak Web traffic hours of 9 am to 5 pm"—and also wrote their own stories. The goal was to increase the flow of original content to the Web, to distinguish *The Washington Post* coverage from what other papers and the major news agencies produced, McCartney said. Ideally the newspaper's reporter wrote the early file for the Web. "We want to take advantage of the beat reporter's expertise, sourcing, and credibility." When a beat reporter did not have time, the reporter telephoned notes to the desk, where a writer produced a story under a double byline. "This arrangement encourages beat reporters to file for the Web while relieving them of the burden if they're too busy." If necessary, continuous news department editors wrote stories on their own, "doing as much independent reporting as possible, and citing wires or other secondary sources." (McCartney 2004)

Dan Bigman, associate editor of NYTimes.com, said the continuous news desk at *The New York Times* had been a catalyst for changing newspaper journalists' opinions about online, and vice versa. "The continuous news desk has changed the culture," Bigman said. In August 2005 the New York Times Company announced that its print and online newsrooms would merge when the company moved to new headquarters in 2007. Online commentator Mark Glaser suggested this was the beginning of a philosophical change that would echo through the newspaper business. Publisher Arthur Sulzberger, Jr. and the man in charge of NYTimes.com, vice-president of digital operations Martin Nisenholtz, had been planning the merger for a decade (Glaser 2005).

USA Today started its 24-hour newsgathering service for the Web in December 2005 and *The Chicago Tribune* followed a month later. Ken Paulson, editor of *USA Today*, said he hoped the print edition would enhance the online edition, and "those online will help bring their talent to the newspaper." It was, he said, "a combining of talent." Charles Madigan, editor of continuous news at the *Tribune*, said this form of news was his paper's new primary focus. "We needed some vehicle to provide a constant stream of news to the Tribune Web site." (quoted in Strupp 2006: 23) Joseph Russin, assistant managing editor for multimedia at *The Los Angeles Times*, said his paper created an extended news desk to get immediacy on the paper's website. "The extended news desk takes stories—wire or *LA Times* reporters' stories—and rewrites or edits the items and gets them on the website." The desk allowed the site to get ahead of stories. "We compete with *The New York Times* and *The Washington Post*. In order to be more competitive we needed to be more current." Russin said a strong push for the desk came from national and international reporters who wanted their stories published faster (Russin 2003).

Elsewhere in the world, similar forms of journalism are emerging. *The Inquirer* is one of the most innovative media groups in the Philippines. J. V. Rufino, editor-in-chief of Inquirer.net, regards his team of 15 multimedia reporters as a "testing lab" for the future of *The Inquirer* newspaper. All his team are multimedia reporters: They take photographs at news events and shoot video as well as write stories for online. The Web team typically produces about 120 breaking news items a day. Rufino tells his multimedia reporters that they are the future. Meanwhile, a lot of the younger reporters at the newspaper have said they want to get involved with multimedia. In Singapore, a team of a dozen producers assemble content for Straits Times online, mobile, and print (STOMP). STOMP is part of Singapore Press Holdings, the major newspaper company in the city whose flagship is *The Straits Times*. The newspaper has a Web site that mostly contains content from the newspaper. Much of STOMP's content is multimedia and focuses on a younger audience (Quinn, personal observation).

These news organizations are innovative. Elsewhere in the United States, we see relatively little original content, based on research from Columbia University's Steve Ross. More than a quarter of media respondents admitted that less than 10 percent of their Web content was original, while only 13 percent of respondents whose organizations had a Web site said the bulk of their Web content was original. "In general, however, original content—that is, content on the web site that has not previously been broadcast or published in print—seems to be increasing faster for newspapers (from a low base) than for magazines and broadcast." Ross did note that more newpapers were allowing their Web site to scoop the print publication. "Routine scooping by the web sites has increased greatly in recent years, but [the 2001] jump was the greatest of all: 45 percent of print respondents said the Web site routinely scoops the print publication." Three out of ten newspaper respondents said they never or almost never allowed the Web site to scoop (Ross 2002: 18–19).

Around the world, print newsroom staff still represents the bulk of any editorial team, because the bulk of advertising still appears in print form. Online numbers remain low relative to total editorial staff numbers. Some examples from Australia help illustrate this point. News Ltd was the country's biggest newspaper publisher until May 2007, publishing seven daily and seven Sunday newspapers. Its two dailies in Sydney, *The Australian* and the *Daily Telegaph*, have more than 700 people on their editorial staff while its online arm, News Interactive, has only about 60 journalists across its range of sites: news.com.au, foxsports.com.au, homesite.com.au, carsguide.com.au, and careerone.com.au. The other News Ltd sites associated with capital city mastheads each had about 10 dedicated journalists, although that number was expected to grow. The Fairfax group became the country's biggest newspaper publisher in May 2007. Bruce Wolpe, Fairfax's director of corporate affairs, said the organization had about 850 people on its editorial staff across *The Sydney Morning Herald* and *The Age* in Melbourne (Wolpe 2006). But the stable of online sites for Fairfax Digital in Sydney and Melbourne employed only about 40 journalists. For both media groups the online news sites relied on the print publications for content. This is likely to continue until the bulk of advertising transfers from print to online. Even then, advertisers will still prefer the "stickiness" of paper forms of advertising. Sites owned by media companies attracted almost all of the online audience for news in Australia. As of mid-2006 Fairfax Digital had 33 percent of the total audience, and Publishing and Broadcasting Ltd 30 percent. News Interactive had 25 percent, and the national public service broadcaster, the Australian Broadcasting Corporation, 11 percent (Jury 2006: 71).

Boom in Online Advertising

Internet advertising revenue in 2006 boomed around the world. In Australia, for example, income from Internet advertising in 2006 was $732 million, compared with $135 million 5 years earlier. Annual growth of 20 percent was expected for the rest of the decade, with revenues reaching $1.5 billion by 2010. Internet advertising represented 8 percent of the total market, was growing at 60 percent a year, and was about to overtake radio in the number three position behind newspapers and television. Print media revenues in 2006 were worth about $4.4 billion, up 14 percent on 2001.

In the UK, online advertising grew 40 percent in 2006. For the first time that year, the Internet received a larger share of advertising revenue than did the country's national newspapers. In 2006, online represented 14 percent of total advertising spent in the UK, the highest proportion anywhere in the world. It was double the percentage in the United States. *The New York Times* identified the UK as the "barometer" for online advertising trends worldwide. Media reporter Steve Shipside said in terms of online advertising, the UK was "the shape of things to come." Newspapers were expected to benefit indirectly because of the technologies developed that allow people to skip television advertising, rendering TV advertising less attractive than online and print. The expected boom in the advertising was likely to be in the area of multimedia and cross-media areas, predicted Earl Wilkinson, president of the International Newspaper Marketing Association (Shipside 2007: 22–23).

Fragmenting Audiences

The audiences that journalists reach out to are also changing. People are consuming more and more media, and that media are consuming more of people's time. News has become a 24-hour process, as audiences consume news from more sources. India has eight 24-hour all-news channels. In early 2007, various countries had set up or were contemplating 24-hour news channels. The 2004 *Communications Industry Forecast* reported that Americans spent 10.04 hours a day with media, an increase of almost an hour a day since 1998. Analysts at merchant bank Veronis Suhler Stevenson, which produces the annual report, predicted that Americans would spend more than 11 hours a day with media by 2008 (Quinn 2005b: 21).

People use many different forms of media during the day, often multitasking. We will see major changes in the way journalists work as they seek to accommodate fragmenting audiences, and also reaggregate those fragments through convergence. Research groups such as the Carnegie Foundation and the Pew Center note that people aged 18–24 and 25–34 tend to get most of their news from the Internet, and rely less on traditional sources such as newspapers. In the past, analysts assumed that people started reading print newspapers as they got older and took out a mortgage. This will not happen for people aged 18–24 and 25–34. As the twenty-first century evolves, people in this age range will continue to get their news online, as will the generations after them.

The way that people get their media is also changing. Audio on the Web has the potential to replace radio as we currently know it in the first decade of the twenty-first century. Similarly, video on the Web could replace television. The company that gave us Skype launched an Internet-delivered television channel called Joost early in 2007. Skype has already challenged the business models of telecom companies by offering free phone calls via broadband. And international calls via Skype to land lines and mobile phones to most of the Western world cost about 2.5 cents a minute. The business models for traditional commercial broadcasters are similarly shaky, which means the revenue sources for journalism associated with those broadcasters becomes problematic. How can *60 Minutes* on CBS continue to conduct expensive investigative work if advertising revenues plummet? With personal or digital video recorders (TiVo is the best known name in the United States; Foxtel's iQ in Australia), people record programs on a giant hard disk. The technology lets people skip advertisements as they play back programs. Given that TV and radio get much of their revenue from advertisements, the arrival of Internet-based TV or radio makes their business model look ill over time. Some commercial broadcasters have tried to stop the spread of personal video recorders. In November 2006, Australia's two biggest commercial TV networks, Channels 7 and 9, refused to air commercials for a model of LG plasma television screen with a built-in digital video recorder. The Multi Channel Network, which represents the major cable-TV providers, also tried to censor the commercials. When the advertisements were eventually aired, the offending line "And when you replay, you can skip the ads" was replaced with "And when you replay, you can skip straight back to the action" (Quinn 2007: 13).

Journalists and Technology: Some Context and History

Before we look at the new tools of journalism in the twenty-first centry, it helps to look backwards. The great British prime minister Winston Churchill once noted that people who fail to learn from history are condemned to repeat the mistakes of history. This section considers how journalists have adopted technology over the past two centuries. It is hoped we can learn some lessons from that history.

News and information traveled slowly in the eighteenth and nineteenth centuries compared with the early twenty-first century. The American Declaration of Independence of July 4, 1776, for example, was not reported in England until more than 6 weeks after the event, on August 21. It took almost two weeks for news of Nelson's victory at Trafalgar on October 21,1805, to reach the people in England. Geoffrey Blainey, in his classic history of Australia *The Tyranny of Distance,* noted that until the 1870s:

> The main job of Australian newsmen had always been the boarding of incoming ships and the collecting of the latest English newspapers [until]...the submarine cable [the telegraph] replaced incoming steamers as the fastest carrier of news (Blainey 1982: 222).

Telegraph wires linking Adelaide, Melbourne, and Sydney were joined on October 29, 1858, and the Sydney to Brisbane link opened three years later. But it took another 30 years before the same capitals were united by rail, and even then track gauges varied. Once international telegraph links arrived in 1872, telegraph operators fed the news from overseas to an increasingly news-hungry audience. The operator's life was lonely, as Blainey noted:

> Out in the centre of Australia stood a line of small stone fortresses where lonely telegraph operators lived more than a hundred miles [160 km] from their nearest neighbour. Relaying the messages by code on to the next repeating station, they heard Europe's latest news before it was heard in Sydney or Melbourne (Bainey 1982: 222).

In the United States and UK, the "stimulus" for the telegraph was expansion of the railways. Samuel Morse's code was first used with the telegraph in the United States in 1844. Morse invented a hand-operated key or switch that allowed operators to stop and restart electric signals, which enabled them to send either a short or long signal (a dot or a dash). These dots and dashes were put together in various combinations to form letters and numbers, and it remained the basic form of telegraphic communication for more than a century. On January 3, 1845, a newsworthy incident occurred that made the telegraph famous in England. John Tawell murdered his mistress in the town of Slough, about 14 miles (24 km) west of London. Slough was one of the stations on the Great Western Railway. Dressed as a Quaker, Tawell fled by train to the anonymity of London. But police arrested him at London's Paddington station. Historian Jeffrey Kieve said transmission of Tawell's description by telegraph to Paddington was largely responsible for his rapid arrest. Publicity around the arrest heightened public awareness of the new device and the telegraph became famous as "the cords that hung John Tawell" (Kieve 1973: 39).

Journalism historian Richard Schwarzlose maintained that the telegraph transformed American journalism "into a news-hungry industry" between the mid-1840s and the American Civil War (1861–1865). Wars tend to heighten and accelerate technological development. Such was the case during the Civil War in the United States. It saw the development of "telegraphese" as journalists rushed to transmit their most newsworthy information over often unreliable telegraph lines. They developed the habit of compressing the most crucial facts into short, paragraph-long dispatches destined for the top of a column of news. This form of writing organizes stories around facts rather than in chronological order. The inverted pyramid format, involving a summary lead, appears to have originated with coverage of President Lincoln's death in April 1865, though that event occurred after the war ended. News agencies had adopted the inverted pyramid format by the 1880s. From the 1870s to 1890s, laws designed to foster education and schools produced a sharp rise in literacy, which boosted the potential audience for newspapers (Schwarzlose 1990).

News agencies evolved around the world because of the development of the telegraph and the public's growing demand for news. Because of increased literacy, the number of newspapers grew. This produced a need for more content, which meant news agencies flourished. What is now the world's biggest news organization, Associated Press, was founded in New York in 1848. Julius Reuter's motto of "follow the cable" led him to establish financial news bureaus throughout Europe, and he established a London office in 1851. That date is generally considered the founding date for the Reuters news agency. An Australian engineer, Donald Murray, invented the printing telegraph or teleprinter (a fusion of telegraphy and typesetting) in 1899. Christopher Lathan Scholes, editor of the *Milwaukee Sentinel* from 1861 until his retirement in 1863, built the first effective typewriter in 1867. By the early 1900s, typewriters accounted for half of all office machinery sold.

Technology and Journalistic Mindset

The telegraph increased the speed at which journalists worked. This in turn changed the journalistic mindset. The telegraph meant that news arrived all the time, rather than in isolated blocks such as when a ship or train arrived. Media historian Jeffrey Kieve noted how newspaper editors "had to make up their minds quickly and be ready to rethink in the course of a single night, as news no longer came all at one time, but continuously" (Kieve 1973: 72). News of the defeat of Napoleon III in 1870 showed how the time element in newsgathering and reporting had contracted. The Prussians defeated Napoleon III's army on September 2, 1870. Two days later, the French people proclaimed a republic in Paris. The *New York Tribune* published the story of the republic on September 6. Compare this relative speed with reportage of other major events described earlier in this chapter. And then consider how quickly news is reported in a world of satellite phones, e-mail, and mobile phones.

Reporters increasingly came to rely on the telegraph, just as modern journalists have come to rely on computers to produce newspapers. *The Sydney Morning Herald* reported on March 17, 1859, that interruptions of only a day or two were regarded "as an intolerable annoyance." Modern day journalists dread a computer crash. Such is the need for reliable technology that IT departments have grown considerably in the past decade to ensure that computers seldom crash. Journalists have come to rely on technology to do their job. On October 5, 1859, *The Sydney Morning Herald* noted that the telegraph was "one of those improvements which, when introduced, cannot be parted with again, or arrested in its progress. From being a novelty and a scientific curiosity, it becomes a social necessity, and we shall soon come to feel that it would be as possible to do without our post offices as without our telegraphs" (quoted in Livingston 1996: 51).

Sir Isaac Pitman invented shorthand in 1837 and gradually it became accepted as a journalists' tool. The Gregg form of shorthand, invented by John Robert Gregg, was introduced in 1888. Gregg is still used, particularly in the United States. Charles Dickens was a journalist before he became a successful novelist, beginning his career as a Parliamentary reporter on *The True Sun* in London in 1831. While a solicitor's clerk, Dickens spent the two years before starting as a reporter teaching himself shorthand. In his autobiographical novel *David Copperfield*, Dickens celebrated his mastery over shorthand: "I have tamed the savage stenographic mystery."

Alexander Graham Bell is credited with inventing the telephone. He and his assistant, Thomas Watson, applied for a patent in 1876. Initially it was seen as a way to transmit music and as a way to check if someone was home so they could receive a telegram. On January 10, 1878, the *Geelong Advertiser* in Australia ran a story about a group of men and women in Melbourne who listened to violin and flute music transmitted several hundred meters via Bell's invention. But it took a while before the telephone became a reporting tool. The telephone linked all European capitals by 1915, and war boosted adoption. The first automatic exchange in the Southern Hemisphere opened in Geelong in 1912; it was only the second in the British Empire. The telephone replaced the telegraph for everyday domestic communication from about this point. A new journalism job classification, known as the rewrite person, subsequently emerged in the United States. By the early 1920s, newspaper correspondents in the various capitals telephoned their home offices regularly in the evenings to dictate their reports, although they experienced some technical difficulties.

Within a decade, the clarity of the connections was nearly perfect. From about this time, the telephone produced changes in journalists' job descriptions. American journalism introduced "legmen" who collected news in cities and phoned it to the city desk where "rewrite men" in the office tailored the news to fit the newspaper's personality. Newspaper historian Anthony Smith said the telephone switchboard transformed the nature of reporting in the 1920s and 1930s:

> Until the switchboard arrived, it was almost impossible for a multi-sourced form of information to pass along the telephone, for example, the results of a large number of football games played simultaneously in different parts of the country or the results of a national election (Smith 1980: 79–80).

Many newspapers used pigeons for communicating complex stories, and carrier pigeons were common until about the 1930s. Peter O'Loughlin, formerly Associated Press' bureau chief for Australia and the South Pacific, said communications were the single most important aspect of a reporter's job, apart from getting the story. "If you could not find a way to get your story out you may as well not have been there." While covering the Olympics in Japan in 1964, he said he was "amazed" to see Japanese photographers carrying baskets of carrier pigeons into the press room at Enoshima where he was covering the yachting. The photographers used them to fly film back to Tokyo 50 miles (80 km) away: "It was quicker than road or rail and more reliable than any other communications available. Over the two weeks I was there I often wished I had brought some myself, so often did the communications collapse" (O'Loughlin personal communication 1996).

The facsimile existed as a concept from about the 1920s but did not get embraced as a reporting tool until the 1970s and 1980s. Glenn Mulcaster, a senior reporter at Melbourne's *The Age,* remembered working as a copy boy at a regional daily in the mid-1980s where the paper had only one fax machine. "When I first started work my paper had one fax machine. That would have been 1986. Faxes were well in use in offices, but not in newspapers." The fax provides a useful reference point for the adoption of the Internet in newsrooms, in the sense that the fax is an example of an innovation that journalists have adopted thoroughly. But it took more than a decade for the innovation to reach saturation levels in newsrooms. By the middle of the first decade of the new century, e-mail had effectively replaced faxes in newsrooms.

As telephone technology improved, so its impact on journalism increased. Telephone interviews became a standard reporting process. In the 1920s, stories were labeled telephone-assisted reporting. We face a similar situation with CAR. When will computer-assisted reporting be described simply as reporting? Australians could not direct-dial overseas until 1976. A year later two teenagers, Steve Jobs and Steve Wozniak, built and sold the world's first personal computer, the Apple. IBM made its first PCs in 1981. The World Wide Web and browsers did not exist until 1993. Within a decade, the Internet was common in newsrooms in westernized nations. Christopher Callahan, assistant dean of the College of Journalism at the University of Maryland, described the Internet as the "most important reporting tool since the telephone."

The technological pace of change since the start of the twenty-first century has been furious. Most businesses have broadband and household adoption has boomed around the world. Broadband is important because numerous studies have shown a direct link between broadband access and number of hours online. Ross noted in 2002 that two-thirds of American journalists used cell phones for reporting, and 57 percent carried laptops. A quarter used personal data assistants (PDA) such as the Palm Pilot or Blackberry (Ross 2002: 25) or a host of new names that became available in 2005. Since then the adoption of cell phones and PDAs by reporters has increased. It is rare to find a reporter at a western newspaper who does not have a cell phone.

Journalism professor Bruce Garrison noted that technology "changes the way things get done." The invention of the typewriter, for example, "changed the way people thought during the writing process" (Garrison 1995: 12). Brant Houston, executive director of Investigative Reporters and Editors, has similarly pointed out that computers change reporters' thinking patterns: "Working with computers requires a different way of thinking. It is more methodical and initially less intuitive" (Houston 1996: 7).

This section has outlined the history of journalism to help us understand where it is going in terms of CAR. One of the lessons of history is that journalists have had to learn to think more quickly and work faster. It is likely that the pace of change will be even faster as we move further into the twenty-first century. This means we need better educated journalists to cope with change and the mass of information that threatens to dominate our lives. The issue of ethics training also becomes more important. A reputation for quality takes many years to develop, but can be destroyed almost overnight by an ethical breach. Journalists need the reliable moral compass that ethics training provides, and that training must be offered before any potential ethical breach occurs. It is difficult to be ethical on the run. The clock is always ticking for journalists. Chapter 2 considers the tools that reporters have adopted in the past few years. Other chapters in this book discuss newer tools that, used well, could save us time.

References

Blainey, Geoffrey (1982). *The Tyranny Of Distance: How Distance Shaped Australia's History*. Melbourne: Sun Books.

Brown, Merrill (2005). "Abandoning the News" in the *Carnegie Reporter*, Vol. 3, no. 2, Spring 2005.

Garrison, Bruce (1995). *Computer-Assisted Reporting*. New Jersey: Lawrence Erlbaum & Associates.

Glaser, Mark (2005). "GrayLady.com: NY Times Explodes Wall Between Print, Web" published in *Online Journalism Review* at http://www.ojr.org/ojr/stories/050809glaser on 9 August 2005 [accessed 1 July 2006].

Houston, Brant (1996). *Computer Assisted Reporting: A Practical Guide*. New York: St. Martin's Press.

Jury, Alan (2006). "Likely Targets in a Remade Landscape" in *The Australian Financial Review*, 14 July 2006, 71.

Kieve, Jeffrey (1973). *Electric Telegraph: A Social and Economic History*. Devon, UK: David & Charles.

Livingston, K.L. (1996). *The Wired Nation Continent: The Communication Revolution and Federating Australia*. Melbourne: Oxford University Press.

MacLean, Sheena (2005). "Print Learns to Love the Web" in *The Australian* Media section, 28 April 2005, 18.

Maier, Scott (2000). "Digital Diffusion in Newsrooms: The Uneven Advance of Computer-Assisted Reporting" in *Newspaper Research Journal*, Vol. 21, Issue 2, 95–110.

Mayer, Henry (1964 reprinted 1968). *The Press in Australia*. Melbourne: Lansdowne Press.

McCartney, Robert (2004). "Continuous news at *The Washington Post*." Presentation to the Online News Association annual conference, Los Angeles, 12 November 2004.

Mulcaster, Glen (1998). Personal interview 24 September 1998, Melbourne.

Murdoch, Rupert (2005). Speech to the American Society of Newspaper Editors on 13 April 2005. Found at News Corporation Web site http://www.newscorp.com [accessed 14 July 2006].

O'Loughlin, Peter (1996). Personal interview 11 November 1996, Sydney.

Quinn, Stephen (2001). *Newsgathering on the Net*, Second edition. Melbourne: Macmillan.

Quinn, Stephen (2005a). *Convergent Journalism: An Introduction*. Boston: Focal.

Quinn, Stephen (2005b). *Convergent Journalism: The Fundamentals of Multimedia Reporting*. New York: Peter Lang.

Quinn, Stephen and Bethell, Paul (2006). "Connected but not Online: A Snapshot of Generation Y in Australia" in *Asia Pacific Public Relations Journal*, Vol. 7, 2006, 51–61.

Quinn, Stephen (2007). "Fast, Fancy-Free Internet is Rapidly Overtaking Traditional Media Thinking" in *The Age*, 14 January 2007, 13.

Ross, Steve (2002). *Change and Its Impact on Communications*. New York: Middleberg Euro RSCG and Columbia University Graduate School of Journalism.

Ross, Steve (2005). *Rebuilding Trust: Rebuilding Credibility in the Newsroom and Boardroom*. New York: Euro RSCG Magnet and Columbia University Graduate School of Journalism.

Russin, John (2003). Comment heard during convergence panel discussion at Online News Association annual conference, Chicago, 15 November 2003.

Schwarzlose, Richard (1990). *The Nation's Newsbrokers*. Evanston: Northwestern University Press.

Shipside, Steve (2007). "Champion the Virtues of Multimedia" in *Newspaper Techniques*, January 2007, 22–24.

Smith, Anthony (1979). *The Newspaper: An International History*. London: Thames and Hudson.

Smith, Anthony (1980). *Goodbye Gutenberg: The Newspaper Revolution of the 1980s*. New York and Oxford: Oxford University Press.

Strupp, Joe (2006). "Across the Web/Print Divide" in Editor & Publisher online, 23 March 2006 [accessed 12 July 2006].

Wolpe, Bruce (2006). Quinn personal interview, 14 April 2006.

2

Generating Ideas and Finding Experts

If we break the newsgathering process into its most fundamental elements, we see three parts to the process: a journalist gets an idea, finds information to develop that idea (via interviews, online research, and documents to name a few of the sources), and then writes the story. The newsgathering process is more sophisticated than this simplistic view, but for the moment we will use it to kick-start the process of finding ideas.

Fledgling journalists often report problems with the first stage of the process, generating story ideas. Even seasoned reporters occasionally find their minds blank. When deadlines loom, it is easy to select stories in press releases or from the usual agenda of council meetings, traffic accidents, or other emergencies. But real news is sometimes far removed from the traditional PR-generated agenda. Stories produced by computer-assisted reporting (CAR) win prizes precisely because they are scoops and not part of the agenda that every other newsroom receives.

Newspaper historian Anthony Smith has wisely noted that newspapers can only publish "available material." That is, a newspaper cannot be a "mirror of reality" but can only be the result of the "potential of its sources." Print publications depend on the caliber of their sources of information and data and the quality of their reporters. We can extend this idea to all media, and not just newspapers. Smith noted that much of the historical literature about newspapers assumed that journalists had an equal range of information sources. "[But] in fact, journalism in any given period has functioned mainly as the processor of *certain available* (our emphasis) kinds of material" (Smith 1978: 208). Smith concluded that a newspaper's chief function was the "selection, arrangement, and reformulation of information passing to it through regular channels" (Smith 1977: 181–182; Smith

1978: 209). CAR provides journalists with an opportunity to broaden the sources of information, and to make those sources part of the "regular channels" that publications access.

This chapter offers ways to use CAR to generate story ideas that are not part of the PR-generated news agenda and how to find experts to interview. To look for story ideas, we need to visit some established parts of the Internet that perhaps people have ignored in the past or did not know existed. It is important here to emphasize that technology is only the start. The technologies listed below will help you find story ideas, but journalists also need to wear out shoe leather walking the beat and talking to contacts face to face to get a complete story.

Ways to Generate Story Ideas

We begin with something called a listserv. The odd name harks back to the days when computer files only had eight character names, because that was the available number of characters. A listserv is also known as a mailing list because it contains a list of names and addresses similar to those an organization might use for sending publications to its members or customers.

Think of a listserv as an electronic magazine. You join the same way you subscribe to the print edition of a magazine by providing your name and address. In the case of a listserv, you need an e-mail address. You send an e-mail to subscribe to a listserv and content soon arrives in your e-mail in-box. Make sure you keep the e-mail that welcomes you as a member, because it will contain details of how to unsubscribe. This may be useful if you go on vacation or are out of the office for an extended period. Set up a folder in your e-mail account, perhaps called "unsub," to store these important e-mails. We are assuming our readers have a unique e-mail address and know how to send and receive e-mail and organize and store e-mail in separate folders.

The Internet is an interconnected collection or network of computers around the world; hence the name, which is an amalgam of *inter*national *net*work. It started as four connected computers in 1964 in the United States and has spread around the world. Within a generation (about 30 years), the number of computers holding Internet files, known as servers, grew by 50 percent a year. By 1998, the world had about 29.7 million servers, each containing anywhere from a handful to hundreds of thousands of pages or sites. Almost a decade later, the number of servers had jumped to 28 million and is expected to rise to 45 million by 2010. It is almost impossible to count the total number of sites on the Web because of the number of sites added and removed each day. Tips for effectively searching those pages for information are discussed in Chapter 5.

A listserv distributes e-mails to all members of that list. Every time someone sends an e-mail to a listserv, every other member receives a copy of the e-mail.

Similarly, every time someone replies to anything on the listserv, everyone gets a copy. Some mailing lists are very active. It is best to join only one or two that relate to your beat or area of interest. Otherwise an onslaught of e-mail may clog your in-box and infuriate your IT support staff. Veteran CAR reporter Bill Dedman points out that journalists can join and leave a listserv any time, often for one story. "You can subscribe to a mailing list about, say, heart attack treatment or government purchasing or some other arcane subject, learn a lot that will help you prepare for an interview, and then unsubscribe." Dedman says all reporters should be on one or two mailing lists about subjects they are monitoring, constantly getting on and off as subjects change.

Listservs are often moderated. Think of moderators as you would a copy editor or section editor—someone who checks on the quality of content. Moderators are granted special powers to keep discussion civil, which means that debate is kept on track and focused. Some listservs reflect the generous nature of the Internet, in the sense that members are willing to answer a stranger's question. You may be surprised what you find if you ask a question to the members of a list. Remember to identify yourself as a journalist, and ask people if they are happy to be interviewed or quoted. Some of the best listservs for CAR journalists are the discussion lists for Computer-Assisted Reporting and Research List (CARR-L), Investigative Reporters and Editors (IRE-L), and the National Institute for Computer-Assisted Reporting (NICAR-L).

How do I locate a listserv? Go to Tile at http://www.tile.net/lists/. Think of it as a search engine for listservs. Tile is also a search tool for finding newsgroups (discussed in the next section).

Search for subjects via key word in the box at the top of the screen. If you know the name of the list, click on the appropriate letter in the alphabetic list further down the screen, then use Control + f to find specific text. Use control + f to find text anywhere on any Internet site. Next, type the word you seek in the dialog box that appears. Once you find a list you would like to join, follow the on-screen instructions. This process involves sending an e-mail to a computer, which controls the flow of e-mail on the list. You will need to reply once to this computer. Remember, some lists have a lot of traffic so limit the number to which you subscribe. Also remember to keep the instructions on how to leave the list.

Listservs have other uses. For example, the NICAR listserv is popular among CAR enthusiasts because it offers a place where people can get technical help to problems they encounter with data sets. Responses to questions arrive right away, making it an excellent tool for journalists working on deadline. Ideas and ethical issues are discussed on the IRE listserv.

Join a listserv in an area that interests you. Lurk for at least a week to get a sense of the tone and then post questions to it. Lurking is an Internet term to describe the act of monitoring the content of a list but not getting involved. It is an ideal way to check the qualifications of the people who contribute and the quality of their discussion. Think of it as similar to sitting in a public space like a café and listening to the conversations around you. Often lurking will stimulate story ideas. Send private e-mails to those who appear most knowledgeable. The only limit to using a listserv for generating ideas is the limit of your imagination.

Newsgroups

Newsgroups live on a part of the Internet known as the Usenet (see Figure 2.1). They are the online equivalent of a newsroom bulletin board. Often the information is old, which makes a mockery of the word "news" in the term newsgroup. The caliber of information varies from useful material to lunatic ravings, with a tendency toward the lunatic end of the continuum. Think of newsgroups as an example of the concept of freedom of speech gone berserk. We recommend getting a private e-mail address from one of the free services (Gmail, Hotmail, or Yahoo, for example) if you want to avoid using your work e-mail address. These addresses are also useful when you are on the road, or if you seek anonymity. A site called Newsgroups.com provides a guided tour about how newsgroups work, at http://www.newsgroups.com/whatisusenet.htm.

You can search newsgroup archives via Tile at http://www.tile.net/news (see previous section) or Google at http://www.google.com. For the latter, select the "groups" link above the box in the center of the screen. Note that newsgroup information goes back to the early 1980s. Other useful newsgroup sites include

Figure 2.1

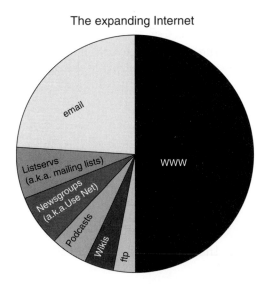

The expanding Internet

Yahoo and Cyberfiber (http://www.cyberfiber.com/). A handful of newsgroups are moderated. In this situation, the messages that you submit are not distributed to the Usenet but instead are e-mailed to the newsgroup moderator for approval. Moderators ensure the messages that readers see conform to the tone of the newsgroup.

Here is an example from the Usenet showing how a journalist used it to find information. Stephen Aquino posted this message to the newsgroup: alt.journalism:

> I'm writing an article on the disparities of what journalism programs teach versus the realities of working on an actual publication. Are editors satisfied with the new crop of grads? Is there something in particular lacking? Are new grads shocked and confused after getting their first job? How do J. educators avoid the pitfalls of theory versus practice. I'd like to get comments from all three types before Oct 1. Please include your credentials and be sure to tell me if you agree to be quoted.

A writer named Skipper Press, author of the *Writer's Guide to Hollywood Producers, Directors & Screenwriters' Agents*, replied: "I find that many college grads don't even have good spelling and grammar skills. I've taught writing skills to them. Instead of wanting to be good journalists or authors they're writing screenplays and grabbing at the platinum ring of the Hollywood carousel. You can find my credentials at the resume web site below." Again, newsgroups demonstrate the high level of generosity of people on the Internet. As ever with information coming from people you do not know, it is important to exercise some caution. See chapter 7 for help in evaluating information found on the Internet.

How to Generate Story Ideas

Open Google Groups and type a word or phrase into the text box. You may want to use a current news story or the name of a person currently figuring in the news. Or you may choose to insert the name of your local mayor, or a leading business person or church figure, or a local sportsperson. It helps if a person's name has an unusual spelling, because the data on these sites go back several years, in some cases to the early 1980s. For example, a search using the key word "wispelaere" produced more than 900 hits about a former Australian intelligence officer, Jean-Philippe Wispelaere, who was detained in Washington on espionage charges for allegedly trying to sell American intelligence secrets to another country. This worked because of the unusual spelling of his name. Common names like Smith or Jones will produce far too many hits. If the name you seek information about is relatively common, the "advanced groups" option with Google Groups helps to reduce the number of hits to something manageable. The advanced option for search tools is also discussed at length in chapter 5.

News Filters

News filters are software programs on the Internet and commercial services that help you find information. They all work the same way—type key words about your topic and the filter searches for you. Software in the filter stores your profile and uses it to check the stories, blogs, or Usenet messages it reads. When the software finds a story, blog, or posting that contains your key words, the program sends a link to your e-mail box.

When setting up an alert, choose your key words carefully. They must be specific enough that you get relevant hits, but not so specific that possible stories are missed. Find out how the filter works. Some will just match key words character by character, so the key word "labor" will not find "labour." It will generally save you time in the long run if you read the help or frequently asked questions (FAQ) section carefully. The filter with the biggest reach is the Google alert option.

Google alerts are automatically e-mailed to you when Google finds results based on your search terms or key words. At this time Google alerts were in beta form, which is computer-speak for still being tested. As of April 2007, Google offered four types of alerts: news, Web, blog, or newsgroup, or a combination of all four called "comprehensive." This is the best option to choose for the most coverage. It works by sending a news alert as an e-mail with a link to the site. Once you set up an alert, it will only be activated after you reply to an e-mail from Google to confirm that you want to establish such an alert. This is to stop people from sending silly alerts to your e-mail address.

The Google alerts home page (http://www.google.com/alerts) offers a list of possible uses for Google alerts: monitoring a developing news story, keeping current on a competitor or industry, getting the latest on a celebrity or event, and keeping tabs on your favorite sports teams. You can probably think of other possible uses for Google alerts. Many government agencies and nonprofits also offer e-mail alerts. Commercial services have e-mail alerts that use public records. For example, 10kwizard.com and its ilk will alert you when a company files a report with the U.S. Securities and Exchange Commission. These sorts of alerts give reporters a head start over less technologically savvy colleagues. Other useful alerts include the following list:

CNN Alerts

CNN offers free e-mail alerts of breaking news, but you need to register; see http://www.cnn.com/email/. You select the topics that interest you and CNN delivers news updates and story links from its sites to your e-mail address. It is an easy and free way to track people, places, companies, and hobbies. The "take the tour" link on this site explains how to set up an e-mail alert.

BBC Alerts

The BBC also offers e-mail news alerts as well as desktop alerts, although the latter are only available for PCs using Windows. Install software for desktop alerts from http://news.bbc.co.uk/1/hi/help/3533099.stm. To register for breaking news alerts you click on the link at the bottom of the page and insert your e-mail address and password. Whenever a big story breaks a message will be sent to your e-mail in-box and a link to the relevant section of the BBC News Web site. You can also sign up for a range of e-mail news services about heavyweight BBC programs such as Newsnight and Panorama.

Australian Alerts

Australia's national broadcaster the Australian Broadcasting Corporation, modeled on the BBC, offers a free e-mail news service called NewsMail. It was developed in response to requests from users for an e-mail service to keep them informed of the major events of the day. NewsMail provides news updates twice a day, each morning and afternoon Australian time, to the e-mail address you nominate. A special news update is sent for major stories. To access this service go to http://abc.net.au/news/services/, fill out the form, and click the submit button.

Some news and information sites will also send you a text message alert about forthcoming programs. You can also set up feeds to have information sent to your desktop or mobile phone. These are discussed in the section on RSS in chapter 3.

How to Generate a Story Using Alerts

Choose a topic for a profile or backgrounder. Create an alert using Google or one of the other options. You should do this about two weeks before you plan to start writing. Open a blank word-processing file and copy and paste information into that file as it arrives. At the end of two weeks you hopefully will have sufficient information with which to write a profile or backgrounder. If nothing else, you will at least have enough information to develop your story further. Alerts are also useful because they provide results from trade publications that do not get wide circulation. Experts who could figure prominently in the story you may write are often quoted in those articles. The *Geelong Advertiser*, a daily in Victoria, Australia, has inserted the keyword "Geelong" into a series of news alerts for several years. Editor Peter Judd said alerts generated scores of stories for the newspaper.

Home Pages

All journalists should read the print and online versions of magazines about their areas of interest and all journalists must visit places where news is being generated, such as the mayor's office or the local police headquarters. With a computer it is easy to visit the online equivalent by monitoring the home pages of people or organizations that relate to your beat. You can usually find an organization's URL by "guesstimating"—or looking for the URL in press releases about the organization. For example, if you have the defense beat you would naturally monitor the home pages of each wing of the armed forces, along with the Department of Defense. But do not allow technology to become a replacement for shoe leather; make sure you also visit places on your beat.

Follow the News

An easy way to generate story ideas is to monitor reliable news organizations around the world to cherry-pick ideas based on how journalists in other countries have done stories. Remember the Greenpeace motto (borrowed from Gandhi) of thinking globally but acting locally. Read overseas news sites (see the list below) and find a local angle. If you find news in a language other than English, Babelfish will translate for you. The results are basic. One of the authors often monitors news from the Gulf Arab states using Google's Arabic translator. See http://babel.altavista.com. Google also offers translation services at http://www.google.com/language_tools.

Useful Online Sites of Major News Organizations

ABC (America)
http://abcnews.go.com/

Australian Broadcasting Corporation
http://abc.net.au/news/

Canadian Broadcasting Corporation
http://www.cbc.ca/

CBS
http://www.cbs.com/

CNN
http://www.cnn.com/

NBC
http://www.nbc.com/News_&_Sports/

Reuters
http://today.reuters.com/

The BBC
http://news.bbc.co.uk/

Assignment Editor
http://www.assignmenteditor.com/

This is a huge site that some journalists set as their home page. Links in blue are free; links in red require a subscription for $50 a year or $15 for three months (as of April 2007).

Newspapers of the world
http://www.actualidad.com/

This home page has an image of a map of the world. You simply click on a region to read its newspapers.

The Paperboy
http://www.thepaperboy.com/

This home page is bold and ugly, but the content is useful. A link at the top of the page allows you to search newspaper archives from around the world. It offers similar sites in the UK and Canada.

Topix
http://www.topix.net/

Topix describes itself as the Internet's largest news site, claiming links to more than 360,000 topics from more than 27,000 sources. It includes mainstream media and blogs. Topix says it aggregates twice as much content as Google News.

Totalnews
http://www.totalnews.com/

Totalnews has a simple interface—a graphic of a compass—and a vertical list of news categories such as business and entertainment. The site was being upgraded as this book was being written.

Read Archives

Some news organizations charge a fee for their archives. Volunteers from the news division of the Special Libraries Association maintain a series of sites that tell you how to access American papers and how much it costs. The site points out which archive services are free. Find them at http://www.ibiblio.org/slanews/internet/archives.html.

Daily Events

One way to generate story ideas is to monitor sites that have almanacs. For example, InfoPlease offers a daily almanac at http://www.infoplease.com/daily. The same rule applies: think globally but act locally. You may discover that Friday of next week is national cheesecake day. This gives you time to write a feature on the subject. Use almanacs when you are scheduled to work on a slow news day such as a Sunday, a public holiday, or Christmas. Almanacs give you time to prepare stories for those slow news days. You can search for almanacs via most of the major search tools. The Yahoo! Almanac at http://dir.yahoo.com/Reference/Almanacs/ is comprehensive.

Covering Humanitarian Emergencies

The Reuters Foundation offers an excellent service for journalists called MediaBridge (http://www.alertnet.org/mediabridge/). It is a set of tools and services designed to make life easier for reporters, fact-checkers, and editors when covering humanitarian emergencies. New additions in 2007 included "hotspot mapping" at http://www. alertnet.org/map/index2006new.htm, which lets reporters search, scan, and zoom in on the world's crises through an advanced mapping system, and "e-learning" at http://www.alertnet.org/thefacts/elearning/index.htm, a group of training modules on topics ranging from how aid works to understanding famine.

Refdesk

One of the most comprehensive sites for journalists has to be Refdesk, which describes itself as the "single best source for facts." Find it at http://www.refdesk.com/.

Finding People and Experts to Interview

Once you have a story idea you need information to help develop that story. Use the Internet to find experts and spokespeople to interview. Find them via both e-mail and databases on the Web.

Make Sure Your E-mail Reaches Its Destination

In a world saturated with data, sometimes e-mails do not reach their destination. Sometimes reporters need proof that an e-mail arrived. ReadNotify is an inexpensive service based in Australia that provides written proof of mailing, delivery, and reading. It also lets you know if the e-mail has been forwarded and the location of any readers. Use it to retract an e-mail or to get it to self-destruct after being read. The use in investigative reporting is obvious, but it will also be a big help with a skeptical editor. Journalists can sign up for a free two-week trial to test it. See http://www.readnotify.com.

Experts Via E-mail

All journalists should be aware of the U. S. based ProfNet, run by PR Newswire, which links reporters with expert sources. Created in 1992, ProfNet calls itself "an online community" representing more than 11,000 news and information officers in 4,000 organizations in North America, Europe, Africa, and Asia. It also has a database of more than 21,000 expert profiles maintained by members on four continents.

Reporters, information officers, and experts can meet each other via e-mail (profnet@profnet.com), the database of expert profiles (http://profnet.com), or expert tip sheets. When registering you will need to provide evidence that you are a journalist. Thereafter, ProfNet's services are free. ProfNet said it was poised for rapid international growth and hoped soon to be able to offer experts in a wide range of countries. "For the time being, however, we are able to offer significant numbers of profiles only in the US, Canada and United Kingdom."

The simplest way to use ProfNet is via e-mail. Journalists should store a template in a world processor and paste a copy into an e-mail each time you need help. You could use something like this format:

> Dear ProfNet,
> My name is (your name). I am a reporter with (insert your news organization). I am writing a story about (insert details) and am looking for an expert in this or a related area who is willing to be interviewed. Please get back to me by (insert your time frame for receiving information). I would prefer details by e-mail, but you can reach me at (insert your fax or phone numbers).
> Thank you in advance.
> Yours sincerely, etc

The above is only a template. You will need to modify it for each query. Make sure your request is specific and that it demonstrates you have already done some research. Detail what you have read or what you think you know. Detail exactly what you want to find out. Do not simply ask for an interview. Say what you need to find out, says Bill Dedman: "How often are children under 14 treated as adults in the criminal courts in homicide cases?" Most important, says Dedman, do not simply ask for an expert in a subject. Ask for a professor who has done research on that subject. This shows you want hard facts, not opinion: "What you're trying to overcome is the professor's fear that you're a student wanting the professor to do the homework. Show that you've done some work, but have good questions to ask."

Web Databases of Experts

Increasingly, organizations are placing lists of experts on Web sites, rather than printing expensive (and dated) brochures and books. Universities are good sources for experts. Most major universities house research centers or units, and most academics in them are happy to discuss their work with journalists. A good example was the Center for War, Peace, and the News Media at Boston University, which continues to be especially useful during the Iraq war (http://www.bu.edu/globalbeat/experts.html).

In countries like Australia, the UK, and the United States, you can usually find an online version of the media contacts directory from a university's home page. Some of the best in Australia include:

Australian National University
http://info.anu.edu.au/mac/Media/Experts_List/index.asp

Macquarie University
http://www.pr.mq.edu.au/journalists.htm

University of Melbourne
http://www.researches.unimelb.edu.au/mediacontact/

University of New South Wales
http://www.unsw.edu.au/news/pad/media/mediaexperts.html

University of Technology, Sydney
http://www.experts.uts.edu.au

University of Wollongong
http://www.skills.itc.com.au/index.asp

A list of Australian experts can be found at: http://www.expertguide.com.au.
You will find plenty of databases of experts at think tanks and universities in the United States and Canada. Here is a small list:

American Press Institute
http://www.americanpressinstitute.org/pages/toolbox/expert_sources/expert_sources/

Ask an Expert
http://www.refdesk.com/expert.html

Canadian think tanks
http://www.journalismnet.com/canada/lobby.htm

Internet Legal Research Group
http://www.ilrg.com/

Soros Foundation
http://www.soros.org/initiatives/esp/resources/experts

University of British Columbia
http://webservices.publicaffairs.ubc.ca/clients/pa/apps/experts/public/index.php

University of California
http://www.universityofcalifornia.edu/news/experts.html

University of Missouri
http://www.missouri.edu/~news/experts.html

University of Toronto
http://www.bluebook.utoronto.ca/

University of Virginia
http://www.virginia.edu/facultyexperts

Because American universities are large, you may need to locate a specific research center and look for experts within that center. For example, Stanford University's library provides an extensive list of available research topics at http://library.stanford.edu/collect/alphasub.html.

Universities in the UK also have plenty of expertise. It is probably best to start with the better known universities, such as:

London School of Economics
http://www.lse.ac.uk/resources/experts/

University of Cambridge
http://www.cam.ac.uk/mediaguide/

University of Leeds
http://www.leeds.ac.uk/media/

University of Oxford
http://www.ox.ac.uk/media/

It is relatively easy to create your own list of university experts by using a search tool such as Google.

Web Sites Listing Experts

News researcher Kitty Bennett at the *St Petersburg Times* collected this huge list of experts for her newsroom. Her Directories Online tends to be North American in focus but easy to search via key word (remember to use control + f to search some of these large files). See http://www.ibiblio.org/slanews/internet/experts.html.

YearbookNews is the online edition of *The Yearbook of Experts, Authorities, and Spokespersons*. Find it at http://www.expertclick.com. It has a search engine built into the home page.

Google Scholar is an excellent place to find scholarly and refereed articles and items in magazines like *Columbia Journalism Review*. Scholar sometimes finds articles without a Web link, but offers ways to use the Google search tool to find the article you seek. See http://scholar.google.com/.

Make Free or Inexpensive Phone Calls Worldwide

It is possible to make free and untimed international and national phone calls using a technology called voice-over Internet protocol, or VOIP. The best known VOIP software is Skype. To use a service like Skype the people on both ends of the call need a broadband Internet connection plus a microphone and speakers. They must use the same software and be registered with the service. To start, download a small and self-installing piece of software and sign up for the free Skype service at www.skype.com. In April 2006, Skype announced it had 100 million registered users. On any given day in 2007 about 8 million Skypers were online. If the other person does not have Skype, it is still possible to phone them cheaply by depositing money into an account via credit card. Calls to non-Skype users in most developed countries cost about 2.5 cents a minute. Late in 2006, the U. S. broadband management company Sandvine said Skype accounted for almost half of the VOIP calls in North America. Early in 2007 Skype was working on providing video phone calls, voice-to-text, and voicemail-to-e-mail translation. It is relatively easy to have your Skype calls transferred from your computer to your cell phone.

Suggested Reading

Run by and for journalists, FACSNet offers an excellent list of resources in its database. You need to register for this free service to get access to the database. http://www.facsnet.org.

The National Press Club in Washington has assembled a superb list of online resources for journalists. Find it at http://npc.press.org/library/resources.cfm.

Use the week ahead site from BBC Monitoring to plan stories around the world. Find it at http://www.monitor.bbc.co.uk/and choose a relevant region.

MediaBridge is an excellent service for journalists provided by the Reuters Foundation. Find it at http://www.alertnet.org/mediabridge/.

References

Smith, Anthony (1977). "Technology and Control: The Interactive Dimensions of Journalism" in *Mass Communication and Society* edited by James Curran, Michael Gurevitch, and Janet Woollacott. London: Edward Arnold.

Smith, Anthony (1978). *The Politics of Information: Problems of Policy in Modern Media.* London: Macmillan.

Blogs as a Newsgathering and Reporting Tool

Blogs represent some of the more interesting developments for the publishing world since the arrival of the Web more than a decade ago. The question of whether blogging is journalism is relevant and is discussed in Chapter 4. But if anyone should blog, it should be journalists. Yet non-journalists threaten to overwhelm the "blogosphere", leaving journalists isolated in their castles of print. The "blogosphere" consists of all the content built by blogs, moblogs, video blogs, vodcasts, and podcasts (these terms are defined later in the chapter).

In 2005, the Pew Internet & American Life Project reported that by November 2004 blogs had established themselves as a key part of America's online culture. About 8 million American adults said they had created a blog, representing about one-quarter (27 percent) of Internet users. Some of this huge growth was the result of political blogs written during the 2004 presidential campaign (Lenhart 2005: i–ii). By the middle of 2006, the number of American bloggers had soared to 12 million, or 2 in 5 Internet users. About 57 million adults said they read blogs (Lenhart 2006: i). To put that 57 million into perspective, it is 7 million more than the average weekday circulation of all America's daily newspapers. As of early 2007, about 75,000 new blogs were born each day. Each day of the week bloggers added about 1.2 million new entries, known as posts, which means about 50,000 updates were appearing each hour. Associated Press is the world's biggest news organization in terms of words produced each day. When CEO Tom Curley told the Online News Association's annual conference in November 2004 that "we thought we [AP] had the big pipe" he was conceding that bloggers were producing more content than journalists (Curley 2004).

Blogs have been around since 1997 but their profile rose in 2002 after blogs became involved in some major news stories. See the breakout for a short history of the major news stories associated with blogs. In 2004, some Democratic presidential candidates used blogs and the Internet to raise both money and their profiles. That year Merriam-Webster, the dictionary publisher, chose blog as its word of the year.

Blogs have boomed because they are easy to set up and maintain. A "blogger" creates an account via the Web with a free or paid blogging service. It is as simple as filling in a form. You can update your blog as often as you like if you have Internet access. One of the authors of this book updates his blog via mobile phone. Anyone with access to the Web can read the blog. Wright Bryan, a Web producer with America's National Public Radio Web site, described blogs as the human voice and imagination amplified by the power of the Web. Blogs offer a new frontier to journalists. "War, politics, and pop culture are all obsessed over and reported on by bloggers. You name a topic and someone somewhere probably has a blog about it." The blogs to watch, Bryan said, were the ones that arose in areas where news was happening. "Whether it's revolution in one of the former Soviet republics or war in Iraq, someone with a front-row seat is blogging about it." These blogs represent unfiltered news available to a global audience. "This is the public taking over where the professional journalist can't or won't go," Bryan said.

Blogs and News: A Short History

December 1997: American artificial intelligence programmer Jorn Barger used the term weblog for the first time to describe his site www.robotwisdom.org.

December 2002: Trent Lott resigns as Senate Majority Leader over allegations of racist comments. Much of the outrage is generated in blogs.

March 2003: A 29-year-old architect, Salam al-Janabi, publishes a blog, Salam Pax, from Baghdad about the impact of war on his suburb. It receives worldwide recognition.

September 2004: The Kryptonite bicycle lock company spends $10 million upgrading locks. Initially the company denied people could open the locks with a Bic pen. But bloggers posted video of people opening locks with Bic pens, and the company lost credibility.

October 2004: CBS anchor Dan Rather apologizes after bloggers challenged his allegations about President Bush's military service. Rather later resigns, and several senior editor staff are fired.

December 2004: BBC receives 25,000 e-mails in the first week after the December 26 tsunami hits southeast Asia.

July 2005: Moblogs provide first images of the bombings aboard a London bus and underground subway. Video from a mobile phone appears on air 20 minutes after being e-mailed to Sky News.

August 2005: Blogs carry much of the real news about the aftermath of Hurricane Andrew in New Orleans.

July 2006: Technorati.com records 50 million blogs, up from 27 million in February that year. That same month commuters in Mumbai, India provide images with their mobile phones of the carnage after seven bombs exploded on suburban trains.

This chapter suggests ways that reporters can harness this form of media. But first, what is a blog? The word is an abbreviation of weblog, itself an amalgam of web and log. It is the same concept as the log a ship's captain maintains while at sea. Thus a blog is a type of Web site where entries are written, or posted, the same way you would update a journal or diary. Blogs often provide commentary or news on a specific topic, but the largest group consists of personal diaries. The big difference when compared with traditional diaries is that people share their blogs. They are social in nature. Blogs and their relatives represent part of a media revolution known as social networking, participatory journalism, or citizen reporting. This concept is discussed in Chapter 4. A blog, then, could be defined as a personal online journal. With blogs, the most recent item is displayed first. A typical blog combines text, images, and sometimes sound with links to other blogs, Web pages, and other media related to its topic. The word blog can also be used as a verb, meaning to add an entry to a blog. More members of the blog family are discussed in the next section.

Moblog is an amalgam of mobile phone and blog. People produce these blogs using cell phones. They send or post images and text to the Web by sending an e-mail (sometimes called a multimedia message, or MMS) from their phone to a Web site set up like a blog. The e-mail's subject line becomes the headline and the message text the body of the story. Software places the attached photograph in the posting as a thumbnail image, and the software allows people to click on the image to get a full-size image. The German newspaper research company Ifra runs industry conferences around the world, and its journalists produce moblogs at these conferences. Some of the best examples of moblogs can be found at Ifra sites, such as the coverage of the Publish Asia conference in March 2007 at http://www.ifra-nt.com/multiblog/publishasia. One of the authors, Stephen Quinn, maintains a moblog to show journalists how simple it is to update one. You can find it at http://qa.bigblog.com.au/.

Video blogs, known as v-logs, are the video versions of moblogs. The simplest form occurs when people take videos with their mobile phones and send them to a blog site, in the same way they post a moblog image. Journalists have been experimenting with video blogs since 2003, using modified Nokia mobile phones. A more sophisticated process involves editing video from portable video cameras, assembling it into packages and short programs, and posting that to a site. Probably the best known of this sophisticated form is Rocketboom (http://www.rocketboom.com). It uses TV news as a model and each weekday bulletin runs for about three minutes. Rocketboom is set in a studio with a presenter but is only available via the Web. Web designer Andrew Baron founded Rocketboom in New York in October 2004. Marketing was by word-of-mouth and by the middle of 2006, Rocketboom claimed to be one of the most popular videoblogs on the Internet "with more daily subscribers for original syndicated multi-media content than nearly any other site, including podcasts." It broadcasts from Baron's apartment, is released at 9 a.m. Eastern Standard Time, and is produced with consumer-level digital equipment. "We differ from a regular TV program in many important ways," Baron said. "Instead of costing millions of dollars to produce, Rocketboom is created with a consumer-level video camera, a laptop, two lights, and a map with no additional overhead or costs." Rocketboom spends nothing on promotion, relying entirely on word-of-mouth marketing, and "close to nothing on distribution because bandwidth costs and space are so inexpensive." Rocketboom makes money through advertisements at the end of the newscast.

One of the best examples of a journalist embracing v-logs is the work of *New York Times* technology reporter David Pogue. You can read his blog, listen to his podcast, or sign up for his weekly video blog at the home page of the paper's Technology section at http://www.nytimes.com/pages/technology/. As with Rocketboom, Pogue creates his videos using a laptop and a consumer-quality digital camera.

A podcast is a do-it-yourself form of broadcasting that became popular about the middle of 2004. You could argue that it is the verbal version of a blog. *Guardian* journalist Ben Hammersley coined the term, basing it on Apple's portable digital music player, the iPod. Listeners download podcast files onto their music players. Podcasting represents another example of personal and convenient media, where individuals choose what they hear rather than relying on radio station schedules. Listeners can automate the download process, so new items are available on their computers soon after they are published. The *New Oxford American Dictionary* chose podcast as its word of the year in 2005. Dozens of American newspapers and magazines embraced podcasting that year, and broadcasters such as the Australian Broadcasting Corporation and the Canadian Broadcasting Corporation offer podcasts. For example, the Australian Broadcasting Corporation has made available podcasts of its Radio National programs since the middle of 2005 (http://www.abc.net.au/rn/podcast/). Some podcasts summarize the day's news; others provide radio-style programs complete with interviews of reporters and newsmakers. In 2005, *Wall Street Journal* reporter David Kesmodel said most American podcasts had small budgets, and were usually hosted by print journalists with "scant broadcast experience." Some newspapers wanted to be seen as innovators with podcasts because they believed they were behind in embracing blogs, Kesmodel said. "But, just as with blogs, it is unclear whether podcasts will become a commercial success or help newspapers gain readers" (Kesmodel 2005).

In London, the *Daily Telegraph* has made available a 20-minute podcast since November 2005. Content initially consisted of reporters or actors reading columns from the print edition. New media director Annelies van den Belt said the project was part of her mission to integrate new media into every part of the paper. Editor Martin Newland said the podcast provided a chance for readers to hear the voices of some of the country's best writers. "Those wanting access to some of the best writing and opinion in the country now have the chance to sample the full 'flavor' of that day's newspaper" (quoted in Ponsford 2005a: 5). In June 2006, Nielsen Netratings reported that the number of American adults who downloaded podcasts outnumbered those who published blogs. About 9.2 million people, or 6.6 percent of adult Web users, had downloaded a podcast in the previous month while only about 6.7 million Americans, or 4.8 percent of adults, had written blogs in the same period, the survey said. These numbers contradict the Pew data outlined at the start of the chapter. Regardless of which data are correct, the numbers show that blogs and podcasts have captured the imagination of the American public.

In the Philippines, the Inquirer.net site launched its podcast network at the start of 2007, focusing on that year's elections and interviewing all senatorial candidates. Editor-in-chief J. V. Rufino said podcasts had proved a runaway success. "We sit the candidate down in our office and we have a set list of questions. It's a panel session with reporters. For our audiences it's like sitting in on a panel interview. It has been very well received. People can listen at their convenience." Inquirer.net records the interview and lets each candidate talk for at least an hour. Rufino adopted this format because he was not satisfied with the sound-bite mentality on local television. Candidates did not have time to discuss an issue fully. "Our podcasts are in-depth. We told the candidates to talk as long as they like, and some talked for 3 hours." The interviews are edited to run for one hour. Rufino said audiences learned a lot from an in-depth interview. "It's the things that candidates say when they relax, what they say unconsciously, that reveals an insight into their character, which is something you lose in a sound bite." The Web site provides the whole interview and publishes the transcript so people who do not have iPods can read it online.

In July 2006, the BBC launched a trial service of video podcasts, known as vodcasts, designed to make BBC News available to people wherever and whenever they want it. The service was designed to build on the considerable success the BBC experienced with its audio podcasting trial. The first vodcast was the Ten Weekly. Content was available in open MP4 format downloadable to video iPods and most other portable video players. The BBC planned a daily vodcast called Breakfast Takeaway, a new daily news briefing aimed at the morning commuter. Adrian Van Klaveren, deputy director/controller of production for BBC News, said news was at the forefront of this trial but a second phase would involve a range of non-news TV content. Vodcasting has become a fact of life globally and it is now possible to download movies and television shows, as well as news.

Profile of a Blogger

In July 2006, the Pew Internet & American Life Project released a portrait of American bloggers, based on a national telephone survey started in November the previous year. It reported that blogging was "inspiring a new group of writers and creators to share their voices with the world." In 2006, about 12 million Americans blogged, and just over half of them were aged 30 or younger. Most bloggers used their blogs as personal journals, and according to Pew, one-third described what they did as journalism. Despite the public nature of what they did, many bloggers saw it as a personal pursuit. Just over one-half (55 percent) used a pseudonym while the rest blogged under his or her own name (Lenhart 2006: ii). Almost two out of four cited their life and experiences when asked to name the primary topic of their blog. Politics and government came a distant second (11 percent), followed by entertainment (7 percent), sports (6 percent), business and news (5 percent each), and technology (4 percent). Faith, religion, or sprituality rated 2 percent in total. Why do they blog, given the vast majority do not make any money from doing it? When asked to list the main reasons, 52 percent said they wanted to express themselves creatively and one-half said they wanted to document their personal experiences or share them with others. Just over one-third (37 percent) wanted to stay in touch with family and friends and one-third wanted to share practical knowledge or skills with others. Making money was last on the list, with 7 percent of respondents citing it as their main reason for blogging. More than half of bloggers included links to original sources and a similar percentage (56 percent) said they spent extra time trying to verify facts (Lenhart 2006: iii).

Bloggers appeared to be more wired than the rest of the population. Four out of five had broadband at home, compared with three out of five of all American Internet users. Almost all (95 percent) got news from the Internet, compared with 73 percent of all Internet users, and more than three out of five went online several times a day compared with one-quarter of other Internet users. Almost three out of four bloggers went online for political news or information, while only one-quarter of other Internet users did so. Bloggers spent an average of two hours a week on their blogs, and were evenly split by gender (Lenhart 2006: iv–v).

How do these American bloggers compare with their Australian counterparts? The McNair-Ingenuity research group conducted a telephone survey a month earlier than the Pew report, in June 2006, and found some differences and similarities. Fewer Australians said they had shared content on the Web—38 percent, or 5.8 million people aged 18 or older—only 4 percent said they had posted to their own blog in the past half year, and only 2 percent had posted a podcast. One out of five had read a blog, 1 out of 11 had listened to a podcast, and one-quarter had downloaded music from the Internet. But the younger demographic figured notably in the number of blog readers and writers. Two out of five people aged 18 to 29 had shared content. And one out of five of that age group had listened to a podcast. Half of this group downloaded music from the Internet in the previous half year. A comparison of the data suggests that Australians are a few years behind Americans, but heading in the same direction (McNair-Ingenuity 2006: 1–3). The significant difference in broadband speeds between the countries should be noted: As of 2006, almost two-thirds of households in America had broadband Internet access, compared with perhaps 28 percent in Australia. In America, broadband means fast access to the Internet, with average minimum speeds of 3 to 5 megabytes a second. In Australia, the telecommunications companies sell maximum speeds of 256 kilobytes a second as "broadband." Given the relationship between broadband speed and time spent on the Internet, the differences in access speed offer a reason whyAustralians are behind their American cousins.

Specialist Bloggers

Specialist bloggers represent the biggest threat to mainstream media, and print publications must learn to respond flexibly to compete with them. *Guardian* special projects developer Ben Hammersley said the vast majority of blogs were online diaries written by teenage girls "about how much they hate their teacher and how much they love their cat." But an increasing number of blogs were written by specialists "who basically write single-subject magazines." Some commentators call these specialists "niche-bloggers" and they were a newspaper editor's biggest nightmare, Hammersley said. In the technology field, a proliferation of niche blogs was providing a steady stream of news and analysis much faster than magazines, with their weekly or monthly news cycles, could achieve. When Apple launched a new iPod just four weeks after another model in 2006, Hammersley said, bloggers were able to cover the newer gadget immediately. Meanwhile, consumer computer magazines were caught with their covers still touting the older product. Some of the niche blogs had high levels of journalism skills and highly targeted readership, which allowed the writers to command high advertising rates. "From a journalistic business point of view, this is both really exciting and really terrifying," he said. "It's really exciting because if you're a specialist in your field you can start your own blog, put Google ads on the site and, if you are consistent and you write well, you could make quite a nice living out of it. It is terrifying [for specialist-subject magazines] because they will always be out of date from now on."

Blogs and Research for Journalism

The main premise of this chapter is the potential of blogs to help reporters do better research and consequently produce better journalism. A willing servant known as RSS is available to all journalists to help you find useful information. Some confusion exists as to what RSS stands for. The most common definitions are "really simple syndication" or "rich site summary." Regardless of which acronym you prefer, RSS is a major boon for journalists. You can have news constantly fed to you instead of searching for it. Content is "pulled" to your computer, as opposed to being "pushed" with e-mail or instant messaging (IM). In chapter 2 we recommended you keep a folder with instructions on how to unsubscribe from listservs for when you need to leave a listserv. It is also much easier to unsubscribe from an RSS feed—a click of a button on a Web site—compared with unsubscribing from "pushed" information such as e-mail newsletters.

A program known as a feed reader or aggregator (also called a news reader) checks a list of sites the journalist nominates and displays any updated articles. The software provides summaries of Web content plus links to the full version of the story. As with e-mail, unread entries are shown in bold. Some feed readers allow you to organize your feeds into categories and save your favorite entries. Small orange buttons on Web sites indicate whether RSS is available. More than 2,000 feed-reading applications are available. They come in two forms: Web-based aggregators that gather feeds for reading in a browser, or desktop news aggregators that can be downloaded and installed on a computer. The latter can be cross-platform, or specific to the Macintosh, Windows, or Linux. Aggregators are gradually being built into portal sites such as My Yahoo! and Google and Web browsers such as Mozilla Firefox, Safari, and Opera. Apple's iTunes serves as a podcast aggregator or "podcatcher." You can pay a few dollars for a feed reader (these come with dozens of feeds pre-loaded) but most are free. Find them by doing a search for "feed reader," "news reader," or "feed aggregator" with a search tool (see chapter 4 for how to use search tools). A comprehensive list is included in the online readings section at the end of this chapter.

One of the biggest Web-based aggregators is Bloglines (http://www.bloglines.com), which Mark Fletcher founded in 2003 and sold to Ask.com in 2005. All journalists should learn how to use Bloglines. Over time you will find a reader that works best for you. Todd Thacker, senior editor for the English-language OhmyNews International in South Korea, recommends RSS to any journalist or "Netizen" with limited spare time. "Remembering to go to a site—any site—on a daily basis is a pain. If you spend as much time as I do online, you'll find your bookmarks list a massive tangle of links, half of which you rarely use." Thacker recommends Google Reader. "Never miss another post" (Thacker 2007).

Search Tools for Blogs

Reporters can use blogs for research, though they should be wary of the caliber of material and exercise the same caution as when using a newsgroup. See chapter 7 for help in assessing information quality and veracity. Chapter 2 covers newsgroups. The potential use of blogs is limited only by a reporter's imagination. A local election looms? Search Technorati (http://www.technorati.com/) or Google's BlogSearch (http://blogsearch. google.com/) to see what the blogosphere is saying about your mayor or local officials. A big game approaches for your local sporting team? Do a similar search to see what is available about the team's star players or manager. Considering a story about your local school? Assess what the blogs say about the principal or teachers. Doing a profile of a business? Search for blogs about the business or the managers.

Technorati.com is one of the leading sites for tracking the blogosphere. It tells us what bloggers consider important and what ideas are attracting the most attention. It claims to report within eight minutes of a blog being published. In November 2005, Technorati was tracking 20.9 million sites and 1.7 million links. A year later the number of blogs being tracked had surged to 60 million. With it you can find out what people on the Internet are saying about you or your company or products. Founder Dave Sifry said the Internet was moving beyond the 1990s metaphor of the world's biggest library to becoming an enormous "river of conversations." "It's a place where we all participate, and the implications are really significant."

Google's BlogSearch is equally powerful. It searches all blogs, not just those published through Blogger (which Google owns). Google says its blog index is continually updated, and allows you to search for blogs written in French, Italian, German, Spanish, Korean, and Portuguese as well as English. The biggest single language group of blogs is Chinese (33 percent), followed by Japanese (25 percent). Only about 20 percent of blogs are in English.

Other tools for tracking the blogosphere include Sphere (http://www.sphere.com), Icerocket (http://www.icerocket.com), and Feedster (http://www.feedster.com). Feedster is a comprehensive tool for searching blogs. It describes itself as "the largest and richest archive of indexed feeds on the Web." How these sites arrived at their results varies and depended on how the site was built. Technorati, for example, based its results mainly on the number of hyperlinks each blog got from other blogs. Technorati is like Google in the way its algorism counts links between Web sites as virtual votes, and sees links between blogs as indicators of an author's popularity. Sifry said this cross-linking was an emerging form of "social currency." Sphere.com analyzes and gives weight to the actual words in each blog posting. It measures the length and frequency of posts to a blog, and how often the individual blogger writes about the subject being queried. To obtain the broadest amount of information on a subject, these sites should be used in conjunction with traditional search tools (discussed in chapter 5).

Other Research Tools: Wikipedia

Journalists should be aware of an online encyclopedia written by thousands of people. It works on the principle of the "hive mind" where the value of something increases in relation to the number of people who contribute to it. Have you ever tried to guess the number of jellybeans in a jar at a county fair or the weight of a prize cow? Much research has shown that the more people who guess the number of jelly beans or the cow's weight, the more accurate the final answer. Wikipedia (http://www.wikipedia.org/) works on the same principle. A wiki is a collaboratively written document published online. Someone writes a wiki entry on Wikipedia, and interested people contribute to the article, commenting on the accuracy and relevance. Over time through this peer-reviewing process, wikis are developed and refined. They are written in a Web browser, always available, and can be updated or commented on by anyone who has access to the Web site. In 2006, the BBC had about 40 wikis on its corporate intranet, about 400 people moderated or contributed to the sites, and about 150 BBC staff wrote their own blogs. Wikipedia's news offshoot, Wikinews (http://en.wikinews.org), publishes stories from a network of volunteer reporters. The caliber of information on all forms of wikis varies considerably. Journalists will need to assess the quality of information because what appears under their byline reflects their credibility. As we said in the chapter 1, credibility is something that takes a long time to develop, but a short time to destroy through ethical breaches or foolishly quoting something from a Web site that is wrong. Chapter 7 offers advice on assessing information quality.

The Yahoo site "Answers" at http://answers.yahoo.com/ is an example of using the hive mind. People post questions to the site, and others answer them. It becomes a moot point as to whether journalists would use content from sites such as Wikipedia or Yahoo's Answers, given questions of credibility and accuracy. These issues are discussed briefly at the end of this chapter and in more detail in chapter 7. One of the reasons that journalists should become involved in blogging is because they are trained to write clearly, act ethically, and are willing to check their facts. This is what distinguishes them from untrained bloggers. Sometimes reporters use their own blog to pose questions to readers, start discussions, or ask for help finding information or sources. The key here is moderation: Reporters should be using up shoe leather talking to their sources and digging for new stories rather than sitting behind a computer all day. They need to balance the time they spend with technology and the time they spend with people.

Profile of a Blogger Turned Columnist

Journalist Ana Marie Cox wrote the gossipy blog Wonkette.com from her Washington home for its first two years before becoming a columnist for *Time* magazine in July 2006. Before then she worked as an editor for online start-ups. Cox said she added content to Wonkette up to 12 times a day. "It starts getting hard pretty quickly. That was in my contract. If you're getting paid to blog, there are certain demands and limitations ... so, 12 posts a day," she told *New York Times* technology writer David Pogue. He put the transcript of his interview with her on the nytimes.com Web site. Cox described blogging as a medium rather than a technology. "It has a very low bar to entry. But the reason why anyone does it, I think, has to do with having an opinion you believe is worth other people hearing, and having something to say ... And I think that's why people get into journalism." Cox said that even when she wrote about things that were controversial, she aimed to make people realize that they should bring skepticism to these kinds of rumors. What are the ingredients for a successful blog? Cox said blogs needed a strong, defined personality with a sense of humor about themselves. "An ability to filter news quickly and to recognize what is interesting to other people. Cox said people had become addicted to rapid updating. "It's almost physically impossible for one person to do that. And so I think that we're probably going to see that the individual, strong-personality blog is not going to be at the forefront, because group blogs are going to be able to do what people expect of blogs better."

Will blogs kill newspapers, Pogue asked. "*The New York Times* will never cease to exist.... But *The New York Times* is going to have to change... all major media are going to have to change to meet the demands of people who have grown used to some of the things they get from blogs.... But, what's kind of neat or inspiring about the blogosphere is that it's very American. The idea that someone could enter into a conversation, based just on having an opinion and an argument. And it's a conversation that includes people who have real power in the world. I mean, that idea is very seductive."

User-Generated Content and Citizen Journalism

Many news organizations invite their audiences to contribute content. A variety of phrases have been coined to describe this concept. Some of the best known include user- or audience-generated content, and participatory or citizen journalism. Regardless of the words used to describe it, the process allows news organizations to harness the creative spirit of these new media forms to produce better journalism. As with blogs, it was a major news event that highlighted the potential of user-generated content. The July 2005 bombings of a bus and underground Tube in London was the catalyst for the acceptance of images and stories from the scenes of the carnage. Helen Boaden, the BBC's director of news, said within an hour of the first blast her London newsrooms received 50 e-mails with pictures and video clips attached. The *UK Press Gazette* reported that the first published image of the bombings appeared on a moblog site. About 3,000 mobloggers posted still and video images to a site called Moblog UK in the days after the bombings. Alfie Dennen, co-founder of the site, said it was the first time moblogging had played a significant part in a breaking news story in the UK. Photographs by amateurs with mobile phones and digital cameras provided the bulk of the pictorial coverage of the bombings. The day after the bombings, the front-page photograph in *The Sun,* the highest-circulating UK daily, came from an eyewitness. A Japanese tourist took the front-page image in the rival tabloid, *The Daily Mirror*. The media weekly *UK Press Gazette* reported that cell phone images taken by survivors on the Underground "were widely used by broadcasters and the national press" (Ponsford 2005b: 19).

Guardian Media reporter Julia Day said the long-predicted democratization of the media had "become a reality" as members of the public turned photographers and reporters. "Claustrophobic videos shot in smoke-filled, bombed-out London underground carriages, photographs of the blasted number 30 bus and horrific scenes of body-strewn roads were among the most powerful images to emerge. All were shot by members of the public, and some of them became the iconic pictures of the day" (Day 2005: 2). John Ryley, executive editor of Sky News in London, said cell phones had produced a "democratization of news." His studio received video, e-mailed by mobile phone, of the bombed Tube at 12:40 p.m. and had it on air by 1 p.m. "News crews usually get there just after the event, but these pictures show us the event as it happens" (Ryley quoted in Day 2005: 2).

Coverage of the December 26, 2004, southeast Asian tsunami and its aftermath was another big story that showed the value of user-generated content. News Interactive, the online arm of the BBC, received 25,000 e-mails in the first week after the tsunami disaster, and nearly two million people looked at the BBC Web site established to help locate missing people. Vicky Taylor, editor of interactivity for News Interactive, said many BBC programs and Web sites used these Web-based bulletin boards to find people to interview, write stories about survivors, and provide updates on searches. "Here was a great opportunity within News to share content sent from our users, viewers, and listeners more effectively, and for it to become a newsgathering base for programs," Taylor said. The BBC's reaction was to establish a "user-generated content" (UGC) desk. It funded a pilot study for three months, employing three journalists to manage content contributed by audiences. By mid-July 2005, the UGC team was receiving 10,000 e-mails, text messages, and video contributions a day. The UGC team subsequently expanded to eight journalists, with staff from each of the main bulletins. "Already the benefits are being seen on screen and heard on air," Taylor said (Taylor 2005: 12).

Hits on the BBC's Web site boomed during and after the tsunami, and even more so after the London bombings. The Web sites of the BBC, Sky News, and *The Guardian* reported significant increases in the number of people going to their sites. On July 8, Guardian Unlimited said 1.3 million people accessed almost 8 million pages, the most on any one day since the site launched almost a decade earlier. (On a typical day, Guardian Unlimited gets 3.5 to 4 million page views.) The same day, the BBC News Web site accounted for almost 29 percent of all Internet news traffic in Britain. The next nearest organization attracted less than 5 percent. BBC TV also rated well. Almost 7 million people watched the extended 6 p.m. bulletin, more than double the 3.3 million who usually watched at that time (Plunkett 2005: 3).

Bloggers in the Timescale of History

Newspapers in the eighteenth century were mostly one-man operations (very few women were journalists), often with links to political parties. The editor was also compositor, printer, publisher, and reporter. The term journalist comes from the Old French word "journal" in the sense of appearing daily (*jour* is the French noun for day). The term originally applied to reportage of current events in printed form, specifically newspapers, but in the twentieth century it came to include electronic media as well. The separation of the roles of reporter and editor began in the 1820s and evolved with the development of the penny press in the 1830s. This and the next decade saw the start of a shift to news about everyday life as reporters covered the seamy side of life: crime, divorce, slum life, and other social problems. During the American Civil War, which started in 1861, reporters provided eyewitness accounts of battles and interviewed generals. In the mid-nineteenth century, the great British writer Matthew Arnold concluded that journalism had the power to "stir people to action" because it makes ideas accessible via newspapers. We could argue that with the arrival of blogging we are seeing a return to the eighteenth-century notion of the one-person operation. A blog is a publishing medium. Blog writers add the ideas. Blogging, then, is the latest evolution of the market place of ideas. The big question is whether blogging is journalism. According to the U.S. Supreme Court it is not. In March 2005, a judge ruled in a case involving Apple Computer and several bloggers who wrote rumors about the company. The judge said the blogs were not entitled to protection in terms of preserving the anonymity of sources because the blogs were not journalism.

Chapter 4 considers the spread of UGC and what has become known as citizen or participatory journalism.

Suggested Reading

The BBC has an excellent collection of articles defining RSS and explaining blogs and related topics. See http://news.bbc.co.uk/2/hi/help/3223484.stm

Read about the BBC's vodcast trials at http://www.bbc.co.uk/newspodcasts.

The editors' weblog from the editors' group of the World Association of Newspapers at http://www.editorsweblog.org contains discussion on whether bloggers are journalists. This site is worth monitoring weekly.

Read a profile of blogging pioneer Jorn Barger at http://web.archive.org/web/20000510161001/www.feedmag.com/feature/cx329.shtml

A full list of feed readers is at http://www.newsonfeeds.com/faq/aggregators.

An overview of new media by Andreas Kluth is published in *The Economist* of 22 April 2006.

References

Curley, Tom (2004). Personal observation at keynote address to Online News Association's annual conference, Los Angeles, 12 November 2004.

Day, Julia (2005). "Citizen reporters" in *Media Guardian* cover story "We are All Reporters Now," 11 July 2005, p. 2.

Kesmodel, David (2005). "Papers turn to 'podcasting' in bid to draw more readers" in *The Wall Street Journal*, 13 May 2005, C1.

Lenhart, Amanda, Madden, Mary. and Hitlin, Paul (2005). "Teens and Technology: Youth are Leading the Transition to a Fully Wired and Mobile World" published 27 July 2005 by the Pew Internet and American Life project. Online at http://www.pewinternet.org.

Lenhart, Amanda and Fox, Susannah (2006). "Bloggers: A Portrait of the Internet's New Storytellers" published 19 July 2006 by the Pew Internet & American Life project.

McNair-Ingenuity Research (2006). "The Future of Media Report" Sydney July 2006.

Plunkett, John (2005). "The Day in Numbers" in *Media Guardian* cover story "We are All Reporters Now," 11 July 2005, p. 3.

Ponsford, Dominic (2005a). "Hear All About It as the *Telegraph* Launches Podcast" in *UK Press Gazette*, 18 November 2005, 5.

Ponsford, Dominic (2005b). "On-the-spot Public Captures the Bomb Terror" in *UK Press Gazette*, 15 July 2005, 19.

Taylor, Vicky (2005). "Vox Pop" in *BBC News Update*, July/August 2005, 12.

Thacker, Todd (2007). E-mail communication, 15 January 2007.

4

Citizen Journalism and
Audience-Generated Content

The first issue we need to discuss is a defintion of the terms that start this chapter. Citizen journalism is a broad term whose meaning is still shifting. We will be quite specific. It occurs in two forms. The first is when members of the public, who are not professional journalists, contribute content that is published on traditional media. This form of citizen journalism reflects one of the basic rules of media known as media-morphosis. New media do not replace old media. Traditional media change to absorb the best of new media (Fidler 1997). This form of citizen journalism includes things like publication of photographs or video taken by amateurs who happened to be at the right place at the right time, such as the London bombings in July 2005. It could also include comment and opinion by a blogger that later appears on a mainstream media news site. Or it could occur when people offer first-hand accounts of events they were involved in, such as the tsunamis on December 26, 2004. Most of the time these people are not paid for their contribution. Citizen journalism in this context is nearly always contextualized, edited, and proofread by professional journalists. The other term used for citizen reporting is "participatory" journalism, but this book will stick with citizen for consistency.

OhmyNews is one of the pioneers of this form of citizen journalism. The site had more than 50,000 citizen reporters as of March 2007, but professional editors still screened the content submitted. Jean Min of OhmyNews International said every story went through an extensive screening and copyediting process before it was published. Citizen reporters "find their stories more polished after proofreading and editorial retouching by professionals." Editors at OhmyNews spent time educating aspiring citizen journalists. "We regularly invite them to our newsroom and give them 'Journalism 101' classes" (personal communication 2007). OhmyNews editors reject about 3 out of 10 contributions each day because of poor writing, factual errors, or lack of news value (Min 2005: 17; Min 2007).

Sometimes good quality blog content appears in mainstream media. The key word is quality. UK journalist Jemima Kiss concedes that the "cream" of bloggers will be experts in their field. "Blogs are often an extension of people's jobs or their passions" (Kiss 2005). It is logical that traditional media should seek out their skills. Indeed, by early 2007, major media organizations like the BBC and CNN were actively soliciting contributions from their audiences. But ultimately professionals will filter the content that appears on mainstream media. Traditional gatekeepers have important skills such as news sense and an understanding of the audience. Min of OhmyNews concurs: "We believe bloggers can work better with professional assistance from trained journalists. On the other hand, we also believe professional journalists can expand their view and scope greatly with fresh input from citizen reporters. News media as a whole can offer more diverse and rich content to readers by tapping into the wealth of Netizens' collective wisdom" (Min 2007).

The second form of citizen journalism occurs when members of the public produce blogs or community Web sites or publications for a specific purpose. In other words, citizens assume the role of journalists. This situation necessitates a debate about who is a journalist. Will citizen journalism mean the end of journalism as we have known it? The answers need to be the topic of another book, but are discussed in a breakout later in the Who is a Journalist section (p. 52) in this chapter. Small citizen journalism sites succeed because they are easy and cheap to set up. The biggest costs are for Internet access and the servers for hosting content, though some groups rent server space. Salaries are often not an issue because people volunteer their time. This means these bloggers do not have the commercial pressure of mainstream media. But most citizens and bloggers do not want to be journalists. Most do not have the time, skill, or energy. But they do want to be heard and respected.

Citizen journalism has arisen in environments where audiences felt neglected by mainstream media. This was certainly the case in South Korea. Many citizens believed the conservative South Korean media ignored them. Notes Min: "They were angry because the mainstream media constantly manipulated the nation's important agenda in politics, the economy, and society for their own taste and purpose. ...Many young Koreans found it made more sense to write for a news media with a strong national brand and formidable presence in the news market than scribble their anger in a puny blog" (Min 2007). We need to introduce a key distinction between citizen journalism and blogging. Citizen journalism focuses on journalism. Blogging is a form of publishing and is often more about expressing opinions. Citizen journalism involves reporting, but not all blogging is journalism. The Pew Internet & American Life Report in July 2006 noted that two-thirds of bloggers (66 percent) did not consider their output a form of journalism (Pew 2006: 4).

Late in 2006, Ben Hammersley became the first multimedia foreign correspondent at *The Guardian*. Before taking this job, he helped set up more than 20 blogs for the paper. "Blogging is not journalism. Blogging can be journalistic. Bloggers can report, analyze, interpret, investigate and explain; blogs can contain journalism, but blogging isn't of itself journalism. Of course, here I'm using 'journalism' to denote the finer aims and traditions of our profession" (Hammersley 2006).

Technologies such as easy-to-use and free blog and podcast software make citizen journalism possible. Shayne Bowman and Chris Willis wrote the important report *We Media: How Audiences are Shaping the Future of News and Information*. They conclude that people are interested in participating and contributing to subjects that traditional media ignore or cover inadequately (Bowman and Willis 2005: 7). The key issue with the second form is sustainability. How can citizen journalism sites find the resources to continue? The first form of citizen journalism is likely to continue because traditional media need quality content, and in many cases they are not paying for it. As of early 2007, the vast majority of user-generated content was not paid for. The second form requires energy and passion to sustain itself, and a form of revenue or business model. Most people lack the time, discipline, or skill to sustain blogs and podcasts beyond an initial period of enthusiasm. Arash Amel, a senior analyst for the media analysis company *Screen Digest*, said no user-generated video site, not even the large ones such as MySpace, has yet to find a reliable source of revenue. "The business model for user-generated sites has been 'build it and sell it and let someone else worry about the business model'." News Corp admitted early in 2007 that its Fox movie studio and television content would be more important than homemade clips for capturing online video advertising. *Screen Digest* expects this market to expand from $1.1 billion in 2006 to $6.2 billion by 2010 (Edgecliffe-Johnson and van Duyn 2007).

Other factors explain the popularity of audience-generated content. While relatively cheap and available consumer technology makes it possible, the main driver is the audience's desire for inclusion, expression, and collaboration. Jim Chisholm, joint principal of the iMedia consulting service, believes audience-generated content is a sign that audiences want to be included. "Our readers want to be noticed, they want to influence, and they want change and to effect it." Chisholm believes the need for good journalism is more important than ever to deal with this "determined cacophany" of voices. "Newsdesks must adapt to, encourge and accept the willing participation of their readers and reporters." All journalists must recognize that communication is a two-way street because "the need to listen is greater than ever before" (Chisholm 2006: 22). Bowman and Willis see collaboration as the driving force behind the "explosion of citizen media" as passionate and motivated people produce new forms of media. "The democratization of media has leveled the competitive landscape and forced dramatic changes in the news business" (Bowman and Willis 2005: 7). They reject the notion that citizen journalism means the end of news media companies or journalism. They see it more as a shift in the area where value is being created. "In the traditional broadcast model, value was created solely by the newspaper or TV station. In the future more of the value will come from creating an infrastructure for citizen participation and nurturing trusted communities." (Bowman and Willis 2005: 9) Some media companies have been more active than others in setting up the infrastructure needed to nurture communities. In Australia, John Fairfax Ltd changed its name to Fairfax Media in 2006 to reflect its move from being a newspaper company to becoming a multimedia group. Fairfax Media established the position of online community editor for each of the its broadsheet flagships in Sydney and Melbourne.

Media commentator Mark Glaser said one of the greatest by-products of citizen journalism was a sense of civic involvement for people who had felt shut out of their own local politics and media. These sites provided "a place for nonprofits and civic organizations to boost community activism" (Glaser 2004). Humans crave community, the sense of belonging that comes from associating with others. Online phenomena such as blogs and podcasting allow people to create and belong to communities of interest around the world. Sociologist Dr. Elizabeth Eddy at the University of the Sunshine Coast in Australia said people most valued communities that provided a sense of purpose and belonging. "These may have a geographical basis such as a neighborhood. They may also involve formal or informal groupings based on hobbies or sports or political affiliations. Communities are maintained via a variety of means, ranging from direct interaction with others through to the Internet" (Eddy 2005).

Wright Bryan, a producer with America's National Public Radio Web site, said blogs represented freedom to writers, offering them a new frontier. "At its best, a blog is a form of personal journalism that opens the public up to a whole new role in the news business. People use it to experiment with form, content, and language. It is the antithesis of a large news organization" (Bryan 2005). Another sociologist at the University of the Sunshine Coast, Dr. Phillip Ablett, agreed that the public was turning to the Internet in response to what they saw as an impoverished and corporate-dominated public sphere. "Nowhere is this more evident than in the creation of Internet sub-cultures or communities and their use of evolving media technologies." The key feature was multiplicity and diversity, Dr. Ablett said. "Some groups are spiritual or cultural, some are 'retreatist' and inward looking, some are faddish and ephemeral, while others are totally reactionary. But they are all arguably evidence of a massive disaffection with the dominant system of corporate media where the flow of information is almost entirely unilateral" (Ablett 2005).

Both forms of citizen journalism described earlier involve the idea of user-generated content where audiences contribute content to traditional media. But it is an ungainly phrase. While in many respects user-generated content is the same as citizen journalism, and the terms get used interchangably, we will mostly stick to the phrase citizen journalism for consistency. Examples of traditional media that have embraced their audiences can be found around the world. In Austria, one of the pioneers is the online edition of *Kleine Zeitung*. Barbara Ebner has been marketing director of *Kleine Zeitung* online (www.kleinezeitung.at) since 2000. The site receives 1.5 million visitors a month. "KZ tries to reach its readers through various platforms and in all sitations of life." Ebner described audience-generated content as a form of reverse publishing. "It's not only about consuming content, but it's also about social currency. News becomes something to talk about at work and home. We give our contributors their 15 minutes of fame." Min of OhmyNews agreed: "People like to develop a reputation. They also want the approval of their peers. That is one of the most precious rewards you can expect on the Web" (Min 2007).

Ebner said mobile and online were the best way to source audience-generated content and print was the ideal medium to play that content back to audiences. Ebner said newspapers had a long tradition of attracting audience-generated content via readers' letters. "What is new are the easier forums to allow audiences to interact such as votes via SMS, online opinion polls, and inviting photographs. The newspaper started a major marketing campaign to tell audiences it wanted their content and used a big red exclamation mark as an icon. Part of the campaign involved an explanation about audience-generated content using print and online. It included a comic strip format to teach people how to moblog. "It must be a hybrid of print and online," she said. "We must do it together because modern media are more and more about multimedia." The paper decided not to pay or give financial rewards for audience-generated content, "though we give the occasional video camera for best photo." That content was marked with the same red icon thoughout the print and online editions. From July to August 2006, readers had contributed four major front-page photographs for the newspaper, and the company awarded a prize for the best summer photo. Just over 6,500 photographs were submitted over 4 weeks and the online site received 80,000 extra page impressions. "Publishing of audience-generated photographs shows our audiences that we appreciate them," Ebner said (personal observation 2006).

Richard Sambrook, director of the BBC's Global News division, said digital technology was fundamentally changing the corporation's relationship with its audiences. It was creating a realignment of that relationship. "I believe that truth, accuracy, impartiality and diversity of opinion are strengthened by being open to a wider range of opinion and perspective, brought to us through the knowledge and understanding of our audience." This meant the journalists' role was to concentrate on how, when, and where to add value through the BBC's strengths of analysis, context, background, and range. "But as we do this we must be open to what members of the public bring to our attention" (Sambrook 2005: 14–15).

The BBC has invested heavily in encouraging its audiences to contribute content through projects such as "Digital Storytelling," which takes the tools of digital media production into communities across the UK, and the BBC's "Action Network," which helps people become more involved in their community. Paul Brannan, deputy editor of the BBC News Web site, said audiences had become a key component of the BBC's daily newsgathering. "Not a day goes by without us actively seeking the public's help in our storytelling." At the same time, audiences daily offer material without being asked. "We're getting pictures, videos, eye-witness accounts, case studies, fresh ideas, angles, sidebars, tip-offs and expert insight." Brannan said the "umbilical cord" between the BBC and its audience was stronger and more instant because of this approach. "And all the incoming material is shared around our organization for use in multiple platforms and outlets." Brannan said one news Web site reader returning to Heathrow airport late in 2006 saw hundreds of pieces of unclaimed baggage after flight disruptions some days earlier and little apparent effort being made to deal with the problem. The story featured in all BBC bulletins and was picked up by several newspapers the next day.

The BBC News Web site's first major story to benefit from audience-generated content was the tsunami that devastated Thailand and southeast Asia in 2004. "But it was the July 7, 2005, London bombings that were a defining moment for the wider BBC. Out of the information chaos and gridlock in the capital the audience came up trumps," Brannan said. Sambrook said that within 6 hours of the blasts, the BBC had received more than 1000 photographs, 20 pieces of amateur video, and 20,000 e-mails. By the next day, the main evening television news bulletin began with a package edited entirely from video sent by viewers (Sambrook 2005: 12). Said Brannan: "The public supplied pictures we couldn't get, including camera-phone shots by a passenger evacuated from one of the bombed trains, shaky video of street scenes and compelling tales of horror and heroism as events unfolded around them." The availability of cheap and compact technology had driven this change. "The ability to capture content and to pass it on in an instant changes the established relationship between publisher/broadcaster and audience." Part of the change required mainstream media to be more transparent about how they conducted themselves (Brannan 2007). It may also necessitate more jobs for journalists as editors, checking the content supplied by audiences.

At *Verdens Gang* (VG) in Norway, the paper provides reporters and citizen reporters with Nokia N70 phones that enable people to record and transmit still and moving images and audio. During the war in Lebanon in 2006, a Norwegian citizen reporter living in Beirut e-mailed video of a bomb flying over the city. Editor Espen Egil Hansen said the video was available on VG's Web site within 10 minutes of arriving, rather than audiences having to wait until that evening's main TV news bulletin. VG has been proactive when it comes to citizen reporting. It set up a site after the tsunami in 2004 so Norwegians trapped in Asian countries could contact their families. The site still existed in late 2006 and was receiving hundreds of messages, images, and comments a day from readers. Indeed, major news events have tended to stimulate the levels of citizen journalism and user-generated content. The 2004 tsunami was a landmark in journalism's history, because it was the first major story in which citizens around the world contributed to a news Web site.

Coverage of the London bombings on July 7, 2005, marked a watershed in the history of British journalism. It was a landmark for the emergence of citizen journalism in the UK, just as the Mumbai train bombings a year later announced its arrival in India. We could subsequently argue that a new news cycle has emerged. Until the arrival of radio in the 1920s, newspapers and news agencies, their loyal servants, had a monopoly on the announcement of news. Their only competition was word-of-mouth. Radio remained the place where news broke until well after television broadcasting resumed at the end of World War II. Television journalists later embraced the live broadcast and dominated breaking news, especially after the spread of 24-hour news channels. It is debatable when people first started turning to the Internet for breaking news. We would argue that big stories in 2005 and 2006 such as the London and Mumbai transport bombings and the disasters in New Orleans have seen the Internet displace broadcasters as the place people go when they want to learn about breaking news. This situation is especially relevant during office hours in developed nations where people do not have access to television. In less-developed countries, breaking news is more likely to be delivered via a mobile phone.

Sustainable Forms of Blogging

The most sustainable type of citizen media, especially in terms of the second form described earlier, will be visual—still and moving images. It is relatively easy to snap photographs with mobile phones and post them to blog sites, especially given the fact that the bulk of mobile phones produced in 2006 and 2007 have a camera. Taking average quality photographs does not require much skill, and technologies like PhotoShop and FinalCut Pro can redeem poor quality still or video images, respectively. Podcasting is similarly easy to establish and maintain. One could argue that unscripted conversations are similar to images in the way they avoid the need for crafted writing. Crafting a good quality article or script requires skill. It takes a lot of effort to create a clear sentence. Good writing requires effort, time, and discipline. Most people do not have those skills. Ultimately, society needs wordsmiths like journalists to write precise content and editors to process the vast amounts of poor quality content in the world. The job of both is to put events into context and make information accessible and manageable to various audiences.

This is why the first form of citizen journalism, the kind that OhmyNews produces, will last longer than most blogs. At the same time, we expect that the second form of citizen journalism that involves images ahead of text will also endure. Google appreciates this point because the company paid $1.65 billion for YouTube in 2006, News Corp shelled out $580 million for the company that owned MySpace, and Yahoo bought Flickr for $30 million. The amateur stories that circulate most widely on the Internet tend to be driven by visuals. An extreme version was the 2005 video of the alleged tagging of the U. S. president's jet. The video attracted more than 80 milllion downloads before it was revealed as a marketing exercise. A similar situation arose late in 2006 when a bystander with a camera phone videoed UCLA campus police using an electric stun gun on a student. Images spread quickly on YouTube and other online sites, as did images of the hanging of Saddam Hussein, taken with a mobile phone, early in 2007. *The Daily Telegraph* in the UK reported that all three major Republican candidates for the upcoming U. S. presidential race had been embarrassed by clips on YouTube. Rudy Giuliani was caught on video expressing support for public funding for abortions for poor women. Today he claims to be against abortion. You can read about it at http://www.telegraph.co.uk/news/main.jhtml?xml =/news/2007/03/14/wtube14.xml.

Blogs for Research

Too many blogs and podcasts are little more than "egocasting" (Rosen 2005) or a form of publication driven by emotion or a desire to showcase one's passions. But we should not forget the vast amount of expertise available to the media in the form of an educated public. Review the section in chapter 3 about Wikipedia and the notion of the "hive mind." Bowman and Willis wisely point out that smart news organizations will find ways to harness the energy of their audiences. They will "discover the right mix of community, comment, commerce and tools" and "leverage the power of the many" so that ultimately mainsteam media "will more tightly integrate citizen content with the core news offerings." Blogs are fine places to go to find people for case studies in feature stories. Aspiring journalists should be aware that editors read blogs when they are searching for new talent. Nick Turner, deputy editor of the *News & Star* in Cumberland in England, employed a dozen bloggers in 2005. They included journalism students, housewives, and people from Cumberland living in the United States.

Never underestimate the global reach of blogs. Traditional media and citizen journalism can happily coexist because one can argue they need each other. Citizen reporters extend the reach of mainstream media, and traditional media give citizen reporters a place where their reporting can be assembled in one place, so audiences have a place to go to find reliable news. Nicholas Lemann, dean of the Columbia University Graduate School of Journalism, writes about the media for *New Yorker* magazine. He believes the two forms of media need each other. "What I haven't seen citizen journalism do yet is provide an ongoing, regular report that

monitors the activities of government business and so on." The key word is ongoing. Lemann sees citizen journalism as a "wonderful add-on" to traditional media
that helps to correct the "flaws in the conversation." But traditional media conduct
the conversation and set the agenda. Lemann points out that audiences do not
have time to read the vast amount of news in the world. Eventually trusted brands
establish themselves as "the folks you can go to because they understand how you
think and give you the kind of news they know you'll be interested in" (Lemann
2007). The authors believe that some of the trusted sources will be blogs, but the
likely long-term winner will be traditional media combined with audience-contrib-
uted content.

Bowman and Willis predict that some media will start to pay for the best citizen
content although they do not suggest a year (Bowman and Willis 2005: 8). See the
section below on OhmyNews elsewhere in this chapter for an example of a successful news organization in South Korea that has embraced its citizens and that pays
for contributions.

OhmyNews

OhmyNews in South Korea pioneered the concept of participatory journalism in
2002. As of March 2007, the Web site had more than 55,000 citizen reporters who
posted up to 200 news articles a day. OhmyNews is the brainchild of Oh Yeon-ho.
During his graduate study at Regent University, one of Oh's professors asked the
class to plan an imaginary new media start-up. He drafted a detailed plan of an
online news medium, with the business model based on the idea that "every citizen is a reporter." After returning to Korea in 1997, he located some investors and
quit his job as a reporter with the weekly magazine *Mahl*. OhmyNews launched
in February 2000. Oh's philosophy of "every citizen can be a reporter" continues.
"Journalists aren't some exotic species, they're everyone who seeks to take new
developments, put them into writing, and share them with others." OhmyNews
does not regard straight news articles as the standard. Articles that include both
facts and opinions are acceptable "when they are good." In 2006, OhmyNews added
English-language pages to its site. Jean Min, director of OhmyNews International,
said the site had 12 copy editors and planned to hire more to cope with the growing
load. "We have a clear editorial policy, which is 'open progressivism.' Copy editors
will sift stories according to their news value [and] story construction," Min said.
"If a story does not live up to a certain quality even if it fits into our editorial
principle, we still reject them or ask citizen reporters to rewrite them." Mainstream
media in South Korea have embraced many of the features of citizen journalism
that OhmyNews introduced. For example, *Chosun Ilbo*, one of the leading conservative dailies, allows readers to leave comments at the bottom of every article on its
online site. Daum, Korea's second-largest portal, is encouraging "blogger reporters"

to submit news to its dedicated news site Media Daum. And SBS, one of the three main Korean TV broadcasters, accepts video news reports from what it calls "u-porters," or citizens with portable video cameras (Min 2007).

Who is a Journalist?

Citizen media challenges the notion of who is a journalist, and generates endless debate on this subject. Alan Kohler is Australia's best known and most accomplished multmedia journalist. He believes the term blog is a meaningless generalization. Many blogs consist of people's online diary entries. Some blogs are content produced by journalists and must be regarded as journalism. "If the distinction between these two breaks down then journalism as a profession is doomed. We have to re-define what journalism is. It's a challenge for journalists to do that, because up to now a journalist was somebody who works for a newspaper or broadcaster and who produces content for them." Until blogs arrived, Kohler said, the market tended to define journalism. "There were a certain number of jobs and if you got one of those [jobs] you were a journalist. If you did not get the job you were not a journalist. It was pretty simple." But the Internet had no barrier to entry so anyone could effectively be a journalist. The profession needed a definition. "It's not like medicine or law where you need a degree and a license to practice. You don't need a qualification to be a journalist. So if you don't need a qualification and you don't need a job with a media organization to be a journalist, what do you need? What is journalism?" Resolution of that question has only just begun, Kohler said. Many people were doing things online that were not journalism but which could be mistaken for journalism. Do we have to broaden our definition of what is journalism to encompass blogs (Kohler 2006)?

The Guardian's Hammersley believes professional journalism is being challenged by dedicated amateurs or freelancers working on their own Web sites. "This is going to shake out quite simply: the best reporters will thrive, no matter where they are, but the worst, and especially the worst professional generalist reporters, will be under a lot of pressure if they want to continue to be paid." Journalists who wanted to make a good living would need to specialize, and to a level of expertise not before seen. "Big Media is always going to exist, because there's an awful lot of added value in editing and commissioning and the putting together of good packages." But traditional media needed to give less emphasis to reporting that was done elsewhere for free. Reviews, for example, were increasingly pointless, he said. "So one side of citizen journalism—the amateur doing local reporting, or specialist reporting for free—will shake itself out. The good ones will start to make money, the bad ones will stop, and the fact you work for a newspaper doesn't shield you from this" (Hammersley 2006).

Mark Jurkowitz is associate director of the Project for Excellence in Journalism based in Washington. He believes that gatekeepers will always be needed to help busy people deal with the flood of information. "Editors are going to play that role." Journalism skills will continue to be needed. "Reporting skills, writing skills, editing skills in any media environment are going to continue to exist." He predicts that citizen journalism will become more professionalized, which will see "some of the traditional forms of newsroom guidance" imposed on new media. "The idea of journalism isn't going to go away; the source of it will change in some ways" (Jurkowitz 2007).

Concerns and Issues Related to Citizen Journalism

The spread of citizen journalism has raised several concerns. Probably the biggest issue in relation to citizen journalism is gaining the trust of audiences and maintaining credibility. Rob Malda founded the "open source journalism" site Slashdot. Trust was something earned over many years, Malda said, because it took time for a site to build the critical mass of a community that could police itself. "No filtering system should be exempt from scrutiny. People forget that network news is a filtering system too.... Our moderation system is really no different fundamentally. We've just lowered the bar for participation on every level. The lowered bar might mean that more individuals make errors, but on a whole [we have to believe] the community will act right" (quoted in Glaser 2004). Journalist and blogger Jemima Kiss suggested that the public's lack of trust of traditional media plus the hierarchical, one-way structure of mainstream news organizations was another reason citizen media was flourishing (Kiss 2004).

Some journalists' unions have expressed concern about the potential loss of work for freelance reporters when newspapers and their online sites invite citizen reporters to contribute. *Guardian* managing editor Chris Elliott told the *UK Press Gazette* in November 2005 that his paper did not pay for reader contributions. The National Union of Journalists in the UK complained about the paper accepting reader contributions to the Web site but later publishing a selection in the print edition. As with many things in life, the market will probably decide. Hammersley believes that bloggers who cannot maintain quality will fail. "The thing is, should a blog fail there's little to no loss. Should a newspaper fail, or even just a section of one, the loss is huge. So bloggers are very free to fail, in a way that big media just isn't at the moment" (Hammersley 2006).

The answer to this issue and the future of blogging and journalism could be provided by the example of a parallel situation with the suppliers of stock photographs. It is part of a phenomenon known as "crowdsourcing." A site called iStockphoto created a market for the work of amateur photographers and as of early 2007, it had assembled the work of about 22,000 contributors, charging between

$1 and $5 for each image. Professional photographers who sell stock photographs cannot compete because the service they offer is no longer scarce, and publishers are no longer willing to pay what professionals charge for their images. Professional quality cameras cost well under $1000. With a computer and PhotoShop, amateurs can create acceptable photographs (Howe 2006). Internet sites like iStockphoto (http://www.istockphoto.com/) combined with database technology make the marketing of images easy. It is the same situation with citizen journalism. Hammersley noted that the Internet meant it was trivially easy for anyone to publish on the Web. As a consequence, professional journalism was challenged by dedicated amateurs or freelancers. "The worst professional generalist reporters will be under a lot of pressure" (Hammersley 2006). Journalists will need to differentiate themselves from bloggers, the reporting equivalent of the suppliers of stock photographs. The best way to do that is through improved quality, the product of specialization and higher levels of expertise, probably gained through higher educational qualifications.

Legal Issues and Audience-Generated Content

If a news organization uses content written by non-journalists, those organizations face potential legal problems. To counter these issues, a news organization has three options: to use journalists to check the content before it is published; to trust the audience and publish unedited; or to find some technology to monitor content, such as identifying and deleting specific key words. The first requires a large number of staff, the second may be perceived as rashness, and the third does not always work because technology does not think but merely reacts. For example, if you ban the word "sex," you ban references to the UK county of Middlesex. Some combination of the three is more likely to work. Some news organizations have adopted innovative approaches. OhmyNews in South Korea requires all citizen reporters to sign a legal document before they start reporting, absolving the site of any consequences if legal problems arise and promising to follow a code of ethics. OhmyNews citizen reporters are forbidden from using a fake identity. The company verifies identities through a government-sponsored authentication process before it grants citizen journalist membership. "OhmyNews puts great importance on the accuracy and credibility of stories. We have trained internal editors who screen, fact check and edit the stories submitted by citizen reporters," Min said. As many as 30 percent of the submissions are rejected for various reasons. These include poor sentence construction, factual errors, or their lack of news value.

Stories that contain claims that potentially damage newsmakers' reputations get more thorough fact checks. Sometimes this entails on-site visits. "We also retain the right to revoke membership of any citizen reporter who is found to have violated the agreement and code of ethics they signed on when they joined

OhmyNews." The site has a committee composed of citizen reporters and other outside watchers. They monitor the OhmyNews main page each day and submit a monthly ombudsman report, which is published on OhmyNews. In the five years since OhmyNews launched in February 2002, the site had only been involved in five legal disputes. "Thanks to the internal screening and editing process, we were able to preserve our credibility as a news media, all without alienating ordinary amateur citizen reporters" (Min 2007).

When Backfence.com, a hyperlocal citizen journalism effort, launched its first two communities in the prosperous areas of Reston and McLean, Virginia, the site asked contributors to sign a "community agreement." Among other things, contributors must confirm that they are the owner of the content, and the content is accurate. Several American newspaper sites do the same. *The Seattle Times* in Washington requires all readers who respond to blogs to identify themselves by their real name and location. "If discussions ever get out of hand," said senior news producer Lucy Mohl, "we simply shut them down; we do not moderate." MSNBC.com, a joint venture of NBC News and Microsoft, introduced a citizen journalism page in mid-2005. Tom Brew, the site's executive editor at the time, said he was aware of the difficulty of confirming facts. "It's a real concern," he said. "We don't want people trying to pull a hoax on us." Brew said the site checked each submission for accuracy either by independent inquiry or contacting the person who sent it. Hammersley of *The Guardian* believes most comments are banal. "Quite a few are offensive, and not a small number potentially illegal. Only a very tiny number of comments left on the blogs add to the piece in question. Open comments always sink to the lowest common denominator over time. It's the combination of anonymity and instant reward that attracts the trolls." Hammersley said his view of humanity has diminished since he started paying attention to the comments: "The loudest voices and the quickest to speak are generally complete assholes. It's a sad fact, but it's why papers have a letters editor. Most of the stuff posted is either drivel or offensive or libellous."

Hammersley admitted it would be foolish to allow comments to be published unmoderated, but it was difficult and time-consuming to edit or filter them. "The only way to do comments is to have solid identity-based registration, to closely filter for certain keywords, to close entries for new comments after a short time, and to have someone post-moderate comments full-time." Hammersley said the vogue in 2006 for wanting a conversation with readers was overblown. "Most readers don't want to have a conversation with you. They want a quality paper" (Hammersley 2006). The issues of quality associated with trust can never be over emphasized.

Richard Sambrook, director of the BBC's Global News division, believes journalism must change in the era of audience-generated content. Journalists must be open to what their audiences bring to the media. Transparency about news selection and the editing process was as important as the journalism itself in retaining public trust, Sambrook said. That is a reason for publication of the BBC editors' blog, where program editors talked about the process of newsgathering and program making. Sambrook argues for a deeper and more analytical form of journalism: "The journalists' role is now to concentrate harder on how, when and where we can add value through our strengths of analysis, context, background and range." This provides an ideal link to the next chapter, which shows you how to use Internet tools to find more relevant and deeper information.

Suggested Reading

BBC editors' blog: http://www.bbc.co.uk/blogs/theeditors/.

Ludtke, Melissa (editor). "Citizen Journalism" in Nieman Reports, Winter 2005.

Project for Excellence in Journalism: Understanding news in the information age. This excellent site has a host of useful resources. See http://www.journalism.org/.

References

Ablett, Phillip (2005). Interview at Sippy Downs, Queensland, 12 November 2005.

Bowman, Shayne and Willis, Chris (2005). "The Future is Here, but do News Media Companies See It" in *Nieman Reports*, Winter 2005, 5–9.

Brannan, Paul (2007). E-mail interview 12 January 2007.

Bryan, Wright (2005). E-mail interview 11 November 2005.

Chisholm, Jim (2006). "The Age of the Reader as Reporter is Here — and We Need to be Listening" in *Asian Newspaper Focus*, September/October 2006, 22.

Ebner, Barbara (2006). Presentation to cross-media workshop at Expo conference in Amsterdam on 10 October 2006. Personal observation by Quinn.

Eddy, Elizabeth (2005). Interview at Sippy Downs, Queensland, 12 November 2005.

Edgecliffe-Johnson, Andrew and van Duyn, Aline (2007). "Online Ads 'Shun User-Generated Video'" in FT.com published 15 January 2007 at http://www.ft.com/cms/s/3494e4ce-a4ca-11db-b0ef-0000779e2340.html.

Fidler, Roger (1997). *Mediamorphosis: Understanding New Media,* Thousand Oaks, California: Pine Forge Press.

Glaser, Mark (2004). "The New Voices: Hyperlocal Citizen Media Sites Want You (to Write)!" in *Online Journalism Review* at http://ojr.org/ojr/glaser/1098833871.php [accessed 14 April 2005].

Hammersley, Ben (2006). E-mail interview October–November 2006.

Howe, Jeff (2006). "The Rise of Crowdsourcing" in *Wired* 14.06, June 2006.

Jurkowitz, Mark (2007). Transcript of "New Media Develops Rapidly" debate in NewsHour on National Public Radio, 1 January 2007. Found online at http://www.pbs.org/newshour/bb/media/jan-june07/media_01-01.html.

Kiss, Jemima (2005). "Citizen Journalism: Dealing with Dinosaurs" posted to www.journalism.co.uk on 26 July 2005.

Kohler, Alan (2006). Interviewed in Melbourne 9 November 2006.

Lemann, Nicholas (2007). Transcript of "New Media Develops Rapidly" debate in NewsHour on National Public Radio, 1 January 2007. Found online at http://www.pbs.org/news-hour/bb/media/jan-june07/media_01-01.html.

Min, Jean (2005). "Journalism as Converstation" in *Nieman Reports*, Winter 2005, 16–18.

Min, Jean (2007). E-mail interview 11 January 2007 and personal interview with Quinn, 21 March 2007, in Seoul.

Pew (2006). Internet and American Life Survey. Found online at http://www.perinternet.org/

Rosen, Christine (2005). "The Age of Egocasting" in *The New Atlantis, a Journal of Technology & Society,* number 7, Winter 2005. Found 29 November 2006 at http://www.thenewatlantis.com/archive/7/rosenprint.htm.

Sambrook, Richard (2005). "Citizen Journalism and the BBC" in *Nieman Reports*, Winter 2005, 12–15.

Skiler, Michael (2005). "Fear, Loathing and the Promise of Public Insight Journalism" in *Nieman Reports*, Winter 2005, 19–20.

Beyond Google: Finding Trustworthy Information Online

If you were searching for a needle in a haystack, where would you start and what tools would you use?

For a basic search you might use your eyes and perhaps the sense of touch—rummaging through the hay until you either saw the needle, or it pricked a finger. If you were extremely lucky and had an idea of where in the haystack the needle had been lost, you might find it relatively quickly, perhaps in a few minutes, or maybe hours. But if you had no idea where it was lost, the search could take days, months, or maybe never end.

But what if you had a powerful magnet, a metal detector, and a portable X-ray machine? The search would be more complex but your chance of success would improve dramatically. The odds would be even better if you could source a little specialist knowledge; perhaps someone who told you the needle was lost in a particular section of the stack.

Much the same can be said of searching for information online: The better your tools, and more fragments of specialist knowledge you gather, the faster and more rewarding the search will be.

Basic Searching

A basic search of the Web is simple—something millions of people do every day. It involves entering a key word, or words, into a search engine such as Google, MSN, or Yahoo! and then scanning the results to see if they provide the information you seek.

The key to success in a simple search is to select the best search engine for the job and to think carefully about the right words to search for—the better those words, the greater your chance of success. In fact, many searchers do not realize that they are searching only the text on particular pages, not any words about the page. What you must do is think about words that are likely to be *in* the text of the document(s) you seek.

And why worry about selecting a search engine? Why not just use Google? The truth is that there is much more to the Web than Google will uncover and there are better search engines for specific tasks. Among other things, Google filters its search results by default. The filter is designed for the admirable purpose of protecting children from stumbling on inappropriate material. But journalists cannot afford to allow even the smallest shred of information to be blocked. Therefore, if you are going to use Google, you need to go to the **Preferences** link on the Google search page and turn all filtering off.

Some search engines also have a locational bias, giving priority to listing results from the particular geographic areas and regions a searching computer is located in. Thus a Yahoo! or Google search from a computer based in the United States, will often return different results from a search initiated on a computer based in, say, the UK, Australia, or India. For those reasons, and others discussed later in this chapter, it is sometimes better to use a meta search engine (one that searches other search engines).

Overall, however, once you are aware of the advantages and disadvantages of particular search engines and have chosen which ones to use for a specific search, there are many advantages in using a simple search. For example:

- It might produce a good result within the first few hits
- It saves time if successful
- It tends to bring up the most popular sites first
- It will list sites that were designed to be associated with the key words you used

But there can also be serious disadvantages in simple searching. It may take hours sifting through page after page of search results to find specific information you seek, or you may never find it. So, just as employing more and better tools and using those tools as efficiently as possible would help find that needle in a haystack, a more carefully thought out approach to online searching increases the chances of a good result.

Advanced Searching

There are two approaches to advanced searching using popular search engines such as Google, Yahoo!, and MSN.

- Use a search engine's advanced options
- Use Boolean search techniques

Advanced search options are under our noses every time we go to most major search engines but, strangely, it is not always easy to see the obvious. Often the options can be found by clicking on a small hyperlink near the search bar where key words are usually entered. Clicking on the Advanced Search link opens a new page presenting a range of options from searching for particular groups of words in the format word AND word AND word, which is Google's default setting; searching for particular phrases; finding single words; and excluding selected words. Google also allows a range of other search modifications including limiting searches to particular file types and date ranges.

Yahoo! has a similar advanced search capacity but it can be harder to find. A visit to http://www.Yahoo.com revealed a basic search bar at the top of the page but no sign of an advanced search. However, if you leave the search bar empty and click on the Web Search button, a new page opens that displays a Yahoo! search page similar to that offered in a basic Google search. And just like Google, it displays a small hyperlink immediately right of the search bar, which opens an advanced search page with similar delimiters to Google's advanced search.

Most good search engines have an advanced search option of some kind, even if you do need to dig down a little from their opening page to find it. The vast majority of those advanced options are based on what is known as Boolean logic. In some instances it is quicker and easier to apply that logic directly than it is to worry about trying to find and use advanced search options. This was the case with MSN search.

Boolean logic is a form of mathematics developed by English scholar George Boole, who died in 1864 at the age of 49. Regarded by many as "the father of computer science" for his contribution to the binary logic by which computers function (Cooksey 1997: 92), Boole also left a formidable legacy known as Boolean search operators. Based on the words AND, OR, and NOT, those operators can be combined with double quotation marks " " to delimit search parameters. Most search engines use AND as their default. Placing AND between words tells a search engine to find Web pages containing each of the words listed in a keyword search. For example, asking a search engine to find the search string global AND warming AND greenhouse AND gas will return one specific batch of results based on the assumption that we want to find Web pages containing all of the words. As an alternative to using the word AND, major search engines will also accept a plus sign as a substitute just as long as the symbol is placed immediately in front of the second and subsequent key words with no spaces. Thus our term global AND warming AND greenhouse AND gas could be replaced with global +warming +greenhouse +gas to produce the same result.

But what if you are a bit vague about the information you seek and need to find a Web page containing only one of your search words? Using the Boolean operator OR you could search for global OR warming OR greenhouse OR gas. That would return a huge number of hits, but it might at least jog your memory so that you could subsequently conduct a more specific search. More specifically, OR can be particularly useful for searching for synonyms that might be associated with a search term. For example, if you are working on a story about a bacteria that survives in refrigerators, you could increase the chance of a successful result by using a search string such as bacteria AND freeze OR ice. That would tell the search engine to find documents containing the word bacteria plus the word freeze or, alternatively, the word bacteria and the word ice.

At the other extreme, you might need to find Web pages that refer to only one word and not other words; For example, if you need to find the word greenhouse and specifically exclude the words global, warming, and gas. To attain the result you want, you would enter greenhouse NOT global NOT warming NOT gas. However, it should be noted that neither Google nor Yahoo! recognize the NOT operator when expressed as a word. They are quirky and prefer the minus symbol (–) immediately in front of the search word to the actual word NOT. Thus to perform our NOT search in Google or Yahoo! we would enter the string greenhouse –global –warming –gas. A search will then return a list of Web pages containing the word greenhouse but none of the words that had the minus symbol immediately before them.

Another powerful tool to help narrow a search involves the use of double quotation marks. These can either be employed alone to find exact phrases or used in combination(s) with the AND, OR, or NOT, as well as the + and – Boolean operators. Entering a search term enclosed between double quotation marks (" ") tells most good search engines to find that exact term or phrase. Thus if we enter the term "greenhouse gas" in Google our search will return only pages containing the exact term greenhouse gas. By combining double quotation marks and other search operators we can obtain even more specific results. For example, searching for "greenhouse gas" + "global warming" will return lists of pages containing both terms, but entering "greenhouse gas" – "global warming" will bring an entirely different result, listing only pages containing the exact term greenhouse gas without the term global warming. Similarly, entering "greenhouse gas" OR "global warming" will bring a vastly different result by listing pages containing one term or the other.

Many of the advantages of complex searching are self-evident, or become so with a little practice. For example:

- Results tend to be specific, or at least much less scattered than those obtained from a simple search
- The number of pages you must open and scroll through is reduced

- You are more likely to find Web pages containing combinations of search words you seek
- Finding specific phrases and terms is relatively easy
- Unwanted information and terms can be eliminated
- Complex searches are much less likely to be influenced by metatags

Web Site Design and Search Engine Bias Affects Results

What are metatags? They are key words and phrases embedded in the code underlying Web sites. They are frequently included by Web site designers in an attempt to make sites as attractive as possible to as many search engines as possible. Similarly, many Web page titles and even Web site addresses have been used by designers in an effort to make their sites rate more highly in search engines than other, sometimes competing and sometimes better, sites and pages.

You can see the metatags, page titles, and all the coding underlying a Web page in Internet Explorer if you click on the View tag at the top left of the Web page toolbar and then on Source. The following example shows part of the coding underlying the Web site http://computerassistedreporting.com, which is a companion to this book:

```
<html>
<head>
<meta http-equiv = "Content-Language" content = "en-au">
<meta http-equiv = "Content-Type" content = "text/html; charset = windows-1252">
<title>Computer-Assisted Reporting</title>
<meta name = "description" content = "Computer-Assisted Reporting, CAR, research links for journalists, journalism educators and students in English speaking countries outside the United States.">
<meta name = "keywords" content = "Computer-Assisted Reporting, Computer Assisted Journalism, Stephen Lamble, journalism links, CAR, CAR links, Computer-Assisted-Reporting.com, journalism research, journalists, slamble, CAR survey, computer, assisted, reporting, links for journalists, computerassistedreporting.com">
```

What that coding tells us is that the site's title is Computer-Assisted Reporting, that its description and metatags include the words computer, assisted, reporting, CAR, journalism, links, and variations on the name of the site's author. The effectiveness of that combination, plus the relevance of the site's name, can be demonstrated when searching for the term computer-assisted reporting in any of the major search engines with the site ranking relatively highly compared with many others on the same topic.

In addition to understanding how metatags, site names, and page titles can drive search engine rankings of Web sites, it is also useful to understand that popularity itself creates a virtual self-fulfilling prophecy when it comes to the results search engines return. Briefly, the more often a searched for page is accessed by visitors, including search engines themselves, the more highly it ranks in the results returned by major search engines such as Google. And, as already mentioned, some search engines also rank sites differently depending on where they are located. That can be demonstrated by entering a search term to search the Web in different national versions of the same search engine. If, for example, the word football is entered in the UK Google site http://www.google.co.uk/> the top ranking results will all be sites dealing with soccer. Enter the same search in the US Google site, http://www.google.com/, and the top search results will refer to American football or gridiron, a very different game. Similarly, a search from the Australia Google site http://www.google.com.au/ returns a list of results in which Australian Rules football ranks highly.

The impact of Web site design and search engine bias have big implications for Web-based researchers. Among other things they mean that just because a Web site rates highly with a search engine does not necessarily mean it will be the best or most appropriate site for accurate and credible information. On the other hand, the fact that someone has taken the time and had the understanding to set up a site so it rates highly could be taken as a sign that its content should be good because it has been assembled by a careful and fastidious person who is conscientious and therefore likely to get things right. Then again, it could be a reflection of the fact that inadequacies in content have been compensated for by careful design and promotion. Also, a site that rates highly in one nation may not rate as well globally. Those factors are considered in more detail in chapter 7, in the meantime they should be kept in mind when evaluating the results of every Web search.

Searching the Hidden Web

Just as design and search engine bias influences search results, so too can the size of a Web site, the way it is stored on a server, and how it is constructed in a physical sense.

The truth is that there are many Web sites that search engines cannot dig down into. Often those sites can only be properly accessed via what is known as a portal. Many of them form part of what is known as the 'hidden Web'—an umbrella term that encompasses huge sections of the Web that many people do not realize exists. This lack of awareness is not because some nerd decided that massive Web-based resources should be deliberately hidden from view. It is simply that many major Web sites are so big and contain so much information that they are built around their own complex network of internal Web sites; in effect a Web too complex for even the most sophisticated search engines such as MSN, Yahoo!, or Google to trawl deeply for information.

Most major government, university, and public corporation sites must be entered and searched through a portal. Many of them actually provide access to other portals within, or at least point to other portals. One prime example is the U.S. Federal Government Web site http://www.usa.gov. That entry page, and the internal search engine it allows access to, opens Web access to literally millions of pages of U.S. state and federal government information and services with much of it accessed through other government portals. The bulk of that information, and the pages it is contained in, is not revealed by even the most clever and efficient search engines. The same can be said of practically every large Web site, the only real entry is via a portal. However, once you have used a site such as http://www.usa.gov to discover a particular portal, for example, the Occupational Safety and Health Administration home page http://www.osha.gov, which is a portal in its own right, you can save that URL in your Favorites list and return there directly next time without having to go through http://www.usa.gov.

To understand how a portal works, it is useful to return to our haystack analogy. In a broad sense, searching the hidden Web involves making judgments not just about key words and search engines, but about which haystacks we should search in if we are to have the best chance of finding a specific needle of information.

If the stack we need to hunt in is a relatively simple affair with a minimalist structure, it will most likely be made up of layer upon layer of hay piled one on the other. To search for our needle we can start at one end of the stack and work through to the other. But what if the stack is a complex structure consisting of many thousands of tightly compacted bales of hay interlocked in intricate patterns? In that case, our only hope of finding the needle would be to go to each bale, open it to unpack the hay inside, then search its content. In that sense, a Web portal that serves as an access point to a large Web site is like one or more complex haystacks containing many separate bales of hay. To have any hope of finding the information we must select an appropriate haystack, isolate each bale, then use our tools to search it. In doing so we can usually employ any, or all, of the search techniques discussed earlier in this chapter. That is because most portal sites understand Boolean logic and many have advanced search options.

So how do you find portals? Often it is simply a matter of common sense and intelligent guessing. If, for example, you believe that a particular government, corporation, or research organization might have information of relevance to some matter you are researching, you would either go directly to its portal site (opening page) or you could use a major search engine such as Yahoo!, MSN, or Google to find the portal for you. Alternatively, you could access what is known as an online search directory (a site containing lists of useful information) such as Computer-Assisted

Reporting at http://computerassistedreporting.com, Bill Dedman's Power Reporting Resources at http://powerreporting.com/, or some of the other sites discussed in chapter 10.

While many portals are relatively easy to find once you know they exist (or suspect they are likely to exist) there are some notable research sites of use to journalists that many researchers overlook. Among them is the Internet Archive or WayBackMachine, as its operators call it. An amazing resource that stores different versions of a large number of Web pages and historic portal entry points dating from the mid-1990s, the site can be used to harvest a plethora of information ranging from how specific staff and officials have come and gone or been elevated or demoted, to financial and corporate information. The archive can be useful for helping find individuals, obtaining background information to inform news articles, and examining corporate mergers or collapses as well as a host of other details including things said or written in the past.

Another use of the WayBackMachine is to see how a person has changed their story over time. For example, *Boston Globe* journalist Walter Robinson used the archive as a resource when he researched George W. Bush's biography. This enabled Robinson to show how details of Bush's military record changed through the years on State Department Web sites.

Other portals of particular use to journalists include court and legal sites, special interest sites relating to a huge range of topics ranging from natural disasters to health and education, aviation to online telephone directories, maps, and graphical representation such as Google Earth, dictionaries, and converters for things such as money and measurement. One point to remember when searching government portals, and one of the major benefits for journalists working in nations where there is not a strong culture of freedom of access to government information, is that CAR methods enable journalists to adopt global perspectives. It is therefore quite likely that journalists in nations where governments are secretive will be able to source information about their own nation by searching portal sites published in other nations. For example, it is sometimes easier for an Australian journalist to find information about military contracts on American Web sites than on Australian Government Web sites. This is a reflection of the fact that there is a stronger, less paternalistic culture of access to government information in the United States compared with Australia, a nation that does not have a Bill of Rights and where freedom of information laws are regularly abused by government officials (Lamble 2003: 51 – 55).

Many media portals, including the online news archives of rival organizations, can be assessed externally from the Web, some for a price. Strangely, while journalists tend to jump online at the drop of a hat for a quick Google search, some overlook the fact that news archives, newspaper archives in particular, can be rewarding sources of information.

Briefly, the hidden Web is an often overlooked but enormously rich resource. Searching sections of it can help you find:

- Original documents
- Documents prepared or created in the past that are no longer generally available
- Photographs and recordings as well as written information
- Court documents
- Government documents both on the Web sites of a reporter's own government and also on Web sites published by other governments
- Statistics
- People

Meta Searching

Just as journalists need to be aware of the hidden Web, they should also develop a sound understanding about how search engines work. Some of those workings have been reviewed earlier in this chapter. Additionally, excellent information is available on the SearchEngineWatch Web site http://searchenginewatch.com/. As explained previously, major search engines such as MSN, Google, and Yahoo! harvest information directly from Web sites and Web pages. Others work in different ways, with some—known as meta search engines or meta crawlers—actually piggybacking their searches on the backs of other search engines.

For that reason, using a meta search can often increase the likelihood of finding a particular piece of information you need because it searches several different search engines at the same time. Examples of meta search sites include: Meta Eureka (http://www.metaeureka.com/), Dogpile (http://www.dogpile.com/), Mamma (http://mamma.com/), Ixquick (http://www.ixquick.com/), Jux2 (http://www.jux2.com/), and Clusty (http://clusty.com/). Meta search engines also tend to gather their results from the home sites of the search engines they piggyback on. Thus, they will often return a different range of results with a different national bias if used from a nation different from where the search engine was established or based.

In a general sense, meta search engines can be highly efficient tools because they cast your search net wider. The downside is that meta searching tends to be less thorough than directly searching several major standard search engines individually. That is partly because searches tend to time out if different sectors of the Internet are congested or running at less than optimum speeds. Boolean searching also tends to be somewhat hit or miss when meta searching because results depend on, first, if the meta search engine recognizes Boolean operators and, second, whether the search engines trawled by the meta search engine will also respond to Boolean codes.

News Archives

Most journalists have direct access to their own news organization's library archives. Whether they take full advantage of that access tends to depend on how sophisticated the archives are. At the top of the spectrum are digital in-house files that contain text and/or sound and video records of every item published or broadcast in the past decade or so. At the lower end, an "archive" may be little more than a dusty pile of old newspapers preserved over an indeterminate period and stacked in a heap somewhere. Between the extremes are bound copies of past newspapers, clip files, film, or microfiche copies of old publications and sound, film, and video archives.

The most accessible and easiest to search are generally newspaper archives. Searching a good computerized newspaper archive is similar to searching an intranet or part of the hidden Web. Computers as everyday work tools, including their application in routine online archiving, have only been used in many organizations since the early-1990s. Therefore, historical news records from before that time are often not available online and must be searched manually.

The information you will find in a newspaper's library files was put there as the result of research and writing by professional communicators—the journalists who wrote the stories. On the other hand, there is a danger that you might accidentally recycle another journalist's mistake(s) by "perpetuating an error made by another journalist" because "past stories may contain errors of fact and spelling mistakes in relation to people's names, place names and dates" (Conley and Lamble 2006: 358). When you do search a news archive, either via the Internet or from an internal news database, it is wise to search the most recent files and additions to that database as well as the older stories. This increases your chances of discovering apologies, retractions, or corrections and discovering if there has been a mistake in the past.

News archives can be particularly useful for checking if someone who is making news today has been mentioned previously in a news report. Sometimes you strike gold. A court report, for example, might mention the type of work the person does (or once did) and/or give general details of the area where they live (or lived). Depending on what sort of profile the person has, a report might also contain information about their husband or wife, former spouse(s), children, interests, businesses associates, criminal background, etc. Information like that could well provide good starting points for building a fresh news story or at least finding a different angle to enhance a new story.

Even if you do not work on a major news outlet with its own comprehensive archive you can still search the archives of other news outlets such as those that can be accessed through the News Corporation Newstext site (http://www.newstext.com. au/) or individual News Corporation newspapers such as the *New York Post* archive (http://pqasb.pqarchiver.com/nypost/advancedsearch.html), LexisNexis AlaCarte! (http://alacarte.lexisnexis.com/partners/int/lexisnews/srchNW.asp?isnew = 1), or Google News Archive Search (http://news.google.com/archivesearch). A particularly useful Web directory with links to news archives in the United States, Canada, and Asia Pacific has been developed by the Special Libraries Association News Division, an international organization for print, Web, and broadcast news librarians and news researchers, journalism, and communications librarians (SLA 2006). It can be accessed at http://www.ibiblio.org/slanews/.

While not always perfect, there are advantages of searching newspaper archives, for example:

- Most of the archives are relatively simple to search by using relevant key words or terms
- Searches can often be limited to specific dates or ranges of dates
- Information in the archives has been prepared by journalists who are trained information gatherers and are likely to suffer damage to their reputations, if not their careers, if their work is not accurate
- Good archives, such as those operated by News Corporation and other large media organizations, contain a wealth of useful information
- News archives reflect news values; therefore they contain categories of information journalists deal with all the time such as crime, human interest, politics, the unusual, entertainment, conflict, health, and international affairs

Searching Within a Web Page

One simple but valuable and often overlooked search tool is at our fingertips in every computer that runs common Web browser software. Using it can literally save hours spent reading through long, and sometimes irrelevant, material.

Say you have searched for a Web page containing key words or phrases you entered in a search engine or portal search box and now you want to quickly check some of the documents that have been found to see in what context the search terms occur in them. Simply open the Web page in Internet Explorer, click on the **Edit** tab or, in later versions, the search box at the top of the page. Then click your mouse on **Search** or **Find on this page** and enter your search term, or even just part of it. Alternatively, simply use Control + f. You will be able to click your way through the document and find each instance of the words or phrase you were looking for.

And that needle in a haystack? Has anyone ever really found one? Enter the phrase "I found a needle in a haystack" in a few different engines and find out for yourself!

Suggested Reading

Conley, David and Lamble, Stephen (2006). *The Daily Miracle: An Introduction to Journalism*, 3rd edition, chapter 15 Computer-Assisted Reporting. Oxford University Press, South Melbourne.

Fogg, Christine (2005). *Release the Hounds*, chapter 7 Tracking Down the Truffles. Allen & Unwin, Crows Nest, NSW.

References

Cooksey, Elizabeth, B. (1997). *Libraries & Culture,* Vol. 32, no. 1. University of Texas Press, Austin.

Conley, David and Lamble, Stephen (2006). *The Daily Miracle: An Introduction to Journalism*. Oxford University Press, South Melbourne.

Lamble, Stephen (2003). "United States FOI Laws are a Poor Model for Statutes in Other Nations" in *Freedom of Information Review*, no. 106, August 2003. Clayton: Legal Service Bulletin Cooperative Ltd. Law Faculty, Monash University, Victoria: 51–55.

SLA. (2006). Special Libraries Association News Division at http://www.ibiblio.org/slanews/ [accessed 2 January 2007].

Multimedia Newsgathering

This chapter proceeds from the premise that some journalists will work as multimedia reporters and hence need to learn how to gather information appropriate for multimedia reporting. The level of multimedia involvement will vary depending on factors such as the size of the news organization, the organization's expectations of reporters, and the specific news situation. For example, solo multimedia journalists sometimes operate in war zones or isolated regions where it is not feasible to send a team. The most controversial form of multimedia journalism involves one reporter who is required to provide content for print, online, radio, and often television. Some people have described this as "platypus" or "Inspector Gadget" journalism. In India they call it Kali journalism, after the multi-armed goddess. Most readers will be aware of the Inspector Gadget cartoon character, where a multitude of tools spring out of his hat. These terms are derogatory and have been used to describe a reporter required to do all forms of journalism but who does all of them poorly. A platypus is a mammal found only in Australia. It has the body and tail of a beaver, and the bill and webbed feet of a duck. It lives in a burrow near lakes and lays eggs, yet suckles its young. Platypus has evolved into a term for a multi-skilled reporter.

Early notions of convergence focused on this "super reporter" who could cover a story for every medium. But the rare exception apart, against tight deadlines it is not possible for one journalist to report well for radio, TV, print, and the Web. The more stories a reporter has to do, the more likely they will miss a deadline or fudge a story. Reporters forced to write stories for every platform will ultimately repeat themselves across platforms. This means they fail to take full advantage of the strengths of each format and the benefits of convergence, which is the ability to tell a story using the most appropriate medium. Critics of convergence have argued a "jack of all trades and master of none" approach degrades journalism. Given time and training, some individuals can perform well as platypus journalists.

This chapter looks at ways journalists can gather research that takes advantage of each medium's strengths..

The size of the news event, and sometimes circumstances, will dictate how many reporters are needed. A solo multimedia reporter can produce good content at routine news events, such as the mayor's weekly press conference. She will be *outgunned at a big news event such as a major fire*, against scores of *mono-media reporters*. The circumstances are key, so the significance of the news event should dictate the level of coverage and the number of people who cover each event. If gunmen take the mayor hostage at the routine press conference mentioned earlier and barricade themselves in the town hall with a dozen employees as hostages, the new circumstances will mean a very different approach to newsgathering and reporting. It will be all hands on deck.

One of the keys to success with multimedia journalism is the quality of the assignment editors (the people who both assign stories and react to changing circumstances). Successful multimedia organizations have a central assignment desk where the assignment editors, who all understand the strengths and weaknesses of each medium (discussed later in this chapter), assess each news event on its merits and send the most appropriate people. It cannot be emphasized enough: The importance of the story dictates the level of coverage and influences the size of the team involved, and the subsequent depth and breadth of the reporting. Teams of reporters will be needed to cover major news events, and some of the team members may have the multimedia skills of a solo journalist. The ability to work in teams will be another of the skills that knowledge workers, including journalists, will need to acquire as we move further into the new millennium.

The online journalist is the most prominent example of a multimedia reporter in the first decade of this century. As print-based newspapers evolve into multimedia companies, the online staff will act as the bridge to the future. This chapter assumes that readers are interested in acquiring multimedia newsgathering skills. It shows how to gather information appropriate for all forms of media. In an ideal world, online news sites will have their own reporters. In reality, much of the breaking news for online sites comes from news agencies like Associated Press or Reuters, or copy shoveled from the parent company's newspaper sites. Chapter 1 discussed how major newspapers such as *The New York Times* have established a continuous news desk so they can use stories from *Times* reporters as breaking news. This is one way to produce unique breaking news. Most newspapers could adopt this process if they wanted unique content, although it will obviously be easier for larger newspapers with their higher numbers of editorial staff.

Unique content will be appreciated. We must remember how easy it is for audiences to research online. They can compare any reporter's story with versions by other reporters at other papers by locating original documents. So discerning readers quickly appreciate that the same breaking news came from a news agency. Readers also have access to archives and powerful search tools, such as those discussed in chapter 5, and we must assume that they are savvy in the way they absorb online news. Journalists thus need to produce original content and market that idea to their publics. They must shun the temptation to modify a sentence or two of agency copy and offer it as a new story. Audiences are also increasingly aware of plagiarism, as several notorious incidents involving big-name reporters in 2005 and 2006 showed. Unique content builds a media organization's brand reputation.

Some Thoughts on Online News

Research by Jakob Nielsen and others has shown that reading from a computer screen is about 25 percent slower than when reading print. This means online should offer less text compared with the print version of a story, to help readers absorb information quickly. Always remember your audience. In a world of information overload, people want online news they can absorb quickly and easily. Sometimes it may be appropriate to offer news in bullet points rather than long sentences or via information graphics and charts. We need to deflate one of the early online myths—that we could put more content online than in newspapers because of the so-called infinite news hole online. Web readers want fast hits of information and news. They do not want to read into eternity. Offer information in easily digestible chunks. In areas of the world where dial-up is standard, online journalism must remain text focused and any images must be kept small. Busy people know what they are looking for and want to access it as quickly as possible. Make pictures smaller and keep headlines more to the point and avoid puns. Cute headlines that work for newspapers are often meaningless online (another argument for avoiding shovelware). Remember the international audience. For many of your readers, English is not their first language. The inverted pyramid format is the most appropriate form with one sentence per paragraph. It is vital to employ simple language. In an information-soaked world, you help your audiences when you provide easily digestible stories.

Journalism professors Nora Paul and Laura Ruhl point out that RSS feeds have changed the online world. We have moved from mass product distribution to personalized news channels (see chapter 3 for an explanation of RSS). Software like Soundslides (see details in Online Readings section) has produced a boom in audio slideshows and a rise in multimedia experiments.

The slideshow is getting a remake with the 'flipbook' style of choreographed image display set to music .... The packaging of series stories with multiple media elements is getting cleaner and more elegantly designed.... Flash and Google maps interfaces are being used to navigate the user through data and information ... (Paul and Ruhl 2007).

Multimedia slide shows that incorporate still images and a voice-over represent one of the easiest and exciting ways to do multimedia online. Journalists need to learn to appreciate the power of the still image combined with either text-based captions or a voice-over. In 2006, Ben Hammersley set up a series of blogs for *The Guardian's* Web sites. He recommends Flickr.com as a storage site for images. Yahoo! purchased Flickr in 2005. A basic Flickr account is free but people can pay $25 a year to use a section of Flickr to store photographs and make them available to Web sites. The fee includes back-up space on Flickr's servers and access to high-resolution originals of photographs. *Guardian* journalists e-mail images to Flickr. The process works like a moblog in the sense that the e-mail's subject line becomes the headline and the text of the e-mail becomes the caption, including a photo credit. Flickr software puts selected images onto *The Guardian's* Web site. Chapter 3 has more information about moblogs.

What is Multimedia?

Multimedia reporting involves new approaches to newsgathering and new ways to tell stories using text, audio, video, and graphics. Print and television news tell stories in a linear sequence. Both have a limited life span and attention span — a newspaper story is often old before it is read and television news is soon forgotten. Multimedia storytelling goes beyond these limitations. Jane Stevens teaches multimedia journalism at the graduate school of journalism at the University of California at Berkeley. To Stevens, multimedia storytelling uses a combination of text, still photos, animated graphics, video, and audio. These are presented in a nonlinear format in which all of the information in the elements merges and is not redundant. It has a longer life span and is a "very different form of storytelling" because it is interactive. "It's a two-way communication system: people can search for information. They send their own text, photos, graphics, video clips and audio to comment on stories or provide additional information" (Stevens 2003). Once a reporter knows what video, audio, still photographs, text, and graphics they plan to use for a story, they need to think about how to find each component. The story starts with newsgathering by collecting information and materials, but we must always remember that the type and circumstances of the news event should dictate the level of multimedia news coverage.

Northrup's Four Stages of News

Kerry Northrup, Ifra's director of publishing, has long maintained that the future of journalism lies in the area of multimedia. In the age of mass audiences and mass media, news consumption was a dedicated activity that people planned into their daily routine. My grandparents read the same newspaper each day and it was their source of news. My parents watched television news in the evening and subscribed to a few magazines. But in our information-soaked world in the early twenty-first century, people get most of their news without really trying, Northrup said. "They pick it up in small pieces here and there through the course of other activities. A few seconds of 24-hour cable news while changing TV channels to something else. The top-of-the-hour radiocast while driving and listening to music or waiting for the traffic report. A glance at the headlines on all the newspapers in the boxes at the street corner. Remarks overheard in the office canteen. News blurbs on the Yahoo homepage while searching for something online. Barely scanned e-mail summaries. A spouse at dinner mentioning something found out." Northrup calls this incidental news consumption. In a marketplace where news consumption is mostly incidental, a successful news provider has to be everywhere all the time, offering the widest practical range of media formats.

To serve their audiences, journalists need to understand this concept of incremental newshandling and working across media. The concept mirrors the way audiences get their news. Northrup said he came to understand the idea of incremental news during Newsplex moblog training courses. A multimedia reporter on the scene would snap a picture with the camera on his/her mobile phone and add text with the phone's keypad before sending it as a multimedia message to a holding site. At the office, an editor (whom Northrup called a storybuilder), would edit the text and release the story to a Web site. That is the first or breaking stage of the story. The storybuilder would call the reporter on the same mobile phone used to take photographs to ask for more facts, descriptions, and quotes. The editor would add these to the moblog entry, and readers would get new information each time they refreshed the page.

Several storybuilders and mobile journalists working together would cover an event in small increments. The overall picture would accumulate over time in the same way as we perceive a mosaic from many smaller pieces. Another type of editor at the Newsplex (whom Northrup called a newsresourcer) would enhance the pictures and text of the moblog with background information. Meanwhile, a top-level editor called the newsflow coordinator would monitor the entire moblog to ensure that the total collection of entries combined to satisfy the requirements of comprehensive editorial coverage. "Looking at the forest more than the trees, so to speak, the newsflow coordinator might reassign a reporter to an aspect of the story that needed more attention. In a fully multiple-media news operation, the newsflow coordinator would also be directing the story coverage in print and on air based in large part on the information being received and disseminated incrementally and in real time through the moblog" (Quinn 2006: xxvii–xxviii).

Over time, different media would cover the story in different ways, depending on the age and circumstances of the story and the relevance of each medium for the story. An organization's multimedia editor would assess the story and would allocate appropriate coverage based on the strengths of each medium. Let's use the example of the mayor held hostage from the start of this chapter. The multimedia editor might assign a television crew to provide live updates or interviews with witnesses. The strength of print lies in analysis and knowledge transfer — the chance to provide deeper and more reflective reportage for later phases of the story. So the newspaper might run stories of previous sieges or profiles of individuals trapped in the town hall. "There is value in having the coverage be a continuum across all media, building on itself while exercising common journalistic standards for quality and credibility," Northrup said. He concluded that this style of newshandling needed a revised workflow in the newsroom, and new ways to gather information (Quinn 2006: xxviii).

Strengths and Weaknesses of Media

All journalists need to appreciate the strengths and weaknesses of the four main media forms: print, broadcast, online, and mobile.

Print allows reporters to go into more detail than other media and provide background information. If readers miss details the first time, they can re-read the story. Print can also offer multiple versions of a big story, taking various angles on the same subject. Print is historic and thus newspapers are a place of record. But newspaper space is limited, dictated by the amount of advertising sold. A newspaper also needs to be delivered and its content is static. Once a newspaper has been published, it cannot be updated so people read news that is often a day or two old.

Broadcasting's big strength lies in its ability to go live as news happens and to convey the emotion of an event. When reported well, audio and video can give viewers a lot of information in a short space of time. Audiences like the idea that they are eyewitnesses to what is happening, and television in particular allows audiences to take in the emotional intensity of an event. But radio and TV are ephemeral. It is easy to miss information if you get distracted. Television requires many people to put together news bulletins and is expensive. Broadcast schedules limit the number of stories that can be covered and the amount of time for each one.

Online journalism offers the immediacy of TV and radio and the space of print. Its main strength is the capacity to be interactive: to foster a sense of connection with audiences. Its news hole is almost infinite, though it is debatable whether this is a strength or weakness. Broadband connections allow for video and audio on demand. But broadband is expensive and in some countries the necessary technology is beyond the reach of most people. Interactive online games and the related forms of journalism are expensive to do well, often requiring teams of people.

Mobile news is fast and interactive, and an easy way to reach younger audiences because mobile phones are associated with an always-on mentality. Many younger people sleep with their phone nearby with the phone switched on at all times. The mobile phone generation has a special relationship with the technology; they personalize their phones with ring tones and pretty cases. But the technology has weaknesses such as the high cost of calls, the problem of lost signal in isolated areas, and the small size of the screen when trying to convey complex information. Mobile phones might best be used as a way to spread radio news.

The Multimedia Newsgathering Process

This section proceeds from the assumption that you are a solo journalist who has to prepare content for all media. How do you gather information in this situation? Some of the basic rules of journalism still apply. Your job is to gather accurate information while remaining bound by legal and ethical codes of conduct. But this process requires a willingness to adopt a new mindset — to think across platforms. When in a hurry, it is best to collect too much information rather than too little. Ideally that information should be in digital form, because it is easier to transport and share. Make sure you date all files and name them fully. All modern word-processing software allows you to use long names. Adopt a formula and stick to it: You should include the minimum of the date, the source, and the subject.

Journalists gather information in two basic ways: Via interviews and through reading documents. Within each of these we find several subsets: interviews can take place by phone, face to face, via e-mail, or text messages. Documents can come in paper or digital form, or from libraries, people, or organizations. This section looks at ways to gather information in the context of multimedia newsgathering. Make sure you carry at least one flash memory drive (at least 1 Gb capacity) at all times. The authors keep theirs with their car and office keys to ensure the memory sticks are always available.

Interviewing

You need to think of an interview as consisting of three stages. Like an iceberg, the major part of an interview is hidden. It is the research you do before you meet the person, pick up the phone, or start typing the e-mail that makes all the difference, especially with longer articles like features. So your mantra should be interviews must be planned and prepared. More than one-half to two-thirds of the work takes place before the interview starts.

Define the Purpose of the Interview

Why are you there? How long is the intended story, and what platforms will your work likely appear on? This will influence how much time you spend researching and interviewing the subject. What is the main platform? What is your deadline? Do you plan to take still photographs or video? Is this person the key interview subject, or only a bit player? Where will you conduct the interview; should you get good location shots? What will be the purpose of the interview: Are you seeking information (light) or entertainment and good video footage (heat)? What do you already know about the person?

Conduct Background Research

The relevant Internet tools are covered in chapter 5. It helps to take a large blank sheet of paper and construct a MindMap. Put the topic in the center, circle it, and then draw six branches from the circle with one of the words who, what, when, where, how, and why on each branch. Then treat each of these words as a separate main topic from which you generate a series of other key words. For example, you could circle who and then branch out key words from that circle for each of the key people involved. Scores of great stories are lurking within public data. You can find stories off the standard news agenda by using deep computer-assisted reporting (CAR) methods (see chapter 11). On the Internet, you can find hundreds of government databases covering issues that audiences are interested in, such as accidents and crime, school test scores, environmental safety, and health. The *Online Journalism Review* points out that Web sites like *The Smoking Gun* attract thousands of readers a day by publishing interesting and quirky news stories found in public records. "Documents also provide a great way to fact-check statements made by an interview subject" (OJR 2007). Indeed, advanced CAR also helps journalists prepare better quality questions for interviews.

It is informative to study the research habits of great journalists such as Ken Auletta, the media writer for *The New Yorker*. Auletta said when researching a story he tried to spend weeks reading about the subject. He creates three digital files: the first is an index of all the materials he collects, the second is a file of people he wants to interview or things he needs to read, and the third is a list of questions to be asked of each interviewee. "Of these files, the most vital for me is the index," he said. Auletta indexed as he reported, noting the names of people others say he should interview and anecdotes or facts to be confirmed. Auletta said he numbered each notebook and document, and placed headlines in the index of things he might want to use. Auletta devised a system for notebooks, documents, and published works: Notebooks get capital letters, with numbers for each page; documents are also numbered; and each published book is allocated a Roman numeral, with each page numbered. "I break it [the index] into subjects — possible leads, chronology, bio, observations [and] themes." After the reporting stage, Auletta studied the index "which I hope helps me climb above the trees." Then he moved the index around the screen of his computer like a deck of cards and organized a narrative. "I write off the index and place a checkmark next to each [index] headline, allowing me to see, when the first draft is finished, what [is] left out and included" (Auletta quoted in Benkoil 2007).

Make an Appointment

Phone the person to arrange a time and place. Confirm the day before or the same morning. You may need to do some marketing: Show them the benefits of meeting you. Avoid use of the word "interview" if the person is a media novice. It is better to use phrases like "meet to talk about" or "an informal chat" because the word interview can scare people who are new to the process. Advise them you will be recording the chat and taking photographs. Again, you may need to persuade them of the benefits of the tape recording (tell them it is good for ensuring accuracy so they are quoted properly). Explain that you need to take video footage to illustrate your story. Implicit in doing a video interview is the idea that people's faces will appear on television or the Web. At times, you may need to appeal to a person's good nature or vanity to allow you to take photographs or shoot video. Tell them you will be as gentle as possible. Keep the tone of the chat light and friendly.

When approaching interviewees, you have a range of ways to contact them — phone, letter, or email. If you phone, consider the best time and place to reach them. Be prepared for voicemail, and think about what you want to say in advance. Be ready to nominate a time to call back. E-mail is less personal than phone, but at least the interviewee can read it when she is free. Many people get hundreds of e-mails a day, so how will you make yours stand out? Keep it short and polite. Be sure to include all of your contact details to ensure a response. With busy people, you may need to send an e-mail request several times, so ultimately it is probably best to phone. It gives you a chance to sell them the interview idea. Sometimes letters of faxes will get more attention because they are rare. Again, keep it concise and polite, and include all your contact details.

Plan the Interview

Plan your list of questions. Beginners will write questions down and have them on a clipboard or notebook as a backup in case they forget what they intended to ask. After a while asking good questions becomes second nature. Use the mind or concept map method discussed earlier to plan your interview. Always over-prepare the number of questions. But also plan how you will deal with a taciturn person or someone who talks too much. What happens if she miscalculate how long she can spend with you or if she is urgently called away? Prepare for that eventuality as well. Being called away is a common trick among people who want to avoid journalists but cannot, because of their position, avoid the media. So they get an assistant to phone them, or program his or her mobile phone to call five minutes into the interview. Be prepared for this situation. The advantage of using video here is obvious: If the subject does scurry away, you can film him avoiding the questions.

At the Interview

You need to prepare some icebreakers for when you meet the person. It is important before you start to compose yourself and remain calm throughout. Keep the tone breezy and friendly. It is said that a dog can sense fear in humans and that is the reason people get attacked. Perhaps humans emit some subtle pheromone the dog can smell. Regardless of the chemical considerations, it is a truism of interviewing that if you are nervous you will make the subject nervous. So you need to devise ways to keep calm. Take lots of deep breaths as you set up your equipment.

Once you start the tape rolling, use the first questions to check basic details such as the spelling your subject's name, title, and contact numbers. Get her permission to be interviewed and the date of the interview at the start of the tape. Also request a business card. The depth of your research shows up as the interview evolves. If you have achieved a good rapport and established a working relationship, you will probably ease into the first questions. Stick to your time and save any potentially sensitive questions (the "bomb") until the last. The reverse applies if you have limited time or you want a reaction on videotape. Good rapport can work wonders, and often will get you through asking even the most sensitive questions. The worst scenario from asking the bomb is being asked to leave, or the person storms off (though both can make for good television). Always make sure you get contact numbers (business cards are most helpful here) at the start of the interview in case the subject does depart abruptly. If you are overwhelmed during the interview and feel you cannot grasp what she is saying because it is too complicated (often the result of being too tense), excuse yourself and go to the bathroom. There you can compose yourself, make some notes, and return ready for the interview.

If you have time, recap and check your notes for anything you may have left out. And always ask if there is anything your subject would like to add. Thank the person when you finish. Listen for the "after-glow." This is the result of good rapport. Some of the best comments come as you are standing at the door or elevator saying goodbye. Sometimes the interviewee, relaxing after the "ordeal" and after you turn off your camera and/or recorder, will offer some interesting insights and quotable remarks. Listen carefully (pulling out a notebook at this point would destroy the mood) and write down the comments after leaving. This last point presents an interesting ethical dilemma: When does the interview end?

Use all your senses to capture a sense of where you are (most interviews take place in the subject's office or home). Appreciate that people love to talk about themselves and the things they are passionate about. Let them do so. Frame questions in a way that encourages feedback: Open questions often start with how or what. Ask things like: Do you have an interesting story about ...? or Describe to me .... Accept that silence is all right. Do not rush into silences. Give people time to think about their answers. Make eye contact and be interested. Sit slightly forward and adopt an open posture. It is OK to say a little bit about yourself. Sometimes this helps people open up. Push for information, but respect the people you interview.

It is best to arrive early for interviews. This gives you a chance to look for suitable establishing shots for your video and request things like mugshots of key individuals and photographs of products. You can also read noticeboards and generally get a sense of an organization's tone and atmosphere. Request documents that you have not had a chance to find during your online research. Make sure you always carry a flash drive so you can take digital copies of files. Sometimes, as is discussed in Chapter 11 on deeper forms of computer-assisted reporting, organizations will only give you access to files if you visit their offices. Know your rights in terms of what kinds of information you can ask for. Bear in mind that you often need to gather data for several platforms.

Gathering Information for Video Packages

This section assumes you are gathering information to make video packages for online sites. The first thing to remember is the power and primacy of the visuals. Think about how distracting the images on a television screen can be even when you are trying to ignore them. When writing for video, appreciate how the image influences everything in the package. Because of the power of the image, make sure that sound is connected to image. Randy Covington, director of the Newsplex at the University of South Carolina, spent 30 years as a TV journalist. He says this visual-audio link is essential for effective video storytelling. "Ensure that what people hear is closely related to what they are seeing at the same time." Think in scenes and ideally storyboard your news story when you prepare. Sometimes because of time pressures, the only place to do this is in the car on the way to the event. It helps to storyboard scenes on blank paper about the size of playing cards. When you need to know what information to gather you can link the information to each scene. And when you assemble your story you can shuffle the cards to find the best structure.

Understand the medium. Remember you have limited time. Online video will often be shorter than for broadcast television so keep the story simple. Ensure your piece has a start, a middle, and an end. Covington says the process of simplifying often leads to inaccuracies, so he urges journalists to be accurate. "Writing for video requires brevity. Perhaps the hardest thing about this writing style is deciding what to leave out." Rich Murphy, chief photojournalist at WFLA News Channel 8 in Tampa, said he aimed to do five things in every story. The first was to "show who did what" and the second involved proving the first with images and sound. This reflects the power of the visuals and the role of sound as a support medium. Murphy advocates finding what he calls a "gee whiz" moment for each story that adds an element of surprise, and connecting viewers to the subjects of stories by getting to know people through good interviews. Finally, Murphy says journalists need to move around and shoot from different angles to provide a variety of shots. In other words, go wide, then medium, then tight, and super tight to establish a story sequence.

Skills for a Multimedia Reporter

What skills does a multimedia reporter need? Ideally your university or media organization should provide training. But if you need to teach yourself the necessary skills, then we recommend these areas: visual thinking, audio editing, writing for radio, writing for online, writing for pictures, and image editing. The European Journalism Centre based in Maastricht, the Netherlands, offers an excellent booklet that teaches all of these skills and a lot more. It is available as a free pdf download from the center's Web site. See the section Online Readings at the end of this chapter for more details.

Appropriate Tools for Multimedia

When discussing what tools to use we get, inevitably, to the PC versus Macintosh argument. Rather than getting bogged down with this issue, remember that computers are simply tools for doing the job. And the most important tool is the brain behind the eyes and fingers that control the shooting or the typing. Both computer platforms have their advantages and disadvantages. One of the authors believes that in terms of producing multimedia content, the Macintosh has advantages over the PC because of the integrated suite of software tools that come free with a Macintosh such as iTunes, iMovie, iDVD and Garage Band. Most PCs come with RealPlayer installed but it is clunky compared with the smooth integration of the Macintosh tools. Final CutPro, the best software for digital video editing, is currently only available for the Macintosh. But Visual Communicator Pro, probably the best single package for producing packages on the desktop, is currently only available for the PC. The parent company, Adobe, produces a cheaper version for online, called Vlogit!

Andreas Pfeiffer, executive director of Pfeiffer Consulting in Paris, conducted a study in April 2006 that compared the cost and productivity of Macintosh versus Windows PCs. The study focused on newspaper production. Pfeiffer found the Macintosh platform cheaper and more productive despite higher reported purchase costs for Macintosh desktop models. The Macintosh was faster to deploy and replace, had fewer security issues, and "so far no spyware" [viruses]. "If we compare Macintosh and Windows computers, we should stop looking at functionality and consider overall productivity and efficiency. While PCs are often faster than Macs in terms of hardware performance, Windows is clearly less productive, and offers a measurably less efficient user interface." Pfeiffer said the Macintosh had significantly less "user interface friction;" that is, its operating system was more efficient. "In this respect, the Macintosh has a clear and measurable advantage. These differences are particularly important in deadline-driven environments." Pfeiffer said the Macintosh was also the clear winner in general user-interface operations and in publishing specific tasks. "The average of 17 publishing-specific tasks is almost two times slower on Windows, the average of 12 common user interface operations (such as cut-and-paste or file navigation) is almost 30 percent faster on the Macintosh. The only program that came out slightly faster on Windows in terms of productivity is Excel" (Pfeiffer 2006: 30). Excel is discussed in chapter 11.

When choosing technology, the decision is simple: Decide what journalism you want to do, and then select the most appropriate tools. If you work for a company that already has a legacy PC or Macintosh platform, then you probably do not have a choice. It is pointless and exhausting trying to beat against the current. If given the choice of starting a multimedia program from scratch, we would always prefer the Macintosh platform because of its integration and its ease of use. This latter factor means that people focus on producing content, not wasting time trying to understand the arcane language of PC error messages. Pfeiffer has pointed out that Macintosh has noticeably less "user interface friction." With technology, diffusion of innovation theory points to the successful adoption of innovations that are easy to use (Rogers 1995: 207).

Journalists Talk Technology

Debbie Wolfe is the editorial technology editor at the *St Petersburg Times*. She also teaches journalism as an adjunct at the University of St Petersburg. Here are her thoughts on technology for podcasting: "After extensive testing of several portable audio recorders, I've purchased a Zoom H4. Additional testing of microphones led me to a Shure hand-held field microphone that's widely used by television folks. For mixing software, I use Audacity — it's free. At the [St Petersburg] *Times*, our staff uses Audacity for podcasting which is why I decided to learn it. It's just the right thing for podcasting. A good number of our reporters use Olympus digital audio recorders — at my recommendation — for field and telephone interviews. Sometimes, the material they gather with these budget recorders is also used for the Web. When the timing works out, one of our Web staff will go into the field with a reporter to capture audio with a more expensive Marantz unit. I think the Zoom H4 provides slightly better audio quality and is a great deal cheaper than the Marantz digital options. There really isn't a standard in the industry yet regarding digital audio recording. Marantz had the tape-based journalism market cornered for years, but not so with digital" (Wolfe 2007).

In the UK, journalists at *The Guardian* use Hipcast (formerly known as Audioblog at http://www.audioblog.com/ or http://hipcast.wordpress.com/) as a reporting tool. Reporters interview people via mobile phones and place audio files on the site. As of late 2006, the basic Hipcast service cost $4.95 a month. A seven-day free trial was available though you need to sign up first and provide credit card details. An option to use Webcams to record video was also available but it and the other podcast choices were more expensive. Those prices ranged from $9.95 a month for the standard podcast plan with 500 Mb of disk space and an unlimited number of podcasts and blogs, to $49.95 a month for the corporate podcast plan with 5 Gb of disk space and an unlimited number of podcasts and blogs. Hipcast lets people record up to an hour by phone or with a Web browser and upload audio or video files. Videos are automatically converted to iPod QuickTime on the fly (Hammersley 2005).

Late in 2006 Ben Hammersley became *The Guardian*'s first multimedia foreign correspondent, one of only a handful in the world. He predicts a "huge change" in the way his newspaper gathers and delivers news by 2008. Converged news requires the reporters in the field, and editors back in the newsroom, to have a new set of skills and equipment. "For reporters, convergence means that filing one finished story a day to their parent desk will not be enough. Instead, journalists on the ground will need to file updates for the online operation, live video for the web site, recorded video for the multimedia desk, live and recorded audio for podcasts, as well as full pieces pulling everything together in time for the first paper edition." Hammersley believes convergent journalism is the product of the maturation of a range of technologies. Key among them is the arrival of lightweight content management systems that allow for unprecedented flexibility in creating authoring and distribution systems, combined with the ever decreasing size and cost of multimedia capture and communication equipment. In the 18 months to the end of 2006, *The Guardian* had focused on exploiting the power of these new content management systems. "We have launched 21 blogs and one major magazine site, with more major operations coming online. We have demonstrated that we can quickly build sites that are both reader and writer friendly and that respond to changing news agendas." It was time to bring that same responsiveness and flexibility to *The Guardian*'s newsgathering and capture by exploiting the potential in new equipment technologies, he said. "Multimedia gear has matured. We can shoot, edit, and publish video and sound from anywhere on the planet with gear that fits into a medium sized backpack." The paper tested the gear in Afghanistan late in 2006 to demonstrate what was possible. The test showed that live breaking news in all media and delivered from any environment was possible. "And it only takes one person. Technologically, therefore, we're ready. But we need to perfect the human systems" (Hammersley 2006). Training will always be important, as will the ability to assess the quality of information the journalist encounters. Chapter 7 considers the latter issue.

Online Readings

Andrew Vigal's Interactive Narratives
http://www.interactivenarratives.org/
Click on the long and short narratives link to see examples of good digital storytelling, and do a local version of one of these stories.

European Journalism Centre tri-medial manual is available from the center's Web site at http://www.ejc.nl/

Jen Friedberg
http://www.jenfriedberg.com/
This site takes a while to load if you are on a slow connection but it is worth the wait.

National Public Radio's multimedia output
http://www.npr.org/
One of the world's best sites for sustained quality multimedia content.

New York Times
http://www.nytimes.com/multimedia/
Another of the world's best sites for sustained quality multimedia content.

newspaper techniques
http://www.ifra-nt.com/
This monthly print and online hybrid publication from Ifra always has useful articles about multimedia (note that the magazine title is in lower case).

Online Journalism Review offers excellent guides to reporting and shooting video
http://www.ojr.org/ojr/wiki/reporting/and http://www.ojr.org/ojr/wiki/video/

Soundslides
http://www.soundslides.com/
This software is popular among journalists for creating audio-visual productions. Download a trial version for a month. It costs $39.95. Another excellent tool is Adobe's Vlogit! It costs $29 a month.

The Knight Center offers some excellent online training materials for multimedia newsgathering.
http://journalism.berkeley.edu/multimedia/

The Poynter Institute's NewsU also has a series of short courses you can use to refresh your journalism skills.
http://www.newsu.org/

The Smoking Gun is another fine place for story ideas.
http://www.thesmokinggun.com/

References

Benkoil, Dorian (2007). "So what do you do, Ken Auletta? *The New Yorker*'s media writer spills the beans on exactly how he does his job" published in MediaBistro online at http://www.mediabistro.com/articles/cache/a9436.asp on 16 January 2007.

Hammersley, Ben (2005). Interviewed in Amsterdam, October 2005, and again by e-mail in 2006.

Paul, Nora and Ruhl, Laura (2007). See their monthly column in *Online Journalism Review* at http://www.ojr.org/ojr/stories/070110paul/

Pfeiffer, Andreas (2006). "In the spotlight Q&A" in *newspaper techniques*, May 2006, 30.

Quinn, Stephen (2006). *Conversations on Convergence: Insiders' Views of Twenty-First Century News Production*. New York: Peter Lang.

Rogers, Everett (1995). *Diffusion of Innovations*, Fourth edition. New York: The Free Press.

Stevens, Jane (2003). "Backpack Journalism is Here to Stay" published in *Online Journalism Review* at http://www.ojr.org/ojr/workplace/1017771575.php on3 April 2003. [accessed 21 January 2007].

Wolfe, Debbie (2007). E-mail interview 20 January 2007.

7

Evaluating Information Quality

You are a journalist, it has been a slow news day and you are hunting for a good story. An e-mail arrives from a previously reliable contact telling you it has just become possible to send a message to a dead person. All you need to do is go to the Web site http://www.afterlifetelegrams.com/AFTERLIFE/index.html, compose a short message, pay a fee of $5 per word, and your message will be delivered in the near future by a person who is terminally ill.

What if another contact tells you about the free online pregnancy test offered at http://www.thepregnancytester.com, the Australian Government's national public toilet map http://www.toiletmap.gov.au/, and the Texas Execution Information Center's Web site http://www.txexecutions.org?

How do you know what is real, what is a hoax, and what is unlikely but true in the online world? After all, one of the strengths of the Internet is also one of its greatest weaknesses—anyone, anywhere can publish just about anything online. There is no requirement for published information to be accurate, credible, true, or responsible. It is also important to understand that the Internet and Web are different from other media. As Bonn University Professor Klaus Grewlich explained some years ago:

> The Internet has inherently global reach, and thus is unlike television, telegraph and telephone, and more like short-wave radio. It has both the one-to-one characteristics of the telephone and telegraph and the one-to-many characteristics of television and radio, and thus is both a conventional and a mass medium (Grewlich 1999: 33).

In addition, television, radio, newspaper, and magazine news media are owned by individuals, corporations, and governments. They are subject to regulation and controls. But the Internet is user driven; no one owns it. It is self-sustaining and you do not need a special license to transmit information, sounds, and images via the Internet. As a result, there is more information available via the Internet than there ever could be on radio, television, newspapers, or, for that matter, from any other repository of information in the history of the world. In 2006, Google claimed that its search engine gave access to more than 8 billion pages of information—a figure that grossly underestimated the number of pages that could be accessed via the Internet because, as explained in Chapter 5, many more pages than Google can access are buried in the hidden Web. These pages are accessed via portals external search engines rarely penetrate.

One portal alone, the U. S. Government's USA.gov, opens access to more than 40 million U. S. state and federal government documents (USA.gov 2006). Most of that information is accurate and the documents are what they say they are. Much the same can be said of information published by other responsible governments, legitimate educational and research institutions, medical societies, and official public libraries.

On the other hand, billions of pages of information published on the web—including that accessed via some portals—is rubbish. It has been put online by individuals promoting a particular point of view, by some who seek revenge, tricksters trying to make money, advertisers peddling their wares, criminals, sexual and social deviates, pranksters, religious and political zealots, terrorists, racial supremacists, fools, and idiots. In short, the Web is as much a haven for evil, warped, and just plain stupid people as it is a forum for the intelligent, ethical, educated, and truly informed.

It should also be remembered that there is a digital divide and not everyone around the globe has Internet and Web access. It is also a fact that humans tend to be egocentric and ethnocentric by believing, wrongly, that others see the world in the same way we do and that they share our values, understandings, knowledge, and ethics. For those reasons, things that are seen as "truths" to some who publish online are not seen as being valid, logical, moral, or acceptable by others. So while it is stating an obvious truth to say that the online world is a vast and wonderful library containing the largest store of information in the history of the world; it is equally true to describe it as a soap box, mad-hatter's tea party, and a vile witches' cauldron bubbling with viruses, worms, rot, and poison.

Journalists are generally educated people well versed in the ways of the world. As such, they could be expected to see and understand both sides of the Internet and Web. So why is it that so many journalists, editors, and news producers have been fooled time and time again by false information gathered online? Journalists are supposed to be skeptical, to fact-check, to only rely on trusted sources, to double-check. They are not paid to be gullible, naive, stupid, and an easy mark for confidence tricksters and those with an axe to grind. But it seems the thrill of the chase and the overwhelming desire to be the first to break that great story has lulled even experienced journalists who should have known better than to throw caution to the wind. Others have paid the price for laziness, being careless with the truth, or their own arrogance. Often journalists who have fallen for the smoke and mirrors of an online hoax have paid a high price—some have been fired and most have been mocked by their peers and the public. At best, their credibility has been shredded.

A good understanding of computer-assisted reporting (CAR) can help avoid disasters. Some of the most essential skills a journalist must learn in dealing with the online world relate to evaluating and checking information. Falling for a hoax is not only devastating for a journalist personally, it is bad for the image of the news outlet they work for and damaging to the image of journalism as a profession whose practitioners should be respected. In the following pages we look at examples of some of the most publicized Internet-related journalistic misadventures of the past few years and then learn how to avoid falling victims ourselves.

Journalists' Mistakes

In 2001, a columnist with the UK newspaper *The Guardian* reported that a study had shown George W. Bush had the lowest IQ of any U. S. president in history. (Norman 2001) The story was picked up and run by other media outlets from New Zealand to New Jersey. It was based on an online report that referred to research at the "Lovenstein Institute." Unfortunately for those who ran with the story, the Lovenstein Institute only exists in the online world and the imaginations of those who created the hoax. The IQ report was a very obvious joke—something it hardly takes a genius to figure out when visiting the "institute's" Web site at http://www.lovenstein.org and discovering other anti-George W. Bush pages, including a "resume" clearly not written by Bush.

In December 2004, the normally highly respected BBC fell for one of the most embarrassing Web-based hoaxes of all time. A producer who had been assigned the task of researching for an article about the 20th anniversary of one of the world's worst chemical disasters—a deadly gas leak at a Union Carbide factory in Bhopal, India that killed thousands of people and maimed more than 100,000 survivors—went to what he thought was the Web site of Dow Chemical, the giant U. S. corporation that had acquired Union Carbide after the accident. He was looking for contact details for a corporate spokesperson to interview. Finding an e-mail address, the producer made contact with a man he believed was such a spokesman. But instead of having visited the Dow Chemical Web site at http://www.dow.com/ during his search, the hapless producer had gone to http://www.dowethics.com/ a fake Web site operated by The Yes Men, an activist group opposed to ways many corporations conduct business. As a result of the mistake, the BBC interviewed an activist from The Yes Men who was only too happy to pretend to be a genuine Dow spokesman. It then broadcast a false report saying a Dow executive had offered to spend $US12 billion compensating survivors of the Bhopal accident.

The BBC later apologized to Dow, its audience, and, tragically, the most cruelly hoaxed of all—the people of Bhopal. Meanwhile, The Yes Men boasted about how the group had provided a spokesman for the BBC interview and how it had used the media to taunt and belittle Dow. News media around the world carried stories about the hoax with a headline in *The Times of India* saying "Bhopal Hoax Haunts BBC, Interview" India's *Central Chronicle* reporting "Jolt to BBC's Credibility Over Dow 'Interview,'" and even *The Age* in Australia sanctimoniously pointing the finger with a report headlined "Bhopal Blunder Hurts BBC" (Holder 2004).

Other notable examples of journalists falling victim to online fraud include the following:

- An Associated Press report in February 2005 that said Iraqi militants had captured an American soldier and were threatening to behead him. The report was based on information and a photo, supposedly of the soldier, posted on a Web site. But within hours of the story being published, it was revealed that the soldier in the photo was actually a plastic toy and no real American serviceman was missing.
- In March 2005, several publications including *The Atlanta Constitution-Journal* ran a story about a man who happened to have many bottles of beer with him when he was trapped in his car by an avalanche of snow and ice. The story said the lucky victim was able to make his way to freedom by drinking the beer then urinating to melt the snow! But the story was a hoax promulgated via the Internet (Regret the Error 2005).
- In December 2005, the *Los Angeles Times* apologized to the Governor of Wyoming for publishing a front page story containing a false "quote" indicating the governor favored the reintroduction of wolves into the wild. In its apology the newspaper acknowledged that the Governor did not make comments attributed to him and that the statement was a hoax circulated on the Internet.
- In February 2006, London's *The Sunday Times* printed an article carrying the bylines of two journalists in which it was reported that naturally blonde women were likely to become extinct within 200 years. Part of the information was erroneously attributed to the World Health Organization, which later published a posting on its Web site denying it had ever conducted such a study (Dobson and Taher 2006).

- In May 2006, more than 20 media outlets across North America including the *Toronto Sun* fell for an Internet hoax and published interviews with a person who said he was a 25-year-old male virgin and that a woman he knew had promised to "help me with my problem" provided there were 5 million hits on his Web site within 30 days.
- In August 2006, veteran Melbourne broadcaster and journalist Terry Lane offered to resign from *The Sunday Age* newspaper after he wrote an anti-war column based on "video evidence of U. S. Army Ranger Jesse Macbeth." Lane had found the video online but did not realize it was a hoax that had been exposed months earlier (Murphy 2006: 3). Lane was later quoted in a rival newspaper, *The Australian*, as saying: "My attention was drawn to what looked like a professionally packaged documentary video in which U. S. Ranger (I now know that that is bogus) Jesse Macbeth recounts his experiences as a soldier in Iraq … I was completely taken in by his fake sincerity. That, I suppose, could be excusable for any person with no responsibility to check bona fides, but in my case I fell for it because I wanted to believe it. That is inexcusable" (Murphy 2006: 3).

Photo Faux Pas

As well as hoaxers attempting to create false "news" online, seeing is no longer necessarily believing as photographs can also be bogus. They are relatively easily altered with the aid of desktop imaging software. That causes particular problems for photo editors and news outlets because, as discussed in chapter 4, many media outlets now encourage input from "citizen journalists" who use digital photography to capture images of breaking news stories and natural disasters. Sadly, the downside is that not all images contributed by supposed "eyewitnesses" are what they are purported to be. Similarly, digital manipulation has made the production and distribution of fake propaganda photos a simple process. Numerous news outlets have been fooled and embarrassed. Some of the more humiliating mistakes include the following:

- One mistake was the publication by *The Boston Globe* on May 12, 2004, of copies of sexually explicit photographs purporting to show American servicemen raping Iraqi women. The horrifying images were on a display board photographed at a press conference with Boston City Council member Chuck Turner. He had called the conference after Congressional hearings about shocking photographs of prisoners at

Abu Ghraib prison in Iraq. Turner was reported in the *Globe's* article as saying: "The American people have a right and responsibility to see the pictures" (Slack 2004). Unfortunately for Turner and the newspaper, the photographs had been exposed a week earlier on WorldNetDaily. com (Gossett 2004) as fakes copied from online pornography sites and distributed by anti-American propagandists. *The Boston Globe* reacted two days after the display board photograph was published by attacking Turner in an editorial in which it said: "Turner's photos appear to match ones found on a pornographic website. Yesterday the *Globe* apologized for including a photo showing the images with the article about Turner's claims" (*Globe* editorial 2004).

- Also in May 2004, Piers Morgan, then editor of London's *Daily Mirror*, was fired after the newspaper conceded photos it had published that supposedly depicted British soldiers abusing an Iraqi were fake.

- In March 2004, *The Washington Post* published a fabricated photograph that purported to show presidential candidate Senator John Kerry speaking from the same platform as actress Jane Fonda. In fact the image was a composite assembled from two different photographs taken in different years at different locations.

- *The Times of India*, Sky News, and Australia's Nine Network were all fooled into running fake photos of what was wrongly claimed to be the December 2004 tsunami, which caused massive loss of life and property along the Indian Ocean coastline in nations such as Indonesia, Sri Lanka, and Thailand. Some of the images they published were actually a 2002 tidal surge in China and other "doctored" fakes of supposedly huge waves featured a city in Chile in the background!

- In August 2006, the Reuters news agency was ridiculed after it published a digitally altered photo supposedly showing the skyline in Beirut after an air strike in which clouds of black smoke had been intensified to make the image appear more graphic than it really was.

It has been argued that many journalists and editors who have been taken in by false information and images accessed or provided via the Internet have failed to apply the same standards to the online world as they would apply in the real world (Pearson 1997: 254). That is largely true, but amazing growth of Internet-based communication technologies and huge advances in digital imaging in the past decade have seen new dangers emerge that were unheard of in earlier generations. On the bright side, however, those same technologies have actually made it easier for savvy journalists to identify hoaxes.

Protecting Yourself

There are four overriding principles journalists should apply when protecting themselves in both the online and real worlds. They are simply to unfailingly trust their own instinct or sixth sense, to use common sense, never take anything at face value, and never make assumptions. As the old saying goes: If something seems too good (or too outrageous) to be true, it probably is.

A good test when checking the validity of information and images in e-mails and on Web sites is to ask yourself: Does it appear to be *reliable*, *accurate*, and *plausible* (RAP) (Quinn 2001: 130). In making judgments carefully consider the following:

Decode the URL

Look carefully at the address of a Web page (its Uniform Resource Locator or URL). After a little practice you will learn to "read" URLs. While not totally infallible (they can be faked, but usually are not), a URL can tell you enough to make you suspicious of a Web site.

After the http://www. in a URL, or in some instances where there is no www in the address just after the http://, the first part of a Web site name appears, and with it the first clue as to whether the site is genuine. For example, the BBC producer who was fooled by the fake Dow Chemical site in the Bhopal hoax should have wondered if there was something wrong when he looked at the Web address. http://www.dowethics.com. Most corporations have relatively simple home page addresses that include their organization's name and not much else. This is because of advertising purposes and because it makes their Web site addresses more search engine friendly. Sub-sections of their sites, like those dealing with specific items such as ethical issues, are normally listed AFTER the initial homepage address in the part of the URL address that is known as a domain name. Similar to a trademark, a domain name must be registered and an annual fee paid to protect it from being used without authority. Thus, the real Dow homepage address is simply http://www.dow.com, while the URL of its Web page dealing with ethics is http://www.dow.com/about/aboutdow/ethics.htm. When interpreting a Web site address it helps if you understand that the forward slash (/) actually means that a separate subsidiary file, or sub-domain, is being accessed within an overall Web site.

Because URLs must be registered, corporations and other organizations tend to simply register a simple domain name reflecting their business name, trading name, or institutional image. That name then literally becomes the key to accessing their home page on the Web. Dow, for example, simply registered http://www.dow.com as its Web address. It did not have to individually register any extensions built onto that base URL because extensions were listed after forward slashes, as in the example of http://www.dow.com/about/aboutdow/ethics.htm. Because of those registration issues, The Yes Men would have found the dow.com domain already registered when they attempted to publish their fake site. Therefore they had to think of and register a new, but similar name. The result was dowethics.com, which is an unlikely sounding name for the main URL of a major corporate Web site. Visitors to the fake site should also have noticed that all links within the site were actually file extensions of the http://www.dowethics.com home page, with subsidiary pages listed after forward slashes in their URLs; for example, http://www.dowethics.com/r/about/corp/corp.htm. To anyone who can read a URL, those clues make it abundantly clear that dow.com and dowethics.com are two totally different domains, hence totally different Web sites.

The next step is to look at the suffix of the URL. That will tell you if the domain has been registered as .com,.org,.biz,.name,.net,.gov,.edu, and so on. Basically, anyone with a credit card can go online and for a nominal fee register a domain with a .com, .org, or .net URL. (Despite the original theory in the early days of domain registration that .com sites would be for commercial enterprises, .org for organizations, .net for networks, and so on.) But .gov (for government domains), .edu (for educational domains), and .ac (for higher educational institutions in the UK and New Zealand) domain names are much harder to register, with registrants having to prove their legitimacy. There are also other specialist suffixes including.mil (for U. S. military sites), .biz (for business sites), .aero (for aviation sites), and .co (for commercial sites in New Zealand and the UK).

Domain name suffixes help us make judgments about URLs. The strict rules about registering .gov, .edu, .mil, and .ac sites mean that they are generally what they say they are. While not an iron-clad guarantee that the content of a site is accurate (school children or some dim-witted university students, for instance, can often post to some .edu sites), the presence of those suffixes at least means the sites that use them have been published by legitimate organizations. It can be a different story, however, with non-restricted domain suffixes such as .com, .net, or .org. In most parts of the world they can be registered by anyone ranging from legitimate users to the sad, mad, and bad.

In fact, one powerful clue to the fact that a Web site is not what it appears to be at first glance lies in the fact that its appearance and URL suffix do not match. For example, http://www.whitehouse.org, while looking at first glance as though it might be legitimate, is totally different from the Web site you will find at http://www.whitehouse.gov, which is actually the real White House Web site. Similarly, http://www.whitehouse.net is another spoof site—one in which the color of the White House changes, but one that can confuse the unwary into thinking it might possibly be legitimate because it cunningly links back to the real http://www.whitehouse.gov site.

The final step in reading a URL is to identify the nation in which it was registered. In all nations except the United States, which does have a national identifier

(.US) but rarely uses it, the final part of the domain name tells us where registration took place. For example, a .nz extension tells us that a site was registered in New Zealand, .ca for Canada, .uk for the United Kingdom, .in for India, .se for Sweden, and .au for Australia. A full list of national identifiers can be found online at http://www.norid.no/domenenavnbaser/domreg.html. It should also be noted that domains without a national identifier are most likely registered in the United States. Those identifiers, or their absence, can be particularly useful because they help online researchers identify what may be legitimate looking sites registered in unlikely places. Seeing a (hypothetical) site name such as http://www.dow.org.rw should send alarm bells clanging loudly because a large organization such as Dow Chemical would be extremely unlikely to register a domain for an organization (.org) in Rwanda (rw).

National identifiers also help to recognize sites registered in tax-haven nations such as the Cayman Islands (ky), Bahamas (bs), and Vanuatu (vu). In some of these nations there is little, if any, government control over fraud, including fake Web content. Examples of Web sites operated from these nations include diploma mill "university" Web sites registered in locations that do not have universities, lottery sites in nations that do not have national lotteries, and high sounding "research institutes" or "corporate" entities with Web sites registered in poverty stricken nations ruled by corrupt regimes. Many fraud, online gambling, and pornography sites were registered in similar locations.

Another thing to look for in a URL is a tilde (~). It usually comes before an individual's user name and indicates that a site is a personal site, which is something that can be good (if the person is a respected expert) or bad (if they are a self-opinionated fool).

Does the Site Look Credible?

Consider the spelling, grammar, punctuation, fonts, and colors used in a Web site. Is the standard of English as high as you would expect it to be? Is the written expression consistent? Misplaced capital letters, a mix of different fonts, badly placed punctuation, and inappropriate word use are all give aways.

Also, look at the overall design of a site. Does it seem old-fashioned or out of date? Or are there too many bells and whistles? When was the site last updated? If it was some time ago, the information it contains might be seriously out-of-date or it might be a sign the site is neglected or fake. One excellent test is to see if a Web site has been linked to by other, credible sites. One way to check this is to identify the key part of the URL and search for it on a good search engine, particularly Google because one of the criteria it uses to rank sites is based on the number of links they have. As explained earlier, the key section of a URL identifying its domain name is the part containing either a portion of a Web site's title or a person's name. For example, in the URL http://www.dowethics.com a Google search for dowethics will quickly indicate that the site is bogus. Conversely, a search for the key part of http://members.optusnet.com.au/~slamble, which is slamble, will show you that the site is legitimate and is in fact a personal site published by one of the authors of this book who has expertise in the area of CAR.

An obvious, but often overlooked, clue is the general content and tone of a Web site. That was another area where the BBC producer who fell for The Yes Men's Bhopal hoax should have been more alert. Among many other things, and even allowing for the fact that the graphics are good, the general tone of the fake Dow site—which contains statements that would be considered outrageous in a corporate context—is nothing like the controlled image one would expect to find portrayed on the Web site of such a big corporation.

Who is Behind the Site?

Every Web site has been put online by a person somewhere. If the site is legitimate that person, or the people they work with, should be readily identifiable. So ask yourself who is behind a Web site you are considering using for research. Does that person have the credentials, authority, and knowledge to have said the things published on the site? Are they really an expert with a PhD, or a bored 16-year-old who is sick of watching television and has built a hoax site as a joke?

Often it is obvious who, or what organization, is represented on a Web site, particularly with government and academic sites. But if your sixth sense starts telling you something might be wrong or if you are not sure about a site for some more obvious reason, there are good ways to start investigating. One is to use a Web-based look up service known as DomainTools at http://www.domaintools. com/. This service links to different sections of the giant WHOIS domain name database in different parts of the world. It provides access to the registration details of most Web sites around the globe. To search for information about a site, you simply enter the part of its domain name that comes immediately after the www and ends with the domain suffix such as .com or .org. An example would be ComputerAssistedReporting.com. A search like that will often provide information about who registered a site and the server where it is hosted. But bear in mind that information on the registers can be false and in some nations it is possible to register domains anonymously; although most legitimate domain registrants have nothing to hide and therefore provide accurate information. If a particular domain name does not show up in a DomainTools search, details might be revealed in nation-specific searches accessed by clicking on specific national identifiers listed in the NORID database at http://www.norid.no/domenenavn-baser/domreg.html. This links to relevant WHOIS and registration information in each nation.

It should also be noted that some information published on the Web appears in pages published by organizations offering free Web hosting. Generally, journalists should be extremely wary of information found on Web sites such as MySpace and other free hosts such as Geospace, Tripod, and Anglefire. Logic dictates that a multi-national corporation, university expert, government, or top research institute is unlikely to put its eggs into such a basket.

Further, it is possible for one domain's URL to redirect to another, different URL. Sometimes the redirection is done openly and transparently for a good reason, but it can also be masked through the use of what is known as a URL gripper. The gripper keeps the originating URL visible in a Web browser's address bar and does not allow the real URL underlying the redirected page(s) to show. An example of the legitimate use of a redirection, without a gripper, can be seen when you go to http://ComputerAssistedReporting.com, which redirects to the home page of one of the authors of this book at http://members.optusnet.com.au/~slamble/index. html. The domain name ComputerAsisstedReporting.com and the redirect were put in place to make it easier for CAR students and journalists to remember the site name, or if they could not remember it, so that at least the site would rank highly in search engines and be easy to find again. But redirects, and URL grippers, are not always used for such altruistic purposes.

Once you have discovered who is behind a site, you need to find a way to check their credibility. If so, are they telling the whole story? Has the author of a secondary quote reproduced it accurately? Are they seeking publicity for some commercial reason, to further their prospects of promotion, or are they a little eccentric? Often a simple online search or a search of a news organization's archive will help. An alternative is to contact the organization a person purports to represent and to speak to them personally or at least to inquire about them. Another good approach is to see if the person is known by other experts in their particular field.

Are there Proper Contact Details?
Just as confidence tricksters who advertise in print media often list their only contact details as a post office box number, e-mail address and/or cell phone number, Internet scammers are usually reluctant to publish street addresses and fixed-line telephone numbers. For that reason journalists should be especially wary of Web sites where an e-mail address is the only contact.

That was another obvious hint in the BBC Bhopal hoax. The sole contact listed on the http://www.dowethics.com Web site was an e-mail address. There was no street address, no telephone number, not even a post office box number! In contrast, the legitimate Dow Web site http://www.dow.com/ lists full street addresses and fixed-line telephone and fax numbers for each of its individual offices in North America, Europe, Latin America, Asia Pacific, Africa, the Middle East, and the Indian sub-continent.

Linking

Another simple test of a Web site's credibility is to see if it is linked to by other credible sites. The idea here is to see if the operators of credible sites have judged a Web site you are interested in as being credible enough to link to from their own site. While the presence of such links is not an infallible indication, it at least means that another person somewhere has thought it worth the effort involved in creating a link.

E-mail, Blogs, and Newsgroups

These Internet resources should be treated with a degree of caution, because each tends to reflect personal opinion, if not the personal musings, of those who use them.

And, just like Web pages, e-mails and their addresses can be faked. That is not to say e-mail is not a valuable tool for journalists. As explained in chapter 3, it can be an excellent way of finding people to interview in person and for interviewing people in different time zones and different parts of the globe. But as that poor BBC producer who was fooled by The Yes Men found to his detriment in the Bhopal hoax, it can also be misused by those who seek to deceive. Often the clues to a false e-mail are similar to those pointing to fake Web sites. The language, spelling, grammar, and word use might be, at least, a little odd. There may be graphics and colors that are not quite right. There may also be cause for suspicion in the address of the sender, which might be either faked, simply be totally inappropriate, or reflect the fact that an e-mail was sent from a more subtlety false, but none-the-less strange, domain address. In terms of faking, and as any effective spammer will tell you, it is a simple matter to cut and paste e-mail addresses in such a way that an e-mail from one addressee appears to have come from another. Similarly, one would hardly expect that a major corporate, educational, or government organization would have an e-mail address such as environmentdeparment@hotmail.com or that a leading expert in quantum physics would have an address such as hotlips@university.org. And, returning again to the Bhopal hoax, there was yet one more hint that the poor BBC producer overlooked. When he went to send an e-mail to the fake Dow Web site to request his ill-fated interview, the e-mail address accessed via the site was info@dowethics.com, an obvious reflection of the fake domain name registered by The Yes Men and their Web site URL.

It is sometimes possible to discover more about the origins of an e-mail by opening it then clicking on its File tab, then in the panel that opens by clicking on Properties, then Details, and then the Message Source button. The information you find will not help much if the e-mail has been sent by a "professional" scammer or if it has come from a spurious domain.

In terms of credibility, blog sites and newsgroups are similar to e-mail. They often contain legitimate information, but they can also contain rubbish and be faked. Depending to some extent on how different sites are set up, it is also often possible for a scammer to post deliberately misleading or mischievous information, comments, and "signatures" on legitimate blogs and newsgroups. Also be aware that many blogs and newsgroups tend to be established by people pushing their own, often highly subjective or emotive, points of view or who are satisfying their own egotistical urges to appear important by self-publishing on the Web. For those reasons, it is wise to regard newsgroups and blogs with caution and as little more than points of contact from where you might, or might not, be able to arrange interviews. In either case it would be most unwise to publish any information posted on a blog or newsgroup without first checking with the person who did the posting, while also checking their credentials.

Plagiarism and the Internet

Conduct a simple search of the Web relating to just about any contentious topic or big news story and you will find multiple copies of the same reports and comments. Often there are so many copies that it is difficult to find or identify the original document. It is therefore a massive understatement to say that the Web is rife with plagiarism and breaches of copyright because nearly all breaches of copyright also involve plagiarism.

There are two dangers for journalists regarding online plagiarism. The first is that they will succumb to temptation themselves. The second danger is that they will attribute information found online to the wrong source—a source that has plagiarized from somewhere else.

Little probably needs to be said about deliberate plagiarism here, except to note that it is simply something ethical journalists do not, and should not, do—ever. Further, ethics aside, a simple Google search for the two key words "journalism" and "plagiarism" points to a more pragmatic reason to be ethical, because it will return more than half a million hits—many of which name and shame former journalists—some of whom were household names until they were caught cheating, were fired, or whose credibility has been wrecked!

Wrongful attribution is a different problem. Every good journalist knows that every quotation, whether direct or indirect, needs to be accurate and needs to be properly attributed. The reality is that with a plethora of information published online and/or repeated in e-mails, the only safe way to attribute is to trace information to its source. The best way to do that is to try to find primary documents and/or the authors of those primary documents. There is nothing quite like asking a source if they did or did not say something, or if they still stand by what they reportedly said at an earlier time. Finding those primary documents, reports, and sources online takes common sense. It involves many of the things already discussed in this chapter such as finding original news reports, looking carefully at URLs, and picking up a telephone and talking to experts.

A Site to be Extremely Wary of

Wikipedia is one Web site that is a minefield for journalists. A site favored by inexperienced and naïve researchers attracted by its high search engine rankings and its encyclopedic tag, Wikipedia represents a brave experiment gone wrong. Established as an open source online encyclopedia to which anyone could contribute, the Web site was hoped to reflect the best of online publishing. The idea was that through mass input and repeated editing and refining entries would become more and more accurate and credible. But the truth is that, while Wikipedia contains some excellent links to other sites, its own entries can be created, changed, or added to by the ignorant, mischievous, stupid, self-serving, and fanatical just as easily as they can be by experts. Examples of manipulation of Wikipedia entries abound.

- In May 2005, a Nashville man wrote a false and highly defamatory biography of U. S. journalist John L. Seigenthaler Sr. which he posted as an entry on Wikipedia. The entry sat online for four months before Seigenthaler heard about it and had it removed. A member of the Committee of Concerned Journalists Steering Committee and a former administrative assistant to Robert Kennedy in the early 1960s, Seigenthaler said there was only one true sentence in the whole entry, but he decided not to sue (CCJ 2005).
- In January 2006, it was revealed that congressional staffers working for members of the U. S. House of Representatives had made more than 1,000 changes to Wikipedia entries in the previous 6 months. The *Lowell Sun* reported that many of the changes were made in an attempt to "enhance entries" while other changes involved the deletion of factual information (Lehmann 2006). While some entries were sanitized by public relations spin doctors to remove unflattering information about members of the House of Representatives, other members were maligned, including one Congressman whose entry was altered to suggest that he "smells of cow dung" (Lehmann 2006).
- Late in 2006, a malicious entry created in Wikipedia included a link to what was supposedly a repair for a damaging computer virus.

But instead of being a fix, the entry actually linked to a Web site that would infect computers with the virus (Moses 2006).

- It was revealed in early 2007 that Microsoft had approached an Australian technical writer to "correct what the company was sure were inaccuracies" in Wikipedia articles. Microsoft reportedly acknowledged it had approached the writer after a spokeswoman said the corporation was "making no headway" in its attempts to flag mistakes to Wikipedia's volunteer editors (AP 2007: 5).

Wikipedia has also been accused of regularly publishing plagiarized material. Another problem is that information and articles posted by leading researchers and academics has been deleted by other, uninformed contributors who have then replaced the original material with entries of their own that contained wrong or misguided information. There have also been allegations that the site and/or entries copied from it have been used to advertise particular products and services. For those reasons, it is wise to regard Wikipedia as nothing more than a site where there may or may not be some good links to general information. Everything found on the site should be corroborated and nothing should be taken at face value.

Conclusion

Although CAR is great for backgrounding yourself for an interview or for conducting other research, proficient users of CAR must learn how to protect themselves and the public they report for by identifying online traps. Journalists must not let themselves be lured into repeating wrong information. They should understand that sometimes people with a particular barrow to push, individuals who make an innocent mistake, or people who just have a plain old-fashioned nasty streak will publish the wrong information online or send wrong information in e-mails.

To avoid the trap of repeating that sort of information by writing it into a news story, journalists need to learn how to assess the quality of information (ask if it is it reliable, accurate, and plausible). Good journalists also cast their nets as widely as possible and try to discover everything they reasonably can about a person or issue from as many different sources as possible. The best protection is to go back to primary or original sources, especially if there is even the slightest doubt about facts or if your sixth sense starts prickling. Finally, there is an adage that many wise old copy editors live by: If in doubt, leave it out!

There are some excellent Web sites that will help you check the validity of information. They include Virginia Tech's Bibliography on evaluating Web information (http://www.lib.vt.edu/help/instruct/evaluate/evalbiblio.html), Virtual Salt's Evaluating Internet Research Sources (http://www.virtualsalt.

com/evalu8it.htm), and Cornell University Library (http://www.library.cornell.edu/olinuris/ref/webcrit.html). There are links to those sites and others on http://ComputerAssistedReporting.com under the heading Verifying Online Information.

References

AP (2007). "Wikipedia Fumes as Microsoft Pays Blogger to Fix 'Inaccuracies'" in *The Australian*, IT Business, 30 January, 5.

BBC (2004). "Cold War Bomb Warmed by Chickens" at http://news.bbc.co.uk/2/hi/uk_news/3588465.stm [accessed 5 January 2006].

CCJ (2005). "Seigenthaler and Wikipedia—Lessons and Questions", Project for Excellence in Journalism, October 1, Committee of Concerned Journalists at http://www.concerned-journalists.org/node/336 [accessed 11 January 2007].

Dobson, Roger and Taher, Abul (2006). "Corrected-Cavegirls were First Blondes to Have Fun" published in *The Sunday Times* at http://www.timesonline.co.uk/article/0,,2087-2058688,00.html on 26 February [accessed 5 January 2007].

Globe Editorial (2004). "Turner's Bogus Photos" at http://www.boston.com/news/globe/editorial_opinion/editorials/articles/2004/05/14/turners_bogus_photos/ on 14 May [accessed 31 March 2007].

Gossitt, Sherrie (2004). "Boston Globe Publishes Bogus GI Rape Pictures Taken from Pornographic Website as First Reported by WorldNetDaily" at http://www.worldnetdaily.com/news/article.asp?ARTICLE_ID = 38464 on 12 May [accessed 31 March 2007].

Grewlich, Klaus (1999). *Governance in "Cyberspace": Access and Public Interest in Global Communications*. Kluwer Law International, The Hague.

Holder, Matt (2004). "We'll Learn from Hoax, Says BBC" published in News Watch at http://news.bbc.co.uk/newswatch/ifs/low/newsid_4070000/newsid_4072400/4072491.stm on 6 December [accessed 5 January 2007].

Lehmann, Evan (2006). "Rewriting history under the dome: Online 'Encyclopedia' Allows Anyone to Edit Entries, and Congressional Staffers do Just that to Bosses' Bios" published in *Lowell Sun Online* athttp://www.lowellsun.com/ci_3444567 on 27 January [accessed 3 February 2006].

Moses, Asher (2006). "Wikipedia Link Led to Virus Site" published in *The Sydney Morning Herald* at http://www.smh.com.au/news/security/wikipedia-link-led-to-virus-site/2006/11/06/1162661592703.htmlon 6 November [accessed 12 January 2007].

Murphy, Padraic (2006). "Age Writer Fooled by Net Hoax Offers to Resign" in *The Age*, 2 August, 3.

Norman, Matthew (2001). "Diary" published in *Guardian Unlimited* at http://www.guardian.co.uk/Archive/Article/0,4273,4224278,00.html on 19 July[accessed 4 January 2007].

Pearson, Mark (1997). *The Journalist's Guide to Media Law*. St. Leonards, New South Wales: Allen and Unwin.

Quinn, Stephen (2001). *Newsgathering on the Net*, 2nd edition. South Yarra, Victoria: Macmillan Publishers Australia.

Regret the Error (2005). "A Real Pisser of a Mistake" athttp://www.regrettheerror. com/2005/03/a_real_pisser_o.html on 4 March 2005 [accessed 5 January 2007).

Slack, Donovan (2004). "Turner Releases Purported Images of Rape by Soldiers" published in *The Boston Globe* at http://www.boston.com/news/local/massachusetts/articles/2004/05/12/2_cite_photos_purported_to_show_abuse/ on 12 May [accessed 6 January 2007].

USA.gov. (2006). "USA.gov's New Search Engine Makes It Easier and Faster to Get the Information You Need" at http://www.pueblo.gsa.gov/press/fgnewsearchengine06.htm [accessed 4 January 2006].

8

Using CAR to Help Develop a Beat

A journalist assigned to a particular news beat (known as a "news round" in some nations) must become an expert in that field. To be effective he or she has to quickly develop trusted contacts and find reliable sources of information. Often, the learning curve will be steep—a process that can be aided greatly through the use of specialized computer-assisted reporting techniques.

In many newsrooms journalists are only assigned to a specific beat after they have proved themselves as a general reporter. In some media organizations there is an unofficial newsroom hierarchy in which specialist beats, some of which are highly coveted, are assigned to experienced and trusted senior journalists. Sometimes one beat, such as court reporting, might be a stepping stone to another more highly prized beat higher up the scale. In many organizations a reporter who has earned the respect of the public, his own editors, and other journalists may work the same beat for decades—perhaps the bulk of his career—eventually holding positions akin to a knowledgeable tribal elder or guru in the eyes of the public.

In nearly all beats, journalists are expected to be motivated self-starters who not only develop and pursue their own news agendas, but who also have the knowledge and contacts to bring their expertise together with reporters from other beats if the occasion demands it. An example of that type of collaboration would be when a political reporter and a health reporter combine to develop a story about the impact of budget cuts on a local hospital and elective surgery waiting lists. A good beat journalist should also be capable of directing others and telling them who to contact and where to find specialist information in the event of massive breaking stories when maybe every person in a newsroom is drawn into a coverage, such as the September 11, 2001 terrorist attacks on the United States.

Depending a little on the nature of their beat, beat reporters are usually expected to file strong stories daily. They are expected to be up-to-date with, or ahead of, breaking news and to regularly set the news agenda. Ideally, they forge ahead of reporters working for competing media outlets by generating their own exclusive stories. They are also expected to be strong feature writers who can produce background and explanatory pieces and work on special supplements related to their area of expertise. In effect, a beat journalist becomes a bridge between one specialist minority group and the general community.

Missing a story, or failing to zoom in on the best angle, is likely to result in a "please explain" from your editor or news producer. And while we are all human and make the occasional lapse, a reporter who does not perform well on a particular beat is likely to find himself or herself transferred back to general reporting and facing a limited future.

Starting Out on a New Beat

There are four key things journalists should do when assigned to a new beat or their first beat. They should quickly educate themselves about the specialist field covered by the beat, immediately start finding and cultivating relevant contacts, learn the "language" of the beat and how to translate that into plain English, begin building a beat database of Internet-based information and links, and keep up to date with relevant news and current affairs online.

A good starting place is to check your own news organization's internal archives for the most recent stories relating to the new area of responsibility. If the organization is small and there is no computerized archive, you can make up for the shortfall to some extent by going online and seeing what can be found in the archives of competing news organizations and on the Web generally.

Educating Yourself about a Beat

You should also attempt to talk to the person you are replacing. If that person is progressing to a more advanced beat within the same media organization she may be happy to help by providing details of her contacts and may even take you around and introduce you to key sources. On the other hand, if the person was moved against his will or if she has been lured away by a competing news organization, she might be less than cooperative in which case you are on your own, just as you would be if the beat is new. In those situations, it is wise to talk to your editor, news producer, or chief-of-staff. They are likely to be experienced journalists who have worked beats themselves in the past and they should at least be able to point you in the right direction, especially as they had the confidence in you to appoint you in the first place.

Just as all journalists must develop and maintain broad understanding of current affairs a beat journalist has to be particularly aware of the latest news, trends, problems, and advances in her or his own area. One of the great strengths of computer-assisted reporting (CAR) is that it can help a journalist who works in just about any specialization within the profession. It can be an invaluable tool for beat journalists because journalism is a highly competitive profession and it is the practitioners who stay ahead of the pack, or who see or hear little things others miss, who build the strongest reputations and careers. CAR can also help you develop a good understanding of what public records and other documents are available that relate to a particular beat. While the degree of access to public information varies between jurisdictions around the globe, any beat that relates in some way to government and government authorities is likely to be underpinned by layers of laws, rules, and public records. It is therefore not only essential to learn as much as possible about those records and what they contain, it is also important to build contacts with the officials who administer them.

Keeping yourself up-to-date with public records, key individuals, professional issues, and new developments in your field of specialization will help you build credibility with sources and also ensure you understand the importance, or otherwise, of changes and unfolding events.

Apart from searching internal archives, a good starting point in relation to a beat is to use simple Web searches to start checking for the names of experts in your region, or even nationally. Simple searching should also help you start developing a sense of the key issues. From there, and as explained later in this chapter, you can build yourself a valuable CAR tool in the form of your own beat database.

Finding Contacts

One of the great strengths of CAR is its ability to help journalists locate experts. However, there are times when traditional approaches, or combinations of CAR methods and traditional techniques, are more appropriate. In terms of covering a beat, it is important to build relationships with people who can help you by providing information, news tips, and background. Obviously, the best way to do this is to get to know particular key individuals on a personal basis. Doing that involves face-to-face meetings. Ideally, the journalist and contact should develop a level of trust, although it can be dangerous for either side and can result in ethical dilemmas and compromising situations if the relationship becomes too close. Mutual trust and respect, but at arm's length, is the best approach.

How you inform your beat with input from sources depends to some extent on the nature of different beats. If, for example, your beat was education, you would find a wealth of information and excellent lists of contacts online at the Web sites of universities, education authorities, and individual schools. You should also be able to find online links listing contacts for parents' and citizens' groups, staff associations and unions, teacher registration authorities, etc. You would also be able to find experts in education-related statistics, latest trends, curriculum design, and teaching methods. In most nations, education is administered by the government and public authorities. You should therefore think about checking with such an authority, for example, the education minister's office, to determine what databases it keeps for administrative purposes. Then you can either ask for portions of the datasets informally or take the formal route and lodge a freedom of information request.

But if your beat was police and crime, you might not find as many good contacts and sources. While that is partly because criminals rarely advertise, it is also partly because police are often secretive and many have little respect—if not disdain—for journalists and media. Therefore, while CAR will help a police beat reporter find "big picture" crime fighting information, statistics, and details police want released to the public, building contacts to support the beat can really only be done by building trust and rapport with individual police officers over time. That said, police department Web sites and the Web sites of census bureaus are often good places to find crime stats that can be downloaded and interpreted in spreadsheets, often using techniques like those described in chapter 11.

At a slightly different level, and looking from a different perspective, CAR methods can still help even if the majority of your contacts must be cultivated personally. This is because a well-informed awareness about issues of concern to people who work in particular occupations, especially when combined with a good understanding of the job-related jargon and culture, enables a journalist to build a rapport with individuals within that occupational group. Sometimes cultivating related experts who are not directly members of the beat's specific occupational group also helps. That can be demonstrated by returning to the police beat example. If a senior detective and/or maybe a regional crime co-coordinator or police chief were reluctant to speak to you as a beat journalist, they can sometimes be turned around if you have built a strong working relationship with a different senior officer or a person outside their direct sphere of influence, such as a well-known criminologist or academic expert in justice and legal studies. It may be that a mutual respect for such a third-party—an expert who you might have first found via a link from, say, a university or criminology institute's Web site—helps break down barriers, particularly if that expert shares the same values and understandings as the police officer whose confidence you wish to gain, or, better still, is acquainted with him or her.

A good beat reporter will actually build different levels of contacts. It is a mistake to focus all the attention of a particular news beat at a local, or micro, level. Sure, people want to know what is going on in their home patch, but they also need to know how what happens at home relates to what has been happening in other parts of their county, state, province, nation, and globally. This is another area where Web searching and e-mail can be a big help in finding contacts and putting local events into a wider context. It also opens many possibilities for comparative articles. News consumers want to know if they are better or worse off than people in other places. For an education beat reporter, for example, that presents opportunities to use CAR to find information and experts to research stories about things such as how literacy levels compare, the proportion of students who go on to university, different approaches to sex and drug education, etc. Similarly, a medical reporter might look at comparative hospital waiting lists in their city or hometown compared with national and international statistics. They should be able to find and interview relevant experts. The point is that there are any number of issues relating to just about any beat where CAR can help find comparative or new information and experts to comment on it. This helps beat journalists maintain freshness in their stories, build their own knowledge, stay ahead of the pack, and better inform those who consume the news they produce.

Learning the Language of the Beat

As a beat journalist, one of your first tasks will be to quickly master the jargon associated with the beat. Again, CAR will help. Every occupation and industry, including journalism and news production, has its own peculiar language, customs, culture, and protocols. "Police speak," for example, is a totally different dialect from "academic speak," and both differ from the jargons of medicine, law, aviation, psychology, or engineering. Different vocations torture the language in their own unique ways and it is highly doubtful if a majority or those engaged in one occupation would fully understand the terminology used be a majority in another. It is therefore imperative that beat journalists quickly become familiar with the jargon, technical language, and acronyms used by those engaged in the field(s) of interest they must report on.

That familiarity should enable reporters to not just interpret what is discussed, but to also literally learn how to speak the same language as those from whom they source their news. They must learn to translate and demystify the jargon so they can write their news reports in plain English which readers, viewers, and listeners find easy to understand.

Again, CAR can help. There are literally thousands of jargon-busting Web sites. To get started on the right track for your beat, it is best to go to a search engine that allows the option of specifically searching in your own region or nation. There are two good approaches from there on. The first is to simply enter the word "jargon" followed by a key word describing your beat. If, for example, you enter the words "jargon" and "police" a search returns thousands of sites dealing with the occupational language of different police services complete with broad regional variations. The same goes for entering jargon and beat-related words such as medicine, law, legal, academic, education, aviation, etc. In some fields, sports for instance, it is advisable to dig a little deeper by searching for the word jargon and then specific types of sport such as golf, tennis, or athletics.

A second approach is to use online searches to help you find meanings of occupational jargon words you have heard or read but do not yet understand. Again, the search works best if you use a search engine that can be limited to searching in your specific geographic region, because jargon or slang words that mean one thing in one region can mean something different in another district. Using this approach it is possible to search for single words and whole phrases (either by enclosing the phrase in double quotation marks or using advanced search options). Be careful of words that mean one thing in one occupation and something different in another; for example, the word beat has different connotations to a journalist, a police officer, musician, street prostitute, chef, or sporting personality.

In addition to searching for topic-specific jargon in the ways described in this chapter, you can find a listing of some good general jargon-busting Web sites at http://ComputerAssistedReporting.com. You would also find it helps to build an inventory of trade magazines, newsletters, and other publications and Web sites that are targeted at those connected with the beat you are covering.

Build a Beat Web Site Database

Most of us have had experience with writing telephone numbers and notes about important information on scraps of paper that we then put somewhere so "safe" that we cannot find them when we need them. Every journalist has had the same problem. The smart ones learn from the experience, particularly after it has caused them trouble when finding essential contact details right on deadline.

One traditional method to avoid such problems is to maintain an up-to-date contact book. Another, newer, approach is to build your own private Web site listing contact details and active hyperlinks to relevant Web pages. An effective beat journalist in the 21st century should have both a traditional contact book and a Web site. The book is portable and does not need electricity or a computer to function so it is great back up. But having your own individualized and private Web site is one of the best assets a journalist can develop.

While building Web sites was once the province of geeks and nerds, this is no longer the case. You do not need specialist knowledge. There are several relatively simple off-the-shelf software programs that do most of the work for you. One of the most popular is Dreamweaver, which is a WYSIWYG (What You See Is What You Get) site-building and page-editing program. There are also some useful public domain software packages available free for downloading from the Web.

But if you do decide to download a freeware software program from the Web, be careful to check and see what strings, if any, are attached. Another very simple free approach is to build a series of Web pages in Microsoft Word. Most recent versions of Word allow users to save documents as Web pages with active hyperlinks that open in a Web browser such as Internet Explorer. Simply go to the File tab at the top left of the screen, then click on Save as Web Page. PowerPoint documents can be saved in a similar way.

Whatever approach you adopt, your beat Web site can sit comfortably on a CD, DVD, or a good quality USB memory stick. This is because basic Web sites do not occupy all that much file space and certainly not more than three megabytes for anything described here.

So how and why would building a Web site help a beat journalist? Simply, it will save a great deal of time, help keep contacts organized, and provide a quick and reliable reference list of active links to key Web sites you use regularly to inform your beat. Further, a private site not stored on your work computer remains your own intellectual property and is portable. If you move from one media outlet to another, you can take it with you. If you feel so inclined, you can also copy and share it, or parts of it, with colleagues. (That was how the companion site to this book, http://ComputerAssistedReporting.com, evolved. Originally built by one of the authors, Stephen Lamble, as a beat site, it evolved as he researched his PhD and was published on the Web as an aid to other journalists.) As discussed in chapter 10, there are a number of similar sites around the globe.

What would you include in a beat site? Ideally the best approach is to build the site so it contains several different sections or pages. One would contain contact details of sources listed in a similar way as in a contact book: Name, fixed line and cell phone numbers, e-mail address and, perhaps, street address details. One of the advantages of listing e-mail addresses is that clicking on them will often open a pre-addressed e-mail window in your default e-mail program. Addresses can be copied and pasted directly from and into e-mails and also e-mail address books.

Other pages should contain headings corresponding to different aspects of a beat. Under each heading you can then copy and paste relevant Web page addresses, URLs from Web sites you will want to return to later, or ones you visit regularly. Next to each copied hyperlink type a brief description of its title or what information it contains. If you are using software such as Dreamweaver, simply type a brief description of each Web site you link to and then use the program to automatically create the hyperlink from a list of browsed pages. Among the sites you would list as links would be the Web sites of relevant experts and institutions, sources of media releases, relevant government Web sites, and any others you find useful.

In some nations journalists who cover similar beats have joined together to pool basic information and tips. The Poynter Institute lists several such North American groups including: The National Education Writers' Association (http://www.ewa.org/), Society of Environmental Journalists (http://www.sej.org/), Religion Newswriters' Association (http://www.rna.org/), and Society of American Business Editors and Writers (http://www.sabew.org/) (Grimm 2004). Also in the

United States, the Investigative Reporters and Editors' IRE Beat Source Guide at http://www.ire.org/resourcecenter/initial-search-beat.html links to many specializations from agriculture and arts to terrorism and transportation (IRE beat 2007). In the UK there are groups such as the British Guild of Travel Writers (http://www.bgtw.org/), Sports Journalists' Association of Great Britain (http://www.sportsjournalists.co.uk/index.php), and Association of British Science Writers (http://www.absw.org.uk/).

Such groups not only provide a degree of peer support for members, they can also serve as points of contact and help identify and find relevant experts. Many also offer useful lists of links and some have newsletters and offer background briefings for members as well as offering access to online archives of members' previously published articles. Adding hyperlinks to any of those sites relevant to your beat to your own list of Web site links is a good idea.

The end product of your Web building does not have to be the most aesthetically pleasing Web site ever constructed — will be a functional tool. It will save time and frustration associated with repeatedly searching for the same key Web sites or trawling your computer's Web history listings so you can go back to that great site you found six weeks ago and that brilliant expert who gave you such good quotes. You will also find that it is simple to keep adding new links and updating earlier ones.

Keeping Up with Beat-Related Developments Online

Keeping an eye on what your opposition is up to is vital if you are covering a beat. You should also do all you can to ensure you are aware of current trends and new developments. Once it would have been enough to keep in touch with contacts and to regularly read relevant newspapers and/or magazines, but today there is also a need to keep up with breaking news online.

There are several different approaches to keeping informed via the Internet. One is to manually trawl through specific news sites looking for press releases and other data. A more productive approach is to target relevant information and have it sent directly to you. The following list outlines some ways this can be done:

- Sign up for topic-specific e-mail mailing lists and newsgroups, then create list-related folders in your e-mail program to store the information.
- Subscribe to Really Simple Syndication (RSS) feeds on Web sites related to the area of interest of your beat. For example, if yours is an education beat, to monitor what is published online by an opposing publication, or any other publication of interest that has RSS feeds, you could subscribe by clicking on the RSS button on the publication's Web site. Updates from the site will be automatically

sent to your computer for viewing by clicking on the Favorites button in your web browser at any time when the machine is turned on.
Major web operatives Google and Yahoo provide aggregated RSS feeds
that combine news threads on the same topic from a range of different
sources and group them into broad categories. There are also personal
weblogs written by experts as well as not-for-profit Web sites that
support RSS feeds.

- Subscribe to specific podcasts on the Web related to topics covered in
  the beat that aggregate stories so they can be replayed at the
  convenience of those who download them.
- Sign up to Web-based online news sites that deliver "tailored news"—
  articles on topics you have nominated from specific regions—every
  time you visit. Good examples here are Google's Personalized News and
  to a lesser extent Yahoo! News, which could only be broadly personalized at the time of writing.
- Subscribe to specific Web-based alerts such as Google Alerts, which
  send e-mail updates advising of the latest news in categories you have
  pre-selected.
- Many government and corporate Web sites and portals have media
  or news sections from where it is possible to subscribe either by RSS
  feeds or e-mail, or both, to particular categories of media releases.
- Regularly enter specific beat-related key words in major search engines
  and meta search engines to find new Web sites and new or updated
  information.
- If you work for a media organization with different outlets in
  different regions or nations, regularly search your own internal archive
  for articles by other journalists that relate to your beat.
- Use the Web to find and make contact with public relations staff in
  government, at universities, corporations, and other organizations of
  interest and ask to be notified about new developments in your specific areas of interest. Most will be delighted about your interest and
  only too happy to oblige.

This chapter has examined practical ways in which CAR can help journalists
develop and work a beat or round. The advice presented here is based on the real-
world experience of the authors, each of whom has seen beat reporters come and go.
Those who have endured, and those most likely to endure in the future, are literally
those who Professor Emeritus of Journalism at San Francisco State University Tom

Johnson has described as being members of the "A-team" of journalism. An early adopter of CAR methods, Johnson categorized publications and news-producing organizations as either "A" or "B" in quality. He made a similar distinction between journalists as displaying "A-team" or "B-team" performance, explaining that:

> The "A-level" publications and broadcasters generally exhibit a richer version of the complex issues for the community, nation and world, and they are willing or able to devote the resources to reporting them. The "B-level" news producers are all those who do not cover the news with the depth, imagination and intellectual grounding as the "A" producers. In similar fashion, editorial staff members in any newsroom are informally classified as on the "A" team or the "B" team. The "A" reporters are brighter and more intellectually aggressive....The "B-team" journalists are, at best, pedestrian in their approach to any story, and they seem to be most secure in the status quo (Johnston 1994: 57).

Johnson's observations have great relevance to the advice discussed in this chapter. Those most likely to join the A-team of today's beat reporters are self-motivated, intellectually aggressive, and savvy about CAR.

Suggested Reading

"A Beat-By-Beat Guide"(2006). Poynter Online at http://www.poynter.org/column. asp?id = 83&aid = 112388 [accessed 26 January 2006].

Scanlan, Chip (2003). "Beat Reporting: What Does it Take To Be The Best?" published on Poynter Online at http://www.poynter.org/column.asp?id = 52&aid = 15521 [accessed 15 February 2006].

References

British Guild of Travel Writers (2007). http://www.bgtw.org/ [accessed 15 January 2007].

Grimm, Joe (2004). "Ask the Recruiter," "Newspaper Beat Reporting?" published on Poynter Online, at http://www.poynter.org/column.asp?id=77&aid=107741 on 1 September [accessed 15 January 2007].

IRE beat (2007). IRE's Beat Source Guide, http://www.ire.org/resourcecenter/initial-search-beat.html [accessed 16 January 2007].

Johnson, J.T. (1994). "Applied Cybernetics and Its Implications for Education for Journalism in the *Australian Journalism Review*, Australian Journalism Education Association, Vol. 16, no. 2, July/December.

Sports Journalists' Association of Great Britain (2007). http://www.sportsjournalists.co.uk/index.php [accessed 15 January 2007].

9

Web Sites and Links for Journalists

Journalists are a strange lot. On the job they are some of the most competitive professionals on earth, often vying for exclusive stories with peers inside their own organizations as intensely as with those working for rival media outlets. But take them out of a newsroom and put them into a university or other setting and they cheerfully start sharing ideas and information.

Some of the most willing to share are retired or semi-retired journalists, many of whom become known for their willingness to mentor and teach new members of the profession. They have reached the zenith of their careers, have solid reputations, fat contact books, and no longer feel the need to prove themselves. Often, they are passionate about journalism and its role in society and believe that they have a duty to pass on the knowledge, wisdom, and understandings of a lifetime. Much the same can be said of a relatively small band of altruistic journalists and journalism academics around the globe who have built Web sites designed to assist their peers and students studying to enter the profession.

Another group of information professionals whose work often informs journalists is librarians. Many of them were early adopters of online technology who were quick to understand the benefits of computer-based research. Some of them drew on their knowledge and research skills to build Web sites especially for journalists. Other librarians focused more widely, publishing information and links on the Web for different types of researchers ranging from scientists to school children. As a result, there are many Web sites built by librarians that offer rich pickings for journalists—pickings that are all the better because librarians tend to be a fussy lot who shy away from information that is not credible.

Just as there are many different types of journalists with numerous different interests who cover scores of different beats and live and work in diverse cultures and political systems in many parts of the globe, Web sites built by journalists, journalism educators, and librarians vary widely in form and content. Some were built and maintained by individuals. Others are the result of collective contributions by many different people. There are sites that resemble, or are, portals that serve as access points to a range of other different Web sites categorized and clustered by topic. Many are simply carefully selected lists of hyperlinks. Others have links grouped geographically, or by beat. Some sites have brief explanations about what you can expect to find when following each link.

A carefully chosen selection of the most useful of those Web sites is listed and discussed in this chapter. Each site is also listed in the companion Web site to this book at http://ComputerAssistedReporting.com. It should be noted that it was not possible, and would not have been desirable, to list every journalism related Web site. The sites that are listed were included because they met specific criteria.

- They were considered to be useful for journalists
- They were judged to be credible
- They were built by real people who were prepared to put their names to their sites
- Information on the sites was offered openly at no cost with no requirement to log in or provide identifying information
- The site was reasonably up-to-date, was active at the time of writing, and the majority of its links were "alive" and working
- The site was judged to be one of the leading Web sites of its kind in the nation it was designed to serve

Chapter 7 explained how the quality of information found online should be assessed. One point that is emphasized is the need to examine the credibility of not just the information, but to also evaluate the expertise of the individual(s) who put that information on the Web. It was pointed out that one major downfall of a site such as Wikipedia was that anyone could publish on the site and anyone could edit entries, whether they were informed or not—expert or village idiot. Conversely, it was suggested that if information was published online by credible experts from respected organizations, it was likely to be reliable, accurate, and plausible (RAP). In that context it is reasonable to believe that Web sites built by reputable journalists, journalism academics, and professional librarians with content that cannot be edited or changed by outsiders should provide links to credible information and that their sites will RAP.

Further, journalists in a hurry need to access no-nonsense Web sites that load quickly. Being asked to identify themselves to unknown Web publishers, forced to sign up, log in, or pay for unseen information that might or might not be useful are all turn-offs. So are sites with music, flashing icons, and obtrusive advertising.

When accessing the URLs listed and described in the following pages, it should be remembered that there is a tendency for Web addresses to change over time, even if sites do not. To compensate for that, and also to make access easier, each of the Web sites listed here is also listed on this book's companion Web site http://ComputerAssistedReporting.com. It is updated regularly—a process that is assisted by readers of this book reporting broken links to the e-mail address listed on the Web site. Similarly, if you find more sites you believe should be included in the Web site listing that are not included here, simply send a brief e-mail to have your suggestion considered for inclusion in the online directory.

The following Web sites are grouped alphabetically by the nations in which they were primarily designed to be of use. Sites considered to be useful in several different nations are listed under the Global heading. It should also be noted that the information presented here is a guide only. The authors and publishers cannot accept any responsibility for what you may or may not find on any site or the accuracy or otherwise of any information you find as a result of accessing any of these Web sites.

Australia

ComputerAssistedReporting.com http://members.optusnet.com.au/~slamble/links/australia.htm

This is the Australian Links page of the companion Web site to this book. It contains hundreds of credible links for Australian journalists, journalism students, and other researchers. The site also has pages of links for journalists around the globe and information about freedom of information around the world.

Internet resources for journalism http://www.library.jcu.edu.au/subjectgds/Fac1/NetResources/jour.shtml

A useful site built by library staff at James Cook University. Links are grouped nationally and internationally. While many of the links can be used by anyone, access to database links is restricted to students and staff from the university.

OzGuide Internet information sources for Australian journalists http://www.journoz.com

An excellent, highly credible, and regularly updated site for Australian journalists, journalism students, and other researchers. This Web site was built and is maintained by university librarian and author Belinda Weaver. Information is categorized and grouped on the opening page, a page that belies the goldmine of information that lies beneath. Links on subsequent pages are succinctly and accurately described, which saves time and makes navigation predictable.

Canada

CARinCANADA http://www.carincanada.ca

This the most significant Web site for journalists in Canada. It has tips and information about CAR as well as links. The site is maintained by a veteran CAR adopter and reporter with *The Hamilton Spectator*, Fred Vallance-Jones. A part-time instructor at Toronto's Ryerson University, Vallance-Jones offers help with freedom of information requests and advice about building databases and has assembled some excellent examples of CAR-based stories and story ideas.

CARinCANADA is also a companion site to a book on computer-assisted reporting written by Vallance-Jones and David McKie. In mid-2007, McKie said it was planned that the Web site would become a portal to a number of datasets in Canada and globally.

McKie is a journalism educator who teaches research methods in the School of Journalism at Carleton University, Ottawa. He is also an award-winning journalist with CBC's investigative unit and has served as president of the Canadian Association of Journalists. He is a co-author of *Digging Deeper—A Canadian Reporter's Research Guide*.

ComputerAssistedReporting.com http://members.optusnet.com.au/~slamble/links/canada.htm

This is the Canadian Links page of the companion Web site to this book.

Julian Sher's JournalismNet http://www.journalismnet.com

This is one of the best journalism Web sites in the world. An excellent and long established site for journalists in Canada and other nations, it was built and is maintained by journalist, journalism educator, and author Julian Sher. An award-winning investigative television documentary producer in his own right, Sher has trained journalists in the United States, Canada, and Europe how to improve their reporting through the use of CAR techniques.

In addition to a huge number of links, many of which are global, Sher's 600-page site has tips on computer-assisted reporting, how to choose the best search engines, news links, lists of experts, contacts, and links for different beats as well as thousands of other bits and pieces of useful information. There are also special sections of the site devoted to Africa, the United States, the UK, Sweden, the Netherlands, Kosovo, and Europe. Part of the site is in English and part in French.

OnlineDemocracy.ca http://www.onlinedemocracy.ca/CAIRS/CAIA-OD.htm

This is a another excellent site for Canadian journalists. It is specifically maintained by David McKie and keeps track of the requests made under Canada's federal *Access to Information Act*. It has links to other freedom of information resources including some in the UK.

Robin Rowland's guide to guide sites http://creativeresearch.on.ca/index2.html

Part of a larger site and a companion to a blog titled *The Creative Guide to Research and Reporting*, this site, although based in Canada, has a global flavor. It reflects Robin Rowland's diverse interests and the fact that he is a journalist, journalism educator, Web producer, television producer, photographer, and author.

The Sources Directory http://www.sources.com/home.htm

A Canadian media and political directory that is largely subscription based, but there are some good free links to be found under the Links and Resources tab on the home page and in links to federal and provincial government information. There is also an archive of media releases and an up-to-date events calendar.

Europe (except for the UK which is listed separately)

European Journalism Centre's Resources http://www.ejc.net/resourcesl

This Web site provides access to reference material and other links, although many of the sites it links to are actually based in North America. It also contains tips for journalists and some good information about journalism education and training.

European Journalism Training Association's useful links http://www.ejta.eu/index.php/website/links/

The European Journalism Training Association aims to stimulate European cooperation in journalism education and to develop a professional approach toward journalism teaching. Its members represent 51 journalism training and education institutions in 23 European nations. The Association's links page is a directory with some odd links, some of which needed updating, but the site does provide good links to its member institutions, many of which have Web sites with their own useful links pages.

JournalismNet Europe http://www.journalismnet.com/europe/index.htm

This is the European section of Julian Sher's brilliant JournalismNet Web site which is described in more detail under the preceding listing of Canadian sites.

Online News Resources in Europe http://www.ojr.org/ojr/lasica/1017820248.php

A Web directory published by the Annenberg Center for Communication at the University of Southern California, this page of links from Online Journalism Review appears to have been designed as an aid to North American journalists wanting to explore online journalism resources and news in Europe.

India

CyberJournalist: Technology, tools, ethics http://www.cyberjournalist.org.in

This is a very useful Web site for journalists in many different parts of India. Built and maintained by journalist Roy Mathew, the site is partly a blog and partly directed toward educating journalists on ethical issues. There are tips, tools, and archives. Journalism links are a little difficult to find at first but there are many of them and they are generally highly relevant and up-to-date.

New Zealand

New Zealand Journalists' Training Organization's journalism links http://www.journalismtraining.co.nz/links.html

This simple links page provides access to major journalism and media regulatory organizations in New Zealand as well as links to institutions providing journalism education and training. There is also an archive and informative demographic information about New Zealand journalists as a group.

Te Puna Web Directory http://webdirectory.natlib.govt.nz/index.htm

A Web site developed by the National Library of New Zealand, this directory of New Zealand and Pacific Island Web sites is a comprehensive, up-to-date, and useful tool for journalists. The database is searchable and can be browsed by subject or alphabetically.

Writerfind—links to resources for writers http://www.writerfind.com/resources/links.htm

While not a Web site designed primarily for journalists, this site is one of only a few in New Zealand that has links specifically designed to assist online researchers. While the site's primary purpose is to serve as a contact point for professional writers and editors and those seeking help from communication professionals, its links are excellent and it contains a wealth of sensible advice for all writers. Built and maintained by freelance writer and academic Nicole Bishop, the site also serves to help freelance writers connect with those offering work.

Southern Africa

Africa South of the Sahara http://www-sul.stanford.edu/depts/ssrg/africa/guide.html

While hosted by Stanford University in California, this directory of African sites is probably the most comprehensive listing of its kind on the Web. The site is searchable and can be browsed by nation and by topic. There are also sections about evaluating online information and comprehensive links to breaking African news stories.

AfricaFiles links http://www.africafiles.org/links.asp

The African links on this Web page have been provided by the AfricaFiles Network, which is based in Toronto, Canada. The directory is comprehensive and most listings are issues-based.

Journalism.co.za http://www.journalism.co.za/index.php

This a very good Web site specifically designed for journalists working in southern Africa. It was built and is maintained by staff and students working in the graduate journalism program at the University of the Witwatersrand and the Institute for the Advancement of Journalism. Although not the easiest to find, the links directory is comprehensive and useful. There are also sections on reporting tools and ethics, including a page of good CAR links.

United Kingdom

BUBL UK http://bubl.ac.uk/uk/index.html

This is a superb, searchable database compiled by the Centre for Digital Library Research at the University of Strathclyde in Glasgow. It contains a wealth of highly credible online information and a huge number of links to key research sites of interest in the UK and internationally. Information is categorized by nation, subject, and type. There is also a searchable archive dating from 1990. See also the Global section of this chapter.

ComputerAssistedReporting.com   http://members.optusnet.com.au/~slamble/links/uk.htm

This is the United Kingdom Links page of the companion Web site to this book.

Journalism.Co.UK Journalism Links Directory http://www.journalism.co.uk/directory/Research_tools/index.shtml

This is a useful page of research links generally aimed at UK journalists. The page is part of a wider Web site which also has a good cross-section of news, views, and tips for journalists. It also includes a comprehensive glossary of words and terms journalists should understand.

Journalism UK http://www.journalismuk.co.uk

This is an excellent Web site for UK journalists with many significant links. While primarily designed as a resource for print journalists, information and links on the site are useful to broadcast and online reporters and editors too. There are also some good international links in the Global section of this chapter.

Julian Sher's JournalismNet: UK http://www.journalismnet.com/uk/index.htm

This is an excellent, long-established and up-to-date research site for UK journalists. An offshoot of Julian Sher's main North American site, it has links to media and government sites in the UK and also opens the door to a huge number of other links, many of which are global. There are also tips on computer-assisted reporting and how to choose the best search engines as well as a great deal of useful information.

NewsDesk-UK.com http://www.newsdesk-uk.com

Despite a somewhat ordinary opening page and a few outdated hyperlinks, this site actually contains hundreds of relevant links for UK journalists. It also has informative sections on UK media law, journalism training, and job listings.

The Journolist http://www.johnmorrish.com/journolist/indexl

Much more than a site with many useful links, The Journolist is an excellent Web site. It was designed by English journalist and author John Morrish to help reporters, writers, and editors make good use of the Internet. Many of the links on the site are annotated, and there are brilliant practical tips and hints about how to research online, about the invisible Web, UK journalism, and a host of other good information.

United States

American Journalism Review's reporters' tools http://www.ajr.org/News_Wire_Services.asp?MediaType = 13

This is a broad set of links mainly of use to North American journalists. There are also lists of quotable experts and tips on using public opinion polls.

Bill Dedman's Power Reporting Resources http://powerreporting.com

A comprehensive and valuable site with excellent links and "thousands of free research tools for journalists." While the site and its links are U. S. based, many of the links are global in orientation. There is also a valuable grouping of links for a wide range of different beats and good sections on journalism and CAR training.

CIA's World Fact Book https://www.cia.gov/cia/publications/factbook/index.html

While not a reference site built by journalists for journalists, the World Fact Book Web site contains a wealth of information about every nation on earth. Sometimes that information is more accurate and more up-to-date than that found on the government Web sites of particular nations. Overall, the site is a brilliant ready-reference if you need national data in a hurry.

ComputerAssistedReporting.com   http://members.optusnet.com.au/~slamble/links/us.htm

This is the U. S. Links page of the companion Web site to this book.

Digital Librarian http://www.digital-librarian.com

A regularly updated Web site maintained by Cortland, New York, librarian Margaret Vail Anderson, this site is designed to reflect "the best of the Web."

A deceptively simple opening page of hyperlinks gives access to a veritable Pandora's box of links on a comprehensive range of topics including news and journalism at http://www.digital-librarian.com/news.html. While the site is broadly U. S. oriented, there are also many worthwhile links to significant international sites.

Direct search (the invisible Web) http://www.freepint.com/gary/direct.htm

A valuable resource compiled by Gary Price, this site gives access to masses of data either difficult to find or not searchable with major search engines. Price is a librarian and the director of online information resources at Ask.com. He is also founder and chief editor of ResourceShelf at http://www.resourceshelf.com. Another of his sites, NewsCenter at http://www.freepint.com/gary/newscenter. htm, is a compilation of hundreds of global links of use to journalists and media professionals worldwide, which Price says is updated daily.

FACSNet http://www.facsnet.org

A Web site run by FACS, an independent organization with headquarters in Pasadena, California, and offices in Washington, DC, it aims to promote high standards of journalism. FACS provides training and conferences and hosts information pages and links for journalists. The organization's Web site has a section devoted to computer-assisted reporting. It has a search page linking to a wide range of resources related to many beats and topics ranging from agriculture to religion.

Gannett Web resources for newsrooms http://www.gannett.com/go/newswatch/nwwebtips/webresmain.html

This is a clean and simple-to-use Web site with many good links grouped by topics. The emphasis is on U. S. sites of use to journalists and editors. Site groupings, ranging from agriculture to welfare and social justice issues, make this a useful site for journalists across the United States working a range of different beats. The groupings also make it easy to home in on particular subjects.

Journalism and media references and resources http://jmc.sbu.edu/faculty/dwilkins/resources.htmhttp://jmc.sbu.edu/faculty/dwilkins/resources.html

A Web site built by Denny Wilkins from St. Bonaventure University, this is an eclectic list of hundreds of up-to-date hyperlinks of interest mainly to North American journalists, although there are some broad international links. There are also good general sections which include a wide range of writing and copyediting tools and help for "the math and statistically challenged."

Journalism resources from Karla Tonella, University of Iowa http://bailiwick.lib.uiowa.edu/journalism

There are more than 40 pages of heavily U. S. oriented links to resources for journalism educators and journalists at this site. It is a particularly good site for finding links to journalism publications.

Library of Congress http://www.loc.gov/rr/

The U. S. Library of Congress portal opens the doors to a huge amount of online information including a link to the still being established Minerva Web archiving project.

NewsPlace.Org http://NewsPlace.org

A site with plenty of good links built by Associate Professor Abraham (Avi) Bass from the Department of Communication at Illinois University. As well as many pages of links, there are tutorials in journalism-related topics such as grammar, copyediting, and style. On the downside, the site layout is messy and navigation is not as straightforward as on some other journalism Web sites.

Reporter.org http://www.reporter.org

This website is underwritten by *The New York Times* and maintained by the Investigative Reporters and Editors group at the Missouri School of Journalism. There are useful, if basic, links to U. S. journalism organizations, reporting resources, and journalism publications.

Shelton Gunaratne's Internet journalism resources http://www.mnstate.edu/gunarat/ijr/journalism.html

Shelton Gunaratne is Professor of Mass Communications at Minnesota State University, Moorhead. His Web site is a valuable tool. It has pages of links to Web search tools, journalism resources, international communications, listservs, and usernet groups. It also has valuable help sections on writing and editing and the Internet. Directories on this site are comprehensive, clean, and easy to use. There is a useful blend of North American and global links.

Special Libraries Association's top Internet sites for journalists http://www.ibiblio.org/slanews/index.html

A useful site for all North American journalists, this directory is also a valuable resource for journalists working particular beats such as arts, agriculture, medicine, defense, politics, and business. Built and maintained by the Special Libraries Association's News Division and hosted by the University of North Carolina at Chapel Hill, the site's links directory listed here is actually part of a much wider site with good global links described in this chapter's Global section.

***The New York Times* newsroom navigator** http://tech.nytimes.com/top/news/technology/cybertimesnavigator/index.html

This is a messy and somewhat odd and outdated collection of links for journalists and others. The Web site is included here more for its curiosity value than as a leading resource for journalists.

The Journalist's Toolbox http://www.americanpressinstitute.org/pages/toolbox/

This is part of the American Press Institute's Web site. As well as links of use to journalists, the site also contains resources for journalism students and their teachers. Other sections cover topics such as free speech, medical reporting, use of statistics, and covering stories about people with disabilities.

Global

BUBL LINK catalog of Internet resources http://bubl.ac.uk/link/world/index.html

A deceptively simple interface provides access to a brilliant, searchable database containing a wealth of highly credible online information and a huge number of links to key research sites in most nations. Compiled by the Centre for Digital Library Research at the University of Strathclyde in Glasgow, information is categorized by nation, subject, and type. There is also a searchable archive dating from 1990.

ComputerAssistedReporting.com http://members.optusnet.com.au/~slamble/links/global.htm

This is the global Links page of the companion Web site to this book.

Direct search (the invisible Web) http://www.freepint.com/gary/direct.htm

Although primarily U. S. oriented, this site and a series of sister sites associated with it contain many excellent global links with specific sections for Australian and Canadian researchers. There are also many good Asian and European links. There is more information under the United States section of this chapter.

Kidon Media Link http://www.kidon.com/media-link/index.php

A searchable database of links to more than 18,000 newspapers and other news sources from almost every country and territory in the world.

Librarians' Internet Index http://lii.org

While not a Web site designed specifically for journalists, the Librarians' Internet Index (LII) was designed to feature the best and most credible sites on the Web. Administered by the California state librarian, there are over 20,000 searchable entries on the site grouped into 14 main topics and nearly 300 related topics.

London School of Journalism's links database http://www.lsj.org/linksdb/linksdb.php

An up-to-date and globally oriented list of journalism and media related links, although coverage of some nations is patchy.

MediaChannel.org—Journalists' Toolkit http://www.mediachannel.org/getinvolved/journo

Some good international links for journalists in many nations plus tips and job listings.

Special Libraries Association's news archives http://www.ibiblio.org/slanews/index.html

This is a particularly useful Web directory for researchers seeking to access international newspaper archives in many different nations. The directory is just one part of a much wider site built by the Special Libraries Association in the United States. As well as also including a links directory for North American journalists, which is listed in the United States section of this chapter, there is plenty of other content of interest to journalists around the world.

The Journalistic Resources Page http://www.markovits.com/journalism/

A broad range of European and international journalism and academic research links compiled by Swedish researcher Nikos Markovits.

While this chapter has summarized some of the best and most useful Web sites and links directories on the Web for journalists, there are literally hundreds of other credible links grouped by nation and topic found at http://ComputerAssisted Reporting.com.

Happy hunting!

10

CAR and the Law

The Internet and Web are brilliant resources that will continue to revolutionize the ways in which we communicate and research, but like almost everything in life, there are pluses and minuses. Sometimes it is hard to pick the difference. The fact is that while the Internet and Web are a treasure trove for journalists, they are also a legal minefield.

From a global perspective, it might seem logical that the extent to which riches are balanced against legal risks would depend largely on the legal jurisdiction in which a journalist works. But the situation is much more complex than that. One major impact of the Internet and Web is that they make material produced in one nation, which may or may not be legally acceptable in that or other jurisdictions, available globally. In practical terms, that means there might be potential legal dangers in re-publishing information in one jurisdiction that was sourced online from a different jurisdiction with a different legal system.

The fact is that law makers, lawyers, courts, and journalists around the world are struggling to come to terms with the Internet and Web. Part of the problem is that the law is a ponderous machine that tends to move slowly and cautiously, while developments in Internet technology and Web browsers are quick and capricious. As if to make things worse, different lawmakers are developing diverse legal solutions to similar legal issues. Thus, online journalists and computer-assisted reporting (CAR) researchers must not just contend with different laws between nations, but quite often with differences in approach within particular jurisdictions within the same nation.

Laws that Help or Hinder

Broadly, there are two groups of laws that concern journalists: those that help and those that hinder. The balance between each group differs dramatically between nations. In many jurisdictions, particularly the United States and New Zealand, laws that could be classified as helpful to journalists include those relating to Freedom of Information (Lamble 2004: 5-9). Many states in the U. S. also have shield laws, which enable journalists to protect their confidential sources. In a broad sense, journalists and online researchers in the United States also have a huge advantage in the form of the First Amendment to the U. S. Constitution, which protects free speech and media freedom. Although those constitutionally embedded protections are not unique, and can also be found in other jurisdictions such as in Scandinavian nations and South Africa, they are much stronger than anything offered by media freedom and free speech laws that are not constitutionally enshrined. For example, Canada's *Charter of Rights and Freedoms* and New Zealand's *Bill of Rights Act 1990* are statutes, not fundamental constitutional laws. They are therefore more vulnerable to political tinkering. But Canadian and New Zealand journalists are better protected than those in Australia and the United Kingdom, nations in which there is not even a pretence of a codified system of freedom of speech, media freedom, or a Bill of Rights. Laws that potentially hinder journalists, online researchers, and publishers include laws of libel, slander, contempt of court, and sedition. Laws that can both help and hinder include copyright laws. They help because they protect those who write, compose, and create from having their work plagiarized or reproduced without permission and provide for redress if those things do happen. But they are also laws journalists must be careful not to breach themselves when they deal with the work of others.

Systemic Legal Differences

Many readers of this book will be journalists or journalism students working in either a republican presidential system such as the United States or a Westminster-style system such as Australia, Canada, New Zealand, or the UK. Many fundamental legal principles are similar in the United States and the Westminster nations. For example, each has an adversarial judicial system, each embraces trial by jury for serious crimes, and each has a judicial system separated to (at least some extent) from its political and executive systems—a principle known as the separation of powers. Further, each of the foregoing nations has separate criminal and civil legal systems and legal systems based on varying blends of statute law (rules made by legislatures) and case law (court or judge-made law based on precedent).

It is also a fact that all journalists, no matter what legal system they work in, need to develop a basic understanding of the key legal issues in their own jurisdiction. In the past, that level of local legal knowledge was enough because a majority of journalists—foreign correspondents included—wrote news for publication or broadcast in one particular national jurisdiction, their own. But the Internet and Web have changed that. Today, journalists need a sound understanding of the key legal elements in every jurisdiction where they work as well as in all nations where their stories will appear. Further, and even more important, they need to have an understanding of the legal systems and relevant laws in the jurisdictions where they source CAR information. Why? Simply because information they find online in one jurisdiction, where it might have been perfectly legal to publish in that system, might seriously breach the law if repeated, or even mentioned, in a different jurisdiction with different laws and legal traditions. The most hazardous danger areas are examined in the remainder of this chapter.

Defamation—Libel and Slander

Becoming embroiled in a defamation action can be incredibly time-consuming and emotionally draining. It can also cost a fortune and take journalists and researchers away from their work for weeks, months and even years.

So what is this thing called defamation? And what does it have to do with CAR, the Internet, and the Web? Fundamentally, defamation is publishing or broadcasting (which in most jurisdictions includes posting material on the Internet) a story, visual image, or comment that could make others think badly of, ridicule, or shun, a particular person. It is more than simply hurting someone's feelings or wounding his pride. It is the transmission of information that damages a person's reputation and makes other people think less of her. It does not just affect journalists, it can have an impact on anyone. In many jurisdictions, defamation is based on what is known as tort law—a long-standing legal tradition based on the idea that each of us has a duty of care to others, in this instance an obligation not to do or say things that would injure another person's reputation.

Defamation can be either spoken, in which case it is often referred to as slander, or in a more permanent form including printed and online text and visual images, when it is known as libel. There is a distinction in some jurisdictions but not in others. Canada, for example, has a *Libel and Slander Act* and the two are treated differently. The same applies in India, where libel can be either a civil or criminal matter but slander is only considered a civil issue. In other jurisdictions, for example Australia, there is no distinction between libel and slander and each is classified simply as defamation.

As a general rule, however, slander is not regarded as being as damaging as libel because spoken words are gone as soon as they are uttered. On the other hand, written and visual images in print and on the Web persist in a more permanent form and can be revisited, re-read, and re-published. In jurisdictions where the two are treated differently, the major difference is that when libel is alleged, the person who claims they have been defamed does not have to show they have actually suffered damage because the law presumes they have. But a person claiming to have been slandered must prove their reputation really did suffer.

Another important difference between defamation law in different legal systems relates to concepts of guilt and innocence. In most adversarial systems of justice, such as those in the United States and Westminster system nations, an accused person is regarded as innocent until proven guilty. The reverse applies in inquisitorial systems, such as France and some other European and Asian nations including Indonesia, where an accused person is regarded as guilty until they prove otherwise.

The innocent until proven guilty principle is what applies to defamation law in the United States. In the United States, it is up to a person who wishes to sue another for defamation[1] to prove that they have been defamed. But not so in Westminster system nations such as Canada, Australia, the UK, and New Zealand. In those jurisdictions, while the burden of proof in criminal law lies with the prosecution to prove an accused guilty beyond reasonable doubt, the burden of proof is reversed in defamation cases and, as is the case in inquisitorial systems, it is up to a person accused of defamation to either prove their innocence or that they had a legally excusable reason for the defamation. Among other things, that means that a person accused of defaming another who does not act to defend themselves could be found guilty by default and ordered to pay damages and costs. There are marked differences, too, in the standards of proof required in different jurisdictions. In civil actions in Westminster system nations, judgments are based on a "balance of probabilities" in defamation cases, but in the United States the criterion is "convincing clarity," a much more rigorous standard.

There are also jurisdictional differences in relation to the use of juries in defamation trials. Similarly, there are different standards of proof, mixes of common law and statute law and how they apply, as well as actual defenses, the roles of judges and juries in determining damages, etc. In some jurisdictions, there is also a distinction between civil defamation (where one person or legal entity sues another person or entity in a civil court hearing) and criminal defamation (where an alleged defamer is charged by the state with a crime and tried in a criminal court where criminal penalties, including jail sentences, can be imposed).

In terms of defending allegations of defamation, truth is often a stand-alone defense, but not in all jurisdictions. Some, such as Quebec in Canada, link truth and public benefit, meaning it is all right to tell the truth, but only if there is a benefit to the public in the truth being known. In the United States, on the other hand, a statement can be false and still not be considered defamatory. Similarly, public figures generally have much less legal protection from defamation in the United States

---

[1] The person who claims to have been defamed and who subsequently launches a legal action is known as the "plaintiff" in many legal systems, while the alleged defamer, the person who must defend themselves against the allegation, is known as the "defendant."

than they do in Westminster nations. In the United States, public officials and public figures must prove a defendant acted with "actual malice" in defaming them if an action is to succeed. Actual malice was defined in the landmark 1964 U. S. Supreme Court case *New York Times v. Sullivan* as a knowingly false statement that was published with reckless disregard as to whether it was true or false. In essence the court said journalists were human and it was inevitable they would make genuine mistakes at times. That judgment, other U.S. precedents and the U.S. Bill of Rights have combined to create an exceptionally tolerant legal environment for U. S. journalists relative to their counterparts in many other nations. Among other things that means American journalists can afford to take bigger risks in treating information gleaned from the Internet and Web more directly at face value than journalists in nations where defamation law is often draconian in comparison. Some important differences and similarities between defamation laws in different jurisdictions are summarized in Table 10.1.

In the U. S. system, freedom of speech tends to take priority over protection of an individual's reputation, but in most nations which have a Westminster-style legal culture, reputation is more highly valued than free speech. The exception among Westminster nations is Canada, where it was ruled in a landmark common law judgment in 1995[2] that protection of reputation should carry equal importance with the American concept of freedom of expression.

One of the major complicating factors journalists face when dealing with defamation laws in countries such as Australia, Canada, and the United States is that there is no single, national defamation law. Instead, each state, province, or territory tends to have its own laws—some of which are quirky. An idiosyncratic example can be seen in Australia, where "uniform" defamation laws were introduced in 2006 across that nation's eight mainland states and territories. The new laws were enacted to replace a confusing collection of earlier laws. They introduced "truth" as a stand-alone defense to defamation in each jurisdiction and they were generally welcomed by journalists and media outlets. But one state, Tasmania, decided to break from the pack when it came to a uniform approach to defaming the dead. In many jurisdictions around the world, it is recognized that a dead person cannot suffer damage to their reputation, but the Tasmanian government decided otherwise. The result is that a dead body can be defamed (or its estate can take action against another entity for defamation) in relation to an article published or broadcast in the island state of Tasmania, but nowhere else in Australia.

Similarly, some jurisdictions in some nations are prone to dealing with defamation as a criminal offense but there are others where it can only be a civil matter. Further, in the UK, Australia, and some other Westminster system jurisdictions,

---

[2] *Hill v. Church of Scientology of Toronto 1995.*

Table 10.1 A Summary of Differences and Similarities in Defamation Laws and Legal Defenses Between Nations

Nation	Statute Law or Common Law	Civil Matter or Criminal	Burden of Proof	Truth Alone as a Defense	Other Main Defenses	Can Corporations Sue?
Australia	Statute but strongly influenced by common law, "uniform laws" in states and territories, but some differences between jurisdictions	Can be either, but usually civil	Defendant	Yes, plus contextual truth	Absolute privilege, publication of public documents, fair report of proceedings of public concern, qualified privilege, honest opinion, innocent dissemination, triviality	No (unless a small business)
Canada	A mix, varies from province to province	Can be either, but usually civil	Defendant but system leans towards U.S. laws	Yes, in most provinces. Defamatory material presumed to be false and malicious. In Quebec, must be truth and public benefit	Fair comment, qualified privilege, the plaintiff agreed with a defamatory statement, special privilege for reports of comments made in courts and legislature	Yes
New Zealand	Statute but influenced by common law	Civil only	Defendant	Yes, plus contextual truth	Honest opinion, absolute privilege, qualified privilege, special privilege for reports of comments made in courts and legislature	Yes, but only if corporation can prove pecuniary loss

Nation	Statute Law or Common Law	Civil Matter or Criminal	Burden of Proof	Truth Alone as a Defense	Other Main Defenses	Can Corporations Sue?
United Kingdom	Statute but influenced by common law	Can be either but civil more common	Defendant	Yes (but not in Ireland, where there must also be public benefit in telling the truth)	Fair comment, privilege, special privilege for reports of comments made in courts and legislature	Yes
United States	A mix, varies from state to state. First Amendment protection of free speech can also be invoked	Can be either in some states, but most often civil	Plaintiff (or state)	Yes. In addition, a defamatory statement can be false and an action still defensible as long as there was no actual malice	Fair comment, special privilege for reports of comments made in courts and legislature, qualified privilege, public figure defense, plaintiff must prove negligence by defendant	Yes

there is what amounts to a second-tier defamation law in what is known as the law of malicious falsehood—an action in which a plaintiff can sue if a statement was damaging in some way although it was not defamatory.

Another significant problem CAR researchers and lawmakers have with defamation lies in working out where it took place. Is a person defamed in the jurisdiction where a defamatory statement was made, or is it where the statement was downloaded? The issue becomes one of where publication actually took place. That question was of major significance in a landmark Web-related defamation case involving an article published online in the United States which resulted in a defamation action in Australia. The landmark case, *Dow Jones Company Inc v. Gutnick*, arose in 2000 after the online version of *Barron's* magazine, which was published by Dow Jones, carried an article implying that well-known Melbourne businessman and philanthropist Joseph Gutnick was associated with convicted U. S. tax evader Nachum Goldberg. At the time, Goldberg was awaiting trial in New York over allegations of share stock manipulation. The article, which was headlined "Unholy

Gains" also suggested there were "uncomfortable questions" about Gutnick's business dealings with religious charities. Gutnick denied the allegations and launched a defamation action in Australia, specifically in his home state of Victoria.

It was argued that although the article had been published on Dow Jones' Web servers in New Jersey, Gutnick could take the action in the Supreme Court of Victoria because it was in that jurisdiction that he had downloaded the *Barron's* article. Further, his lawyers argued, it was in his home city of Melbourne[3] where his reputation had suffered most damage because many of his friends and business associates lived there. Dow Jones argued that the case should be heard in the United States under U. S. law—a jurisdiction where defamation laws are not nearly as harsh as they are in Australia. After complex legal argument, Australia's top court, its High Court, ruled that Gutnick could proceed with the action in Victoria. Late in 2004, Dow Jones and Gutnick settled out of court after the corporation reportedly agreed to pay Gutnick hundreds of thousands of dollars in damages and legal costs.

In addition to drawing attention to the substantial differences between defamation laws in the United States and Australia, the case sent alarm bells ringing among Internet service providers and online publishers around the world. It was subsequently cited in legal hearings in Canada, the United States, and the UK. What worries online publishers is that a citizen of one nation, with its own peculiar laws and no explicit constitutional guarantee of free speech (such as Australia) was able to sue a publisher in another nation with different laws and where free speech and media freedom are constitutionally enshrined as a basic right (such as the United States). In essence, and although it is still to be fully tested in other jurisdictions, the Gutnick case came to be seen as meaning that an article was not just published in the jurisdiction where it was put online and where it was stored on a server, but that it was also published in a legal sense in every jurisdiction where it could be downloaded.

Those points raise some major questions for journalists. What, for example, would the outcome be if a journalist in the UK, Canada, New Zealand, or Australia repeated information she had found on a U. S. Web site that was not defamatory under U. S. law but was defamatory under the law in her own nation? Could she be sued in her own nation under her own law by a U. S. citizen mentioned in the original U. S. article? And what about the implications in relation to other laws apart from those of defamation?

Finally in relation to defamation, no matter what jurisdiction a journalist works in, he needs to be aware there is also a danger he could be found to have defamed someone in the course of conducting research. For example, asking defamatory questions in e-mails is a trap to be avoided. It can arise when a person a journalist

---

[3] The capital city of the south east Australian state of Victoria.

wishes to interview asks to be sent questions in writing. If there are statements or innuendos in those questions that are defamatory of the person asked to respond, or of another person, that e-mail could become the basis for a defamation action. This could happen because the mere act of writing and sending those questions, especially if the e-mail is seen by a third person—a person other the one who wrote it or who it was addressed to—can be sufficient for a court to decide that the e-mail and the imputations it contained were "published" in a legal sense. Similarly, in many jurisdictions courts have little or no interest in whether defamation was accidental or deliberate. In those jurisdictions, breaking the law by accident is no excuse, which is something many journalists and publishers have found to their chagrin in the past.

How then do you protect yourself from defamation? As already noted, journalists need to develop a broad understanding of defamation laws in the jurisdictions in which they work and will have their work published. In a general sense, there are also steps they can take that should help provide almost global protection. No matter what jurisdiction is involved you will help protect yourself if you:

- Make it a habit to report only facts and apply the principles of good journalism such as objectivity, fairness, balance, attribution, accuracy, clarity, etc.
- Never assume anything, not even the most seemingly insignificant detail. Truth is the best starting point for a defamation defense.
- Be wary of information you find online. Attempt to verify it in another way or, better still, use it to find primary source material. Remember, anyone can put anything online and the majority of those who do so are not guided by journalistic imperatives of accuracy and fact checking.
- Always seek both sides of a story and actively offer a right of reply. No matter how persuasive someone might be, there is always more than one side. The more a story is critical of an individual, the more important it is to contact that person and seek his or her comments on that criticism. If you cannot contact that person, you should at least try, and try in such a way that your attempts can be verified later.
- Be careful when seeking comment. Do not argue and do not make judgmental statements. They could be taken later as a lack of good faith and a sign of malice.
- Distinguish between factual reporting, comment, and opinion. Be careful to base comment and opinion on facts you genuinely believe to be true.
- Write about others in ways that you would expect others to write about you. Be ethical and responsible.

Contempt

Another dangerous trap online is contempt of court. It is an area of law that evolved as a means of upholding the dignity and standing of judicial systems, to enforce court judgments, and promote fair trials.

The concept of open justice—which says justice must not only be done but be seen to be done—is at least notionally a hallmark of legal systems in the majority of democratic nations, but it is a concept tempered to varying degrees by laws of contempt of court. In the U. S. system, contempt of court can be a civil matter or criminal offense, and it is either direct or indirect. Acting insolently in a court, refusing to obey a direction from a judge, or causing a disturbance in a courtroom would be classed as direct contempt. Failure to conform with an order issued by a court, for example, an order to pay alimony in a family court case, would be classed as indirect contempt. In each example, a perpetrator would most likely be cited for civil contempt. Criminal contempt is reserved for more serious cases such as threatening a judge, juror, or witness or perverting the course of justice.

As with defamation, different standards apply to the legalities surrounding contempt of court in the United States compared with the relevant laws in Westminster nations. There are also some important differences between contempt laws among Westminster nations. Those differences can pose major problems for online researchers and online publishers. In fact, in most Westminster system nations there are three different classifications of contempt. They can be broadly considered as contempt in the face of the court, scandalizing a court, and sub judice contempt. In those nations, thumbing your nose at judge or other court official during a hearing would be regarded as contempt in the face of a court. Irrationally criticizing a judge, court official, or ruling in a published or broadcast article could be seen to scandalize a court. And commenting on the supposed guilt or innocence of an accused person while their case was dealt with by the courts would seen as sub judice contempt.

While most courts in most legal systems regard contempt in the face of the court or direct contempt in the U. S. system as a serious matter, approaches to the other two categories are many and varied. For example, constitutional guarantees of freedom of speech and media freedom temper U. S. laws. As a result, U. S. media are free to attack the judiciary generally and particular judges specifically in ways not tolerated in Westminster jurisdictions. Journalists, commentators, and politicians in the United States can say practically anything they like about judges and their judgments. Because of this, U. S. judges are sometimes attacked and lampooned during election campaigns in which would-be-if-they-could-be political candidates rail against the courts and wave the banner of law and order for purely political purposes.

Similarly, and for the same First Amendment related reasons, concepts of sub judice contempt are not as significant for journalists in the U. S. system as they are in Westminster system nations. The term *sub judice* is Latin. It literally means under a judge (or magistrate) and/or before the courts. The main aim of *sub judice* law is to achieve a fair trial for an accused person and to avoid "trial by media." Where they apply, the laws say media must not do anything that would interfere with the process of justice or report anything that might be construed to indicate a person who has been charged with a crime is innocent or guilty. One of the overriding aims of *sub judice* law is to protect jurors from reading, seeing, or hearing anything that might color their thinking and interfere with them making a proper decision based solely on evidence presented in court. Another aim is to prevent publication of information that could potentially contaminate witnesses' memories of events. In Australia, what is known as the *sub judice* period starts as soon as an accused is charged with an offense. But in Great Britain it starts earlier, when legal proceedings are "imminent," and in New Zealand when proceedings are "highly likely." The period does not end until an accused has been found guilty or acquitted (discharged) by a court. If there is an appeal, the period is extended until the appeal ends. During the sub judice period, journalists can only report fairly and accurately on what is actually said in open court. They may not comment on a case or those involved and must especially avoid making any suggestion, either directly or by innuendo, about the supposed guilt or innocence of an accused. They must also avoid publishing any information about alleged confessions, an accused person's previous criminal history or his character, or anything said during a hearing that was said while a jury was absent from a courtroom.

In the United States, a breach of *sub judice* principles can only be punished if public discussion related to a court hearing is believed by a judge to constitute a "clear and present danger" to how that particular hearing is likely to function. But in some Westminster jurisdictions, contempt can be punished if it merely tends to influence those involved in court proceedings. In practical terms, it helps to look at how the different laws function in different systems. In the U. S. system, guarantees of media freedom and freedom of speech have allowed media virtually open slather in relation to reporting details of crimes and commenting on individuals involved, including on their supposed guilt or innocence. From time to time, and especially in high-profile cases, judges try to limit what is said about an accused outside court by issuing "gag orders," but they can only do so if there is a "substantial likelihood" of a fair trial being impossible. However, suppression orders are difficult to enforce in a system where freedom of speech is a fundamental cultural expectation.

Another, probably more effective, way of attempting to achieve fair trials in the U. S. system involves sequestering juries (shutting them away from the public and from news and information by isolating them in hotels where they eat, sleep, and live once they have been sworn in). Based on the principle that if media cannot be restrained from reporting, then jurors can be locked away in places where they cannot access those reports, sequestering still does not protect jurors from the pre-trial publicity that takes place in the often long period between the time an arrest is made and when a jury is sworn in at the start of a trial.

One of the best known examples of how U. S. media are relatively uninhibited in relation to reporting during criminal trials was the notorious O. J. Simpson trial in 1994, which became a media circus. An American movie star and football legend, Simpson was charged with murdering his former wife Nicole Brown, 35, and her friend Ronald Goldman, 25. On June 17, 1994, after being charged with two counts of murder, Simpson led a long, low-speed car chase through Los Angeles in which he was pursued by police and by journalists in television news helicopters who were reporting live. That night, after Simpson had finally surrendered to police and been put in jail, he became the butt of joke after joke broadcast by incredulous media. By the time he eventually came to trial, Simpson was a laughingstock. Worse, trial by media had seen him portrayed at the extremes—either as unequivocally guilty, or as an innocent victim of a race-based frame-up by white police. In a verdict broadcast live on television in October 1995, and despite problems with his alibi and the discovery of damning forensic evidence, Simpson was acquitted by the jury. CNN later reported that at least one juror believed Simpson was guilty, but she also felt the prosecution had bungled the way it presented evidence. Other jurors said they had made a quick decision because they were sick of being sequestered for nine months. Despite the verdict in his criminal trial, Simpson was found liable in a 1997 civil suit for the deaths of Brown and Goldman and ordered to pay $US35.5 million in damages to their families.

In an article after the end of the civil trial *USA Today* reported that:

> The 2½-year-long case has given rise not only to a roster of lawyers, jury experts, writers and others who have appeared on TV to discuss the case, but also to television shows devoted almost entirely to the trial and its legal intricacies.
>
> ...As they did with military experts during the Persian Gulf war, TV networks hired platoons of commentators to analyze the criminal and civil trials. If anything, Simpson's civil trial put more spotlight on analysts because there was no courtroom video footage to fill up airtime. Gag orders also prevented trial lawyers from giving interviews, as they did in the criminal case (USA Today 1997).

The level of reporting and media involvement in the O. J. Simpson trials would not have been tolerated in Westminster system nations. The publication of post-trial interviews with jurors in the high-profile cases also would not have happened in many Westminster jurisdictions. For example, in the Australian state of

Queensland, it is an offense punishable by up to two years' jail to even identify a juror, let alone interview one. If a juror did agree to be interviewed and that interview was published, the journalist who conducted the interview, the publisher, and juror could each be jailed.

The implications for online researchers and journalists are similar to those which apply to defamation. The main problem is that reporting and publication of comment about a court case which might be perfectly normal and safe in a legal sense in one jurisdiction can be considered a serious offense punishable by a jail term in another. In those jurisdictions where sub judice reporting is limited, breaking the rules can also lead to aborted trials, with offending media organizations and individuals ordered to pay associated costs.

Another graphic, if bizarre, example of how U. S. journalists and publishers navigate their nation's contempt laws in ways almost unimaginable to journalists in most Westminster system nations occurred in August 2000 when the online version of Pittsburgh's *Tribune-Review* newspaper published a list of the names of hundreds of "purported callers" to a prostitution service (*Tribune-Review*, 2000). In an article headed *"Tribune-Review* Sees Duty to Release List," the paper referred to a pending criminal case against former Fayette County Commissioner and alleged madam Susanne Teslovich who was accused of running an escort service from her home. Justifying its decision to publish the names, the newspaper took the moral high ground and said: "...the case has generated a tremendous amount of public interest. At the *Tribune-Review*, we feel we have a duty to disclose information that has been made part of the public record by government officials." Then followed not only the list of names, but the originating telephone numbers, the names of businesses if the calls had been made from work, and specific, sometimes enlightening, annotations beside specific names such as "ask prices & location," "Sabina she is running late," "told him to call another agency," "it is his birthday," and "wrong number." In a sequel article published online in January 2001, the *Tribune-Review* reported on a court hearing that stemmed from action it took in a bid to force the disclosure of two names on Teslovich's list which had been suppressed (*Tribune-Review*, 2001). The articles were part of a larger sequence of reports. They demonstrate the point that U. S. journalists expect their purposes to be served by the First Amendment, with the public's "right" to know clearly taking precedence over an individual's "right" to privacy. But it is not only media that use the First Amendment. In 2003, Susanne Teslovich established her own Web site. Under the banner "Madam of the County?," she used the site to argue that she was prosecuted for political reasons. Beside a photograph of a woman wearing a black corset and knee-high leather boots she appealed to readers not to be fooled by "the news media and the press releases from prosecutors" (Teslovich 2003). In a footnote, Teslovich was sentenced to three years in jail for prostitution offenses. She appealed but lost and served her time in Fayette County Prison.

While there was nothing legally wrong with the *Tribune-Review* articles, or of Teslovich's defense of herself, in terms of their publication in the United States or on U. S.-based Web sites, publication in the same forms in a Westminster system nation would have invited legal action for contempt of court. Bald comments in the stories such as "...the escort service run by Teslovich" and "Teslovich, 54, is accused of acting as a madam to a ring of prostitutes under the guise of First Class Entertainment Service, an escort service she operated from her home near the Menallen Township village of Smock" would have breached tenets of sub judice contempt in Westminster nations such as Australia because of their *tendency* to prejudice a fair trial by influencing potential jurors. This is especially true if publication occurs in the time between an accused being charged and their case going to trial (at which point it is generally permissible to report on details revealed in court during the trial, but it is forbidden to make inferences or comments suggesting or implying guilt or innocence).

Even among Westminster system nations, there are wide differences in laws of contempt. For example, the Canadian approach is not as strict as in Australia or New Zealand. The Canadian Judicial Council has published uniform guidelines for judges which refer to tensions between enforcement of contempt laws and the rights implied by the *Canadian Charter of Rights and Freedoms*. Noting that the Charter had, in effect, "abolished" the concept of scandalizing the court, the guidelines clearly imply that the Charter's protection of rights "are not absolute" and are qualified by a "reasonable limits" clause and therefore the "proper judicial use of contempt powers are entirely compatible" with the Charter (Canadian Judicial Council 2001: 2,3). Scandalizing a court is still regarded as an offense in the UK but it is rarely pursued. In Australia, on the other hand, the offense is still enforced, which is something Melbourne attorney Colin Lovitt found to his expense in 2003 when he was fined $US6,600 for calling a magistrate a "complete cretin."

Another difference between contempt laws in Canada and Australia is that, while a charge of sub judice contempt can be laid in relation to a publication that merely "tends" to influence a jury or otherwise impact on the possibility of a fair trial in Australia, in Canada a charge cannot succeed unless the risk to a fair trial is "real, serious or substantial" (Canadian Judicial Council 2001: 9). This more closely mirrors the intent of U. S. law. The focus in Canada is particularly on publication of prejudicial information, such as evidence led at a *voir dire*, if a jury is not sequestered, although that evidence can often be published later. The Judicial Council says that:

> Where the publication is based on sources other than *voir dire* evidence, the question will be, as it is for all forms of sub judice contempt, whether a fair trial has been put at risk. The assessment of risk must take account of the fact that, during its deliberations, the jury should be shielded from media coverage of the case (Canadian Judicial Council 2001: 9).

Thus, Canada's defamation and contempt laws are generally more constraining for its media than equivalent laws in the United States. However, the Canadian laws are less restrictive and more cognisant of public rights than similar laws in Australia and, as will be seen, in New Zealand. In a 1999 discussion paper on the role of juries in criminal trials, the New Zealand Law Commission concluded that, unlike Australia, it was unclear when the sub judice period started (Juries in Criminal Trials 1999: 75). The Commission said that while Australian law defined the period as starting when an arrest had been made or charges were formally laid, a precedent-setting court case in New Zealand appeared to have found that sub judice actually commenced when criminal proceedings became "highly likely" (Juries in Criminal Trials 1999: 78). Confusion over timing aside, the test of sub judice contempt in New Zealand is somewhat more aligned with the Canadian test than the Australian in that it considers "as a matter of practical reality" whether a publication or broadcast "caused a real risk, as distinct from a remote possibility" of prejudicing the administration of justice and a fair trial. Although, as in Australia, an "intention to commit contempt is not essential" (Juries in Criminal Trials 1999: 70). Penalties for sub judice contempt in New Zealand are more likely to be a fine than a jail sentence and are normally imposed on a publisher rather than on a journalist (Juries in Criminal Trials 1999: 70-72). As in Canada and Australia, members of the New Zealand Parliament are warned not to comment on sub judice matters (Natural Justice Before Select Committees: 10). They are also forbidden by standing orders of the House of Representatives from criticizing a judge (The New Zealand Legal System).

In New Zealand, as in Australia, England, and Wales, it would be considered contemptuous to publish details about a criminal record of an accused, to comment on the previous bad character of an accused, to report any alleged confession, and to publish photographs of an accused before a trial if identification was likely to be an issue (McGrath 1998). Under common law, it is also regarded as illegal for a journalist in New Zealand to approach jurors before, during, or after a trial.

Just as laws in many U. S. jurisdictions allow video and still cameras in courtrooms, New Zealand courts allow television and radio recordings to be made during court cases and also allow photographs to be taken inside courts. The in-court media coverage does not allow direct "live" broadcasts and is subject to a strict code of conduct and guidelines endorsed by New Zealand's Chief Justice (The In-Court Media Coverage Guidelines 2003). Overall, however, New Zealand's sub judice contempt laws are seen as similar to those in Australia and the UK, while stricter than Canada's and those in the United States. McGrath summed up a comparison of the four nations thus:

>...the United States view that, as a general principle, the constitutional rights to a fair trial and to trial by jury are, as regards the media, required to accommodate the prohibition in the First Amendment. Canada, perhaps inevitably, is following that lead. There is no apparent restraint by the media in disseminating any information

about a pending criminal trial that attracts the public's attention. The criminal justice system in North America has, as a result, had to adjust to the appetite of the media. Prospective jurors are extensively interrogated, trials are often moved and juries are locked away, in an effort to preserve, as far as possible, the fairness of the proceeding in the face of virtually unrestricted reporting. By contrast in New Zealand, along with Australia and Great Britain, the common law continues to seek to uphold both fair trial and free speech values, first by requiring the media to delay comment that would harm judicial proceedings until the trial is over, and secondly, if the media does not comply, through the exercise of the judicial power to punish for contempt. In doing so, it recognizes that we live in an era in which it is much more difficult for media organizations voluntarily to observe traditional conventions of restraint in reporting on matters of administration of criminal justice (McGrath 1998).

Other Perils

Laws vary between jurisdictions in many other ways too. Crimes committed by juveniles are often treated differently from similar crimes committed by adults. In some jurisdictions it is illegal to identify juvenile offenders but they can be named in others. The age at which a person is no longer regarded by judicial systems as a juvenile generally ranges from 16 to 18, although in some U. S. states it can range up to 24 in relation to some crimes. In many jurisdictions, including most Westminster nations, the names of victims of sexual offenses are totally protected and it is an offense to publish any information that could result in their being identified. Similarly, the identities of victims of crime, especially child victims, are often protected. As noted earlier, jurors are also treated very differently in different systems. Individual jurors can be identified and interviewed in some jurisdictions, particularly the United States, but identifying a juror in other systems, such as some Australian states, is a criminal offense punishable by a jail sentence.

Privacy laws also vary widely. For instance, in some jurisdictions birth and death certificate information and gun registration details are freely available but not in others. The same goes for details of motor vehicle registration, voter rolls, court records, police documents, access to divorce records, criminal history, driving license details, telephone call records, and commercial in-confidence dealings by government.

There are other pitfalls too. Attempting to explain to the FBI, CIA, MI6, or your nation's spy agency that all that hard-core pornography, recipes for making explosives, and arrangements to attend an al-Qaeda training camp are purely for journalistic research may be difficult to say the least. Anti-terrorism laws, particularly those relating to treason and sedition, also pose potential problems. In the United States, for example, the federal offense of "seditious conspiracy" carries a potential jail term of up to 20 years (ALRC 2006). In Australia, it is a jailable offense to publish or broadcast a report that a terror suspect is being held by the Australian Secret Intelligence Organization (ASIO). In the UK, the *Terrorism Act*

2006 makes it an offense punishable by up to seven years in jail to publish information that "encourages" or "glorifies" terrorism (ALRC 2006). A separate section of the same statute also makes "dissemination of terrorist publications" an offense. Other nations which have sedition laws include Malaysia, Turkey, the Philippines, and China including Hong Kong, where "seditious publication" remains a crime inherited from the days of British colonial rule.

So in terms of information relating to terrorism and criticism of governments and powerful officials, be careful what you download and also what you re-publish. You should ask yourself if that material complies with the law in the jurisdiction in which you reside and work. Additionally, does it also comply in the jurisdiction where it was put online? Finally, will it comply in jurisdictions where there will be a new publication which encompasses that information?

Copyright

Copyright is a form of intellectual property protection that online researchers must understand. The idea of intellectual property relates to the ownership and expression of ideas. In broad terms, copyright does not protect ideas, but it does protect the expression of those ideas in a tangible form. That expression can take the form of books, papers, movies, music, works of art, new products and machines, Web sites, poems, computer software, photographs, and new plant varieties. Because the physical expression of intellectual property can have a monetary value attached to it, it can be traded—bought, sold, and assigned.

Online and digital piracy (the unauthorized copying of copyright material such as music, text, and photographs) is a growing problem. UNESCO says its member states have nearly 100 separate laws relating to copyright protection (UNESCO 2006). Overall, however, copyright around the world generally conforms to a set of international treaties, the most famous of which, the *Berne Convention for the Protection of Literary and Artistic Works*, has existed in various forms since 1886. In effect, those conventions mean that copyright is administered in broadly similar ways in each of the world's major judicial systems.

The idea of the treaties is to give the owners of copyright exclusive rights in relation to their material, to protect that material from being used without permission, and to provide an incentive for creators to go on creating new works. After all, if a writer, composer, photographer, or artist cannot make a living from selling their work, there would be little point in them producing it.

In most nations, copyright is free and automatic. Unless she or he has come to some arrangement with another party, a creator is generally the first owner of copyright. The work does not have to have been published and a creator does not have to pay a fee for copyright protection. That protection becomes a right the instant an expression of an idea is created. Contrary to common belief, there is generally no specific requirement for a creator to specifically mark his or her work with a © symbol to show it is protected. The symbol is a reminder, not a legal requirement. In some instances, an employer owns the copyright to material produced by employees, especially if the employees were commissioned, or paid, to produce a particular story and/or photographs. Many employers also own digital rights. In some jurisdictions, governments claim copyright over material published on official Web sites by public servants.

Under current law in many nations, particularly those of the European Union, the United States, and Australia, copyright protection continues for 70 years after the creator dies. In New Zealand and Canada, the time period is 50 years after the end of the calendar year in which the creator died, although different rules and time periods apply in New Zealand for works other than those of a literary, dramatic, or artistic nature. In the UK, the time period is 70 years for literary, dramatic, musical, and artistic work, but it is shorter for some other materials. In the United States, although the current rule is 70 years, the situation is complex in relation to works published at different times in history, with, for example, some works published between 1923 and 1977 protected for 95 years after the death of the creator (Copyright Term 2006).

Once copyright has expired, a work is considered to have become part of the public domain and it may be freely reproduced. Examples include the works of Shakespeare, early novelists such as Defoe and Dickens, and most of the music of the great composers such as Mozart and Beethoven. A living creator may also attach a notice to her work relinquishing copyright and assigning it to the public domain. In most jurisdictions, he may also transfer all or part of his copyright to another person or corporate entity.

The greatest threats to copyright are plagiarism and/or unauthorized copying. Online researchers must be careful not to plagiarize and not to breach another's copyright. In practical terms, that means you can only use a very limited amount of something someone else has created without his or her permission. Otherwise you must seek permission from the copyright owner, and that owner has every right to demand a fee and a perfectly sound legal right to refuse permission for the work to be reproduced. In most instances, however, people will be reasonable. The response might also depend on why you want to reproduce the work. If it is for a good cause, say a charity or publication in the public interest, she might allow you to use material for no fee or a nominal amount. If it is for a money-making venture, such as your latest red-hot novel, she might demand a substantial fee. Those details can be negotiated. The most important thing, however, is that you must get permission in writing. The same laws apply to Web and online publishing as to print.

There are also laws in most jurisdictions that allow copying for educational use. They vary between nations but are often known as "fair dealing" or "fair use" provisions. There is also the fact that some material cannot be copyright. Newspaper headlines are not, neither are single words, names, advertising slogans, nor ideas. There is no copyright on news, facts, or common data such as calendar dates and measurements. Similarly, if a lecture or interview is given "off-the-cuff" without notes, it is generally not copyright. But it would be if based on prepared notes.

In many jurisdictions, a breach of copyright leaves an offender open to both criminal prosecution by the state and liable for a civil action for compensation by the copyright owner. There are numerous examples globally of journalists and other writers who have lost their jobs and or been fined substantial amounts as a result of plagiarism and breach of copyright. As well as suffering the ignominy of exposure as cheats and thieves, they have faced substantial fines and even jail.

In Australia, for example, the maximum penalty for a person found guilty of a criminal offense in relation to a breach of copyright is $A60,500 or five years in jail. A company can be fined up to $A302,500. In the United States, penalties for "willful infringement" by an individual can be as high as $US150,000 per infringement and can also attract jail sentences. In most jurisdictions, those whose copyright has been infringed are also entitled to sue for damages.

Conclusion

Overall, the key message for journalists and other online researchers is that they must have a sound understanding of the law in the jurisdiction in which they work. They also need to learn about and understand relevant laws and how they are applied both in the jurisdictions they gather information from and in the jurisdictions where their work will be published. It is also important when writing material for publication that is critical of individuals in a particular jurisdiction, that writers must present their work in such a way that it would be legally acceptable or "safe" at law in the primary jurisdiction in which the criticized individual resides and does the bulk of their business and/or practices their profession.

Further Reading

There are many good legal Web sites listed online in the companion Web site to this book at http://ComputerAssistedReporting.com.

References

ALRC (2006). Discussion Paper 71, Review of Sedition Laws, Chapter 6, Sedition Laws in Other Countries, Australian Law Reform Commission at http://www.austlii.edu.au/au/other/alrc/publications/dp/71/6.html#Heading152 [accessed 22 July 2006].

Armstrong, Mark, Lindsay, David, and Watterson, Ray (1996). *Media Law in Australia*, 3rd edition. South Melbourne: Oxford University Press.

Canadian Judicial Council (2001). *Some Guidelines on the Use of Contempt Powers* at http://www.cjc-ccm.gc.ca/cmslib/general/contempt_2001.pdf [accessed 29 June 2006].

Copyright Term (2006). "Copyright Term and the Public Domain in the United States 1 January 2006" Cornell Copyright Information Centre at http://www.copyright.cornell.edu/training/Hirtle_Public_Domain.htm [accessed 23 July 2006].

Juries in Criminal Trials (1999). Part two, a discussion paper, Law Society, Wellington at http://www.lawcom.govt.nz/UploadFiles/Publications/Publication_76_159_PP37Vol2.pdf [accessed 30 June 2006].

Kafcaloudes, Phil (1998). *ABC All-Media Court Reporting Information* at http://www.abc.net.au/corp/pubs/legal/court/court_default.htm [accessed 30 June 2006].

Lamble, Stephen (2004). "Media Use of FoI Surveyed: New Zealand Puts Australia and Canada to Shame" in *Freedom of Information Review*, no. 109, February 2004. Clayton: Legal Service Bulletin Co-operative Ltd., Law Faculty, Monash University, Victoria, 5–9.

McGrath, John (1998). "Contempt and the Media: Constitutional Safeguard or State Censorship?" in *New Zealand Law Review*, 2(371), 1989 at http://www.crownlaw.govt.nz/uploads/Contempt.pdf [accessed 19 June 2006].

Natural Justice Before Select Committees: A Guide for Witnesses (2005). http://www.clerk.parliament.govt.nz/NR/rdonlyres/A4F2FA15-FCB9-46E3-A2A4-9C15DACACD86/15948/NaturalJustice2005.pdf [accessed 18 June 2006].

Teslovich, Suzanne (2003) "Madame of the County" at http://madamofthecounty.com/ [accessed 18 June 2006].

The In-Court Media Coverage Guidelines 2003, (2003) Ministry of Justice, http://www.justice.govt.nz/media/guidelines.html [accessed 3 June 2007].

The New Zealand Legal System at http://www.justice.govt.nz/pubs/other/pamphlets/2001/legal_system.pdf [accessed 19 June 2006].

Tribune-Review Online (2000). "Tribune-Review Sees Duty to Release List" published online on 5 August 2000 at http://www.triblive.com/news/headling.html [accessed 5 August 2000].

Tribune-Review Online (2001). "T-R Wins Fight to Move Up John Doe Arguments" published online 22 January 2001 at http://www.triblive.com/live/news/news_story.html?rkey = 83366+sid = 024c45621da4c24d51919c93b71013b2+cat = news-regional+template = news1.html [accessed 25 January 2001].

UNESCO (2006). Collection of National Copyright Laws at http://portal.unesco.org/culture/en/ev.php-<URL_ID = 14076&URL_DO = DO_TOPIC&URL_SECTION = 201.html [accessed 22 July 2006].

USA Today (1997). "No Matter How Simpson Case Goes, Media are Winners" on January 31, at http://www.usatoday.com/news/index/nns189.htm [accessed 18 June 2006].

11

Advanced CAR

Chapter 1 explains that computer-assisted reporting (CAR) can be used at different levels, from the basic to the advanced or investigative. This chapter is about how to use advanced CAR—information-finding and interpreting techniques using statistics and databases. The methods discussed in the following pages should be used in conjunction with the online approaches highlighted in previous chapters and also with traditional journalistic procedures such as interviews.

In essence, the type of journalistic research discussed in this chapter starts with an idea—either your own, or an idea someone else has suggested would be worth investigating. Once the idea has surfaced, the next steps involve thinking about where to start looking for useful evidence and information that explains what, when, where, who, how, and why. Often, but not always, an analysis of relevant statistical data can help. In some nations, statistics can be found in publicly available records with many databases accessible online. Where government records are not accessible via the Internet, access can sometimes be gained simply by asking for information either informally or formally through a freedom of information request. Privately held data can be more difficult to access, but often there is corporate information available in annual reports, reports to shareholders, or in records held by courts or regulatory authorities.

There are wide variations in how freely records can be accessed in different nations and in the effectiveness of freedom of information laws between jurisdictions. These range from laws in the United States, Sweden, and New Zealand which usually allow reasonable access, to laws in Canada and Australia which are restrictive (Lamble 2004: 5–9). Examples of where to find good statistics for advanced CAR analysis are listed under national headings in this book's companion Web site at http://ComputerAssistedReporting.com.

At this point, it is important to understand that there are different types of investigative reporting. As U. S. CAR pioneer Bill Dedman (2007) explains, some investigative reporters, for example, journalists like Bob Woodward of *The Washington Post*, use an interview approach. Others, including people such as Professor Philip Meyer, who employed what he called "precision journalism," sometimes use public records and at other times use surveys (Dedman 2007). Yet others specialize in following money trails, cultivating specialized sources, document analysis, or in investigating individuals of interest. The best investigative journalists use a range of different approaches, casting their nets as widely as possible and in directions different stories dictate. In that sense, CAR is just one more tool. Although CAR has evolved to a large extent in parallel with developments in computing, and particularly since the advent of the Internet and Web, it does not replace traditional techniques but it certainly can strengthen them.

In 1989, Bill Dedman won the Pulitzer Prize for investigative reporting after analyzing Census data and U. S. Federal Reserve records to inform a story in the *Atlanta Journal-Constitution*. His success using advanced CAR inspired journalists around the world. Teams of reporters using CAR methods have won the Pulitzer for investigative and/or public service journalism every year since. CAR stories have won recognition in Canada, too. In 1999, *The Chronicle-Herald* in Halifax, Nova Scotia ran an outstanding series of articles titled "Homicides in Nova Scotia Who's Killing Who," which were based on a statistical analysis by Paul Schneidereit. The series won an Atlantic Journalism award for enterprise reporting, the national Justica award for reporting on justice issues, and was a finalist in the Canadian Association of Journalists' (CAJ) inaugural CAR award. In 2007, Schneidereit was president of the CAJ. More recently, the Canadian Broadcasting Corporation won the CAR award and overall prize awarded by the Canadian Association of Journalists two years in a row (2005 and 2006) for stories on adverse drug reactions.

If you seek the fame associated with the Pulitzer Prize or any other prize recognizing outstanding journalism, it really helps to learn how to use advanced CAR. Even if you do not seek fame, an understanding of statistics and how to analyze them is an important tool for modern journalism. Among other things, it will help you perform high-class conjuring tricks to literally pluck stories out of thin air. Developing stories in this way should help you find a job. Reporting positions are difficult to get. Editors tell us that job applications begin to blur after a while because of the sameness of prospective reporters' approaches. But having an advanced skill like CAR, and some clips to prove it, can mean the difference between being ignored and getting an interview. CAR becomes your unique selling point (USP). You will also get stories no one else can because advanced CAR can give you agenda-setting stories that are off the standard news agenda. Editors love initiative and the unusual. You don't have to wait for a Deep Throat. You can check things out yourself by using a government agency's own computerized records.

Finally, your stories will have more context and credibility. For example, you report on a rabid dog terrorizing a suburban shopping mall. That's a good story. But if you analyze the historic incidence of rabid dog bite reports that you obtain from local public health officials, or you have data that tells readers that rabies and dog bites are increasing and by how much, you have a much better story. You are letting readers know why this story is important. You are putting stories in context and adding depth and breadth.

There are links at http://ComputerAssistedReporting.com to examples of significant statistically based CAR stories. You will see that while those stories include many different topics, they demonstrate the types of results you can achieve by using the techniques explained in this chapter.

CAR and Statistics

Some people study journalism, not rocket science, because they fear statistics, numbers, and mathematics. Do not panic, one of the brilliant things about computers is that they are very good at math and statistical analysis. Once you have mastered a few basic concepts, all of which are based on simple logic, most of the analysis that informs advanced CAR is done for us painlessly by tricky computer spreadsheets and online calculators. In that sense, driving advanced CAR is a bit like driving on the road—you do not have to worry about what makes the engine purr or the gears change, all you must learn is how to steer, work the pedals, and pull the levers!

Those who have been there before you, some of whom were math phobic themselves when they started, will tell you that journalists who have used higher level CAR know there are many advantages in learning a little about statistics and math, including the facts that:

- Good statistics are hard, or impossible, to argue against.
- Statistics can help separate facts from opinions; for example, are things really worse, better, or different from how they were in the past?
- Statistics can often be expressed graphically to add visual impact to a story, for example by using pie charts and bar graphs.

A basic understanding of statistics can also help you identify their misuse and abuse by people who try to bamboozle the public. As Fogg says:

> The ugly side of statistics is that they can be very slippery, so it is wise to understand how the figures were produced (Fogg, 2005: 191).

You should also be aware that sometimes the results of your statistical interpretations, while hopefully highly accurate, may come as a surprise to people who have been fed a diet of officially interpreted data prepared by public relations practitioners, political minders, and politicians.

> They might have seen 'official' figures which were sorted and grouped in a different way so they were presented with a sanitized view. One thing to bear in mind as a journalist is that many public servants are treated as much like mushrooms as the rest of the community. Often the only figures they see are ones put out in media releases by government public relations staff. Sometimes 'real' statistics produced by using CAR methods are as much news to those public servants as to anyone else ...(Conley and Lamble 2006: 367, 368).

Producing those real statistics is often the result of working with spreadsheets. By far the most popular is Microsoft's Excel, which is available alone or (more often) in the Office suite of programs. Spreadsheet software programs are extremely clever because they allow us to assemble data, put it in order, search it, sort it, and filter it. In effect, they let you interview data.

Order of Operations and Brackets

To use a spreadsheet effectively and to avoid silly mistakes there are some simple, logical, math concepts that must be understood. They are just like road rules—obey the rules and accidents are unlikely, but ignore the rules at your peril! The first rule is what is known as the "order of operations." If you think back to junior school, you might remember that the order of operations is a rule that says we must process a math problem in the correct sequence, otherwise our solution will be wrong. Look at this example: $2 + 4 \times 6 \div 4 - 2 = ?$ If we just work our way along the line from left to right and do not take any notice of the order of operations, the answer will be 7, which is wrong. But if we apply the order of operations rule—multiply first, then divide, add, and subtract in that order—our answer will be 6, which is correct. To understand how that works, the calculation can be broken into segments. Without applying the rule and simply working from left to right we would get the following outcome $2 + 4 = 6$, then $6 \times 6 = 36$, $36 \div 4 = 9$, and finally $9 - 2 = 7$, which is wrong. But using the order of operations correctly, the calculation would be $4 \times 6 = 24$, then $24 \div 4 = 6$, $6 + 2 = 8$, and finally $8 - 2 = 6$, which is correct. So remember, we must multiply, divide, add, and subtract in that order.

The next simple concept relates to the use of brackets in a formula and what they mean. Understanding them becomes important when driving a spreadsheet. Brackets tell us what part of a problem to solve first. They should be interpreted in conjunction with the order of operations rule. Basically, the use of brackets adds another dimension to the order of operations because they tell us to calculate the part of a problem that is surrounded by brackets before we tackle any other section of the problem. Where brackets are placed can make a big difference in the result. Returning to our previous example but inserting brackets in different parts of the equation will lead to very different results. We have seen that if we simply apply the order of operations to 2 + 4 × 6 ÷ 4 − 2 = ?, the correct answer is 6. But now we insert brackets thus: 2 + 4 × 6 ÷ (4 − 2) = ? The brackets tell us to work out (4 − 2), which equals 2, before we do anything else. We then follow the normal order of operations for the rest of our problem and find the correct solution, which is 14. That answer was obtained by working out (4 − 2), which equals 2, then in accord with the order of operations multiply 4 × 6, which equals 24, and divide that by the 2 we obtained in the first part of the calculation in the brackets, which equals 12, to which we finally add the first 2, giving us a correct total of 14.

Different results would be obtained by moving the brackets to different parts of the problem. For example, if the brackets were as follows: (2 + 4 × 6) ÷ (4 − 2) the correct solution would be 13. That is because 4 ×6 = 24, 24 + 2 = 26, which would be divided by the result of (4 − 2), which is 2, leaving a final answer of 13. There is no need to get hung up on the numbers at present. The main point here is to understand that the order in which we do things with numbers affects the results we obtain. We should work out what is in brackets first (in accord with the order of operations inside the brackets if relevant), and then use the order of operations for dealing with what is left of the problem. A good grasp of those basic concepts will help Excel do some very powerful number crunching for you.

There are other basic concepts that help us work with statistics and draw meaning from them in ways news consumers can understand. They are averages and medians, percentages, and converting statistics into a comparable form by expressing them in terms occurrences per 100,000.

Average and Median Numbers

Average and median numbers are often used to describe things such as housing prices, commodity prices, voting trends, crowd sizes, and rainfall or temperatures. An average is calculated by adding all the numbers in a list and dividing the result by the number of numbers in the list. Thus if we want to find the average of 3, 9, 7, 10, 14, 2, and 1 we add the numbers 3 + 9 + 7 + 10 + 14 + 2 + 1 to get a total of 46, which is then divided by 7, because there are seven numbers in our list. We get a total that rounds out to 6.6 or the average, which is also called the mean. The disadvantage of using an average is that it can be skewed by the inclusion of either very high or very low numbers in a list. For that reason, it is often better to use median numbers, especially when comparisons are made. The median is simply the middle number in a list, the number at which half the numbers are higher and half lower. It is commonly used when comparing housing prices over time, ages, and salaries. Thus the median of our list 3, 9, 7, 10, 14, 2, and 1 is 7, the middle number after the numbers are put in sequence. When a list contains an even number of numbers, the median is calculated by working out the average, or mean, of the two middle numbers.

Percentages

Percentages are particularly relevant to things like reporting on elections, figures to do with the economy, tourist numbers and occupancy rates, interest rates, population growth, demographics, marks and grades, and rates of pay. Working with percentages becomes easier once you get the idea that you are expressing numbers in relation to 100. Thus one something among a pile of 100 somethings is 1 percent or one in every 100, ten somethings would be 10 percent or 10 in every hundred, and 50 somethings would be 50 percent, 99 somethings 99 percent, etc. All you need to remember about percentages is that they are a very useful way to compare one number as a proportion of any other number by expressing each as a fraction of 100. The two most common percentage calculations journalists should understand and know how to perform are expressing one number as a proportion of another and expressing percentage increases and decreases.

First, how do we express one number as a percentage of another number? Say a factory produced 100 widgets last week but something went wrong on the production line and 25 of the widgets were faulty. As a journalist you need to find out what proportion of the widgets had a fault in them and would have to be recalled. To do that you simply take the total number of faulty widgets produced in the week, 25, divide by the total number of widgets produced, 100, and multiply the outcome by 100. Thus we would have $(25 \div 100) \times 100 = ?$ percent. So, remembering to solve the problem in the brackets first, we have $25 \div 100 = 0.25$, which we then multiply by 100 to get a final result of 25 percent. We can now report with confidence that 25 percent of widgets made last week were faulty. The forgoing example was based on clean convenient figures, but the formula works in exactly the same way when the figures are not so neat. For example, if a baker baked 2500 loaves of bread in the past five days and 72 of those loaves were burnt in the oven, we could work out what percentage were frizzled to a cinder by applying the formula $(72 \div 2500) \times 100 = ?$. Thus, $72 \div 2500 = 0.288$, which we then multiply by 100 to get 2.88, meaning that 2.88 percent (which we would round upwards to 3 percent) of the loaves were spoiled.

It is common to know only part of the data attached to a percentage, which means you need to find more information. For example, you know that 60 percent of 5000 people surveyed about an issue agreed with a proposal. Logic dictates that would mean that the rest, 40 percent, either disagreed or had no opinion. But what if we wanted to find out how many agreed, and how many disagreed or had no opinion? To find the number who agreed, you would reverse the process explained in the previous paragraph and divide the percentage who agreed by 100 then multiply the result by 5000, which is the total number of people surveyed. The formula would be (60 ÷ 100) × 5000 = ?number. Thus, 60 ÷ 100 = 0.6, which we then multiply by 5000 to discover that 3000 agreed. This means that the other 2000 either disagreed or had no opinion.

Journalists also need to know how to calculate percentage increases and decreases. Say the population of Nowheresville increased from 102 to 250 in one year because gold was found in the hills. How would we calculated the percentage increase? First, we need to find the actual increase by subtracting the original population of 102 from the new population of 250. We then express that difference as a percentage by dividing the population difference of 148 by the original number in the population, 102, then multiplying the result by 100. Thus we have ((250 −102) ÷ 102) × 100, which comes down to (148 ÷ 102) × 100, and 1.45 × 100, or an increase of 145.1 percent, which we would round down to 145 percent. As an aside here, note the use of double brackets in our calculation. That is something you will see used in spreadsheet formulas. All it means is that we should solve the calculations in the overall brackets before moving to the rest of the problem. To do that we find the solution to that part of the calculation which is inside the brackets within the brackets, then calculate the rest of the problem in the overall brackets, and finally the remainder of the problem outside the brackets by following the normal order of operations.

Now let's calculate a percentage decrease. Say gold ran out in the hills behind Nowheresville, and a few old-timers had dropped dead from all the excitement, resulting in a decrease in the population from 250 to 94. How do we calculate the percentage decrease? First, we calculate the actual decrease by subtracting the new population of 94 from the previous high of 250. To express that number, 156, as a percentage we divide it by the base population of 250, then multiply by 100. Thus we have ((250 − 94) ÷ 250) × 100, or a 62.4 percent decrease, which would round down to 62 percent.

Now you have come this far and hopefully understood the relevant concepts, it is worth pointing out that if you do not want to work out the math yourself, there are some great percentage calculators online. One is Percentage Calculator (http://www.infoseek.com.au/percentage.htm) and another is NewsEngin's Percentage Change Calculator (http://newsengin.com/neFreeTools.nsf/PercentChange/form-PercentChange). Others are listed in the companion Web pages to this book at http://ComputerAssistedReporting.com.

Comparing Occurrences, Prevalence, or Impact

Another valuable concept journalists must understand is the idea of presenting figures in terms of population, or some other measure such as time or frequency so we can compare the occurrence, prevalence, or impact of different events in logical contexts. One good example would be comparing the number of accidents a particular model of aircraft has been involved in compared with another model by counting the number of accidents per 100,000 hours each model has flown. You can find an example along those lines in the story about ultralight aircraft on the Why Use CAR page of http://ComputerAssistedReporting.com. Another good example, and one that is commonly used, involves comparing occurrences in communities of different sizes by converting figures into a rate per hundred thousand people. To do that you simply divide the number of whatever it is that you are comparing, say the incidence of bird flu, by the number of people living in a particular area and then multiplying the result by 100,000.

Here is an example: For the sake of the exercise let's say there are 192,000 people living on the island of Armageddon and there have been 12 cases of the potentially lethal Asian strain of the H5N1 bird flu reported in the past month. In the same period, there were 9 cases reported among the 90,000 people living on the island of Pestilence. How do we compare the rates? Simple. To work out the proportion per 100,000 on Armageddon, we would divide the 12 cases by the population of 192,000 and multiply by 100,000 or (12 ÷ 192000) × 100000 = ?. The result: 6.25 cases of bird flu per 100,000 people. To work out the incidence on Pestilence, we take the 9 cases and divide by 90,000 and multiply by 100,000, or (9 ÷ 90000) × 100000 = ?. The result: 10 cases per 100,000. Therefore we can now report that there is a much higher incidence of bird flu among the population of Pestilence than on the island of Armageddon. In other words, even though the population of Pestilence is much smaller than that of Armageddon, a larger proportion of Pestilence's population was infected with bird flu in the past month. The next step would be to find some relevant experts and interview them.

Calculators and Symbols

All the calculations considered so far in this chapter can be solved for us in an Excel spreadsheet. If you do not want to use a spreadsheet, there is a very handy little calculator that many people are unaware exists in the Windows operating system. To use it click on Start at the bottom left of your screen, then on Run. In the box simply type calc, hit OK, and off you go. Be aware that in the Windows system the division sign (÷) is replaced with a forward slash (/) while the multiplication symbol (×) is replaced with an asterisk (*).

CAR and Excel

Now that we have dealt with basic math we can look at computer spreadsheets offered in Excel. Why use a spreadsheet? Simply because it is a powerful tool that can help us perform magic by doing all that nasty math stuff for us. It can also sort and group numbers and even names, ages, and brand names. We can also use it to help present our findings visually in graphs and diagrams.

In the following pages, there are relatively simple one- or two-row examples of some of the more useful things a CAR journalist can do with Excel. While the examples are basic and readers who are expert with spreadsheets will be able to skip over them, the intention is that they will help those who are less familiar with Excel understand some of the things that can be done with the software. The examples have also been designed as basic templates that you can take, set up on your own computer, and use as starting points for working with more complex data either entered as you go along or downloaded from online sources.

One important tip in relation to Excel and the steps explained in the following pages is to keep saving your work as you go along, using different file names under the Save As option the Office Button at the top of the page. Then, if the worst happens and something goes wrong, at least you can return to an earlier version of your spreadsheet and all is not lost. Another simple but often overlooked tip is to regard the undo arrow in the toolbar at the top of the page as your best friend. It can help you literally go back in time and recover from apparently horrendous mistakes.

Navigation

The first thing we need to do is to find our way around (see Figure 11.1).

We must understand how to find reference points in a spreadsheet. Excel makes that simple for us by giving each box in the grid what is called a cell address. In

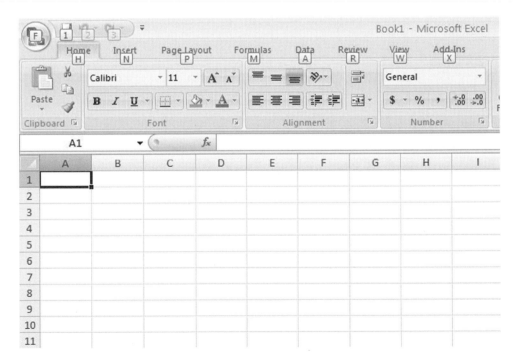

Figure 11.1 Cell A1 highlighted.

Figure 11.1 you will see that there is a bold box in column A row 1. The box is actually at the cell address A1. That address is listed in the toolbar immediately above column A. If you were to click the mouse pointer, which should be a large open cross, in cell D6, that address would show in the toolbar immediately above column A. So would the cell address of any other cell you clicked on.

We also need to learn how to make columns wider. That is done by going to the colored rectangle at the top of the columns where you see A,B,C, etc. Put the mouse pointer on the line at the right side of the column you want to make wider, and click and drag the border line across until the right margin of the column is where you want it. In the Figure 11.2, you can see that the right edge of column D has been dragged to the right to widen it, and that the cell at D10 has been highlighted. It is also possible to automatically adjust the width of a column so that it is no wider than its contents. To do that you put the cursor, or pointer, across the cell boundary line in the colored column heading border. Then, when the cursor automatically changes to a split double arrow, double click the left mouse button. Column B of Figure 11.2 has been automatically resized using this method so that it fits its content.

Figure 11.2
Column D has been widened manually and cell C10 highlighted, while column B was automatically adjusted to fit the width of its content.

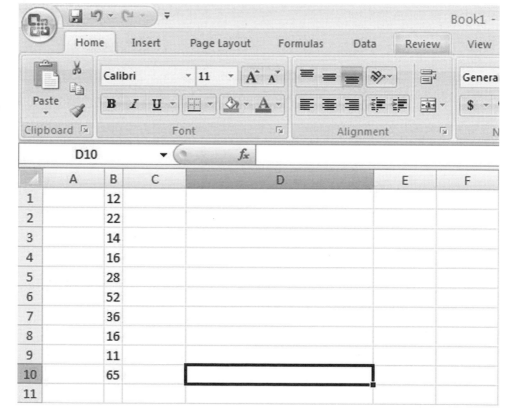

Next, we need to know how to hide unwanted columns cluttering up the screen. You do that by clicking on the letter in the gray rectangle at the top of the column so the column is highlighted and then clicking your right mouse button and selecting Hide from the drop down menu. To "unhide" you click on the tops of the columns on each side of the hidden columns to highlight them and then click on Unhide. You will see that columns E, F, and G are hidden in Figure 11.3, that column I has been widened, and cell H22 is highlighted.

The Formula or Function Bar
After learning the basics of navigating in Excel the next step is to make a spreadsheet work and solve problems by applying commands expressed as a formula.

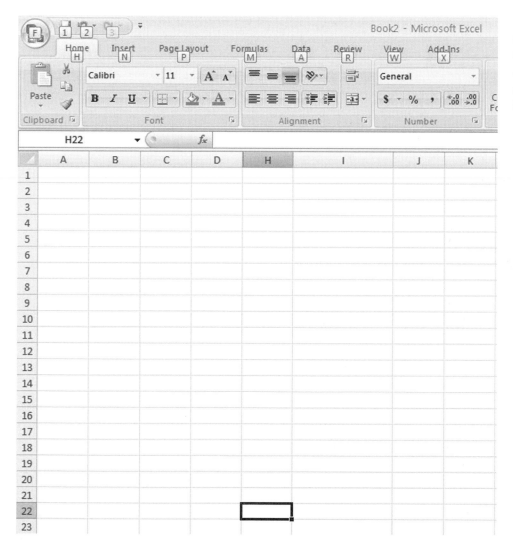

Figure 11.3
Columns E, F, and G are hidden, column I widened, and cell H22 highlighted.

If you look at the top of a spreadsheet, to the right of the cell address toolbar you will notice that there is a blank white space to the right of a small *fx* symbol that looks a bit like the address bar in Internet Explorer. That space is where we tell Excel what to do by inserting a formula. In Figure 11.4 you will see the formula = 2 + 4*6/4 − 2 in the function bar and the solution, 6, in cell A1.

In Figure 11.4, the spreadsheet has been told to calculate one of the problems discussed earlier in this chapter. The problem 2 + 4 × 6 ÷ 4 − 2 = was translated into Windows symbols and the = sign was moved to the front of the problem, thus = 2 + 4*6/4 − 2. After clicking on cell A1 (or any other cell) and entering = 2 + 4*6/4 − 2 in the function bar and hitting the enter key, the correct solution, which is 6, appears in the cell. Excel has automatically taken care of the order of operations and completed each math function in the correct order for us.

In Figure 11.5, there is a different result because Excel has calculated the part of the problem in brackets first, then applied the order of operations to produce the correct solution, 14.

Figure 11.4 The problem 2 + 4 × 6 ÷ 4 − 2 = "translated" into Windows symbols, with the solution in cell A1.

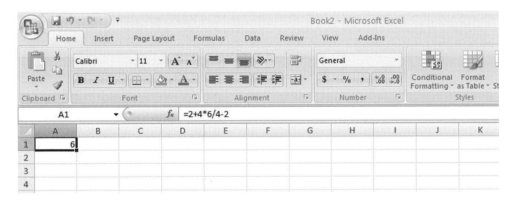

Figure 11.5 Where brackets are placed affects the outcome of a problem.

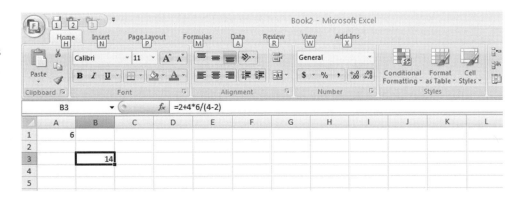

Adding

Adding a column of figures is simple in Excel. Say you have a list of 10 different numbers in column A, starting at cell A1 and finishing at A10. We would simply enter = SUM in the formula bar followed by the range of numbers we want to add using a colon to separate the starting cell and finishing cell and enclosing the range in a bracket (A1:A10). As can be seen in Figure 11.6, our formula would be = SUM(A1:A10). In this example, the total is listed in cell A11, but, as shown in Figure 11.7, it could actually be made to appear in any other cell in the spreadsheet we had clicked on and entered the formula.

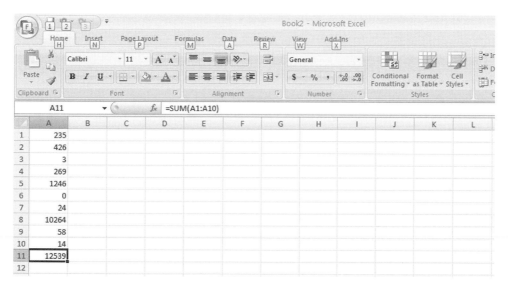

Figure 11.6 The total, or sum, of all the numbers listed from cell A1 to A10 is displayed in cell A11. Note the formula in the formula bar.

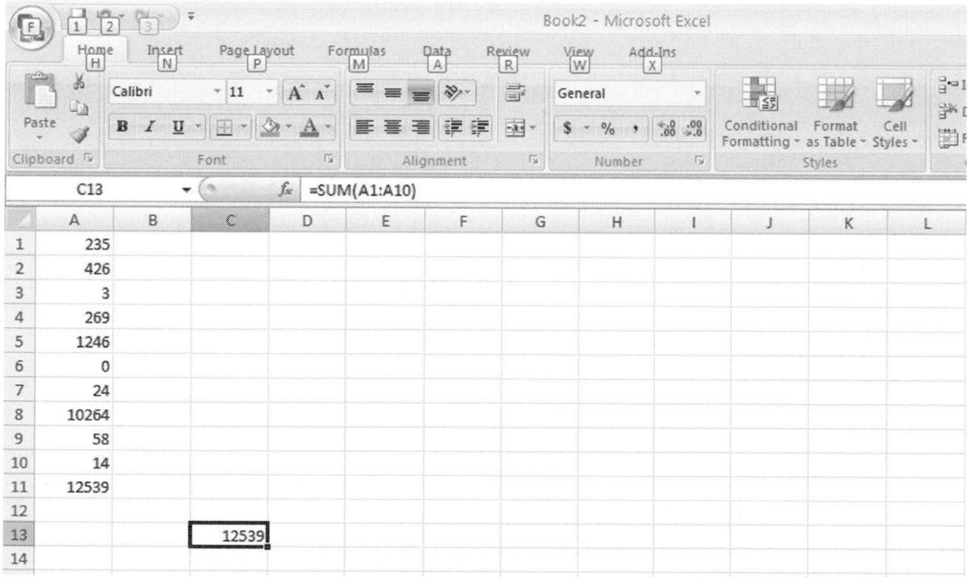

Figure 11.7 Excel will return an answer in any cell where we apply a formula. In this example we have the same result, the total of all the numbers listed in cells A1 to A10, displayed in cells A11 and C13.

Averages and Medians

Calculating averages and finding medians is also simple in Excel. We can take the list of numbers used to calculate examples earlier in this chapter —3, 9, 7, 10, 14, 2, and 1—and enter them in column A of a spreadsheet. If we then click on a lower cell in the same column of the sheet, we can tell Excel to calculate the average. The result can be seen Figure 11.8. After entering the numbers in our list (they can often be simply copied and pasted) from cell A1 to A7, it was then a matter of simply clicking on cell A9, going up to the formula bar and typing in the formula = AVERAGE(A1:A7), and hitting enter. The result, 6.571429, which should be rounded to 6.6, is displayed at cell A9. Note here that the formula is in a special format. Each math formula we use must begin with an = sign. Then there is a command, AVERAGE, an opening bracket, the first cell address in the list of numbers then a full colon, then the final cell address in the list of numbers, and a closing bracket. The opening bracket serves to separate the cell range from the command, the first cell in the range we are working with, in this case A1. The colon means "in the range of" or "from, to."

We use exactly the same process in Excel to find the median in a list of numbers, only we replace the word AVERAGE in the formula with the word MEDIAN. The result can be seen in Figure 11.9 where the average, 13.6, is listed at cell A9 and the median, which is 9, is at listed at cell C9.

Percentages

Excel can also calculate percentages and percentage differences. Let's return to the example seen earlier in this chapter concerning the baker who burnt his bread. Remember, he baked 2500 loaves in the past five days and 72 of those loaves were

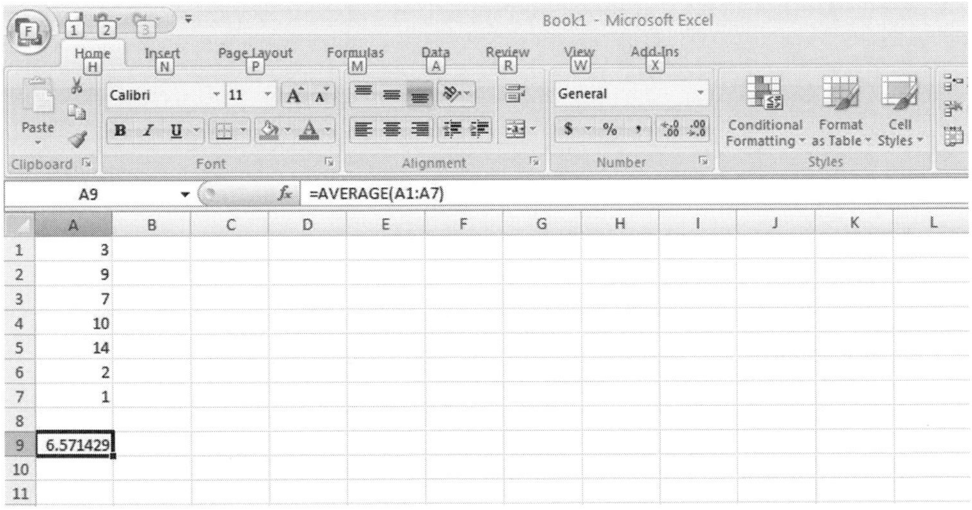

Figure 11.8
Calculating averages is simple. Note that you can use the Number buttons to choose how many decimal points are displayed.

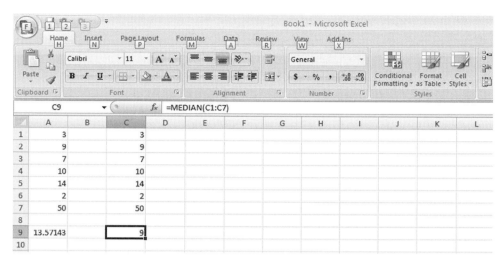

Figure 11.9
In this example, note how the inclusion of one larger number, 50, has skewed the average, leaving the median, 9, as a more accurate indicator of the majority of numbers in the column.

burnt in the oven. We calculated the percentage of burnt loaves by applying the formula (72 ÷ 2500) × 100 = 2.88. As can be seen in Figure 11.10, it is actually easier to do the same calculation in Excel by listing the total number of loaves baked in cell A1 (2500) and the number burnt in B2 (72), clicking on C2 and entering the formula = (B2/A2)*100, which results in the correct answer of 2.88 that would then be rounded upwards to 3 percent.

Percentage Change or Difference

Calculating percentage change is also relatively simple in Excel. Returning to Nowheresville, where the population jumped from 102 to 250 in one year after gold was found, we would calculate the percentage increase in population by entering the base population of 102 in cell A1 and the new population (250) in B2. As seen in Figure 11.11, you could then go to cell C2 and instruct Excel to find the difference between the new population and the old one by subtracting 102 from 250, then dividing the difference (148) by the original population (102) and multiplying by 100.

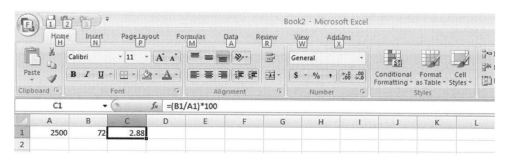

Figure 11.10
Calculating a simple percentage.

Figure 11.11

Calculating percentage increase where A1 was the original number and B1 the new number.

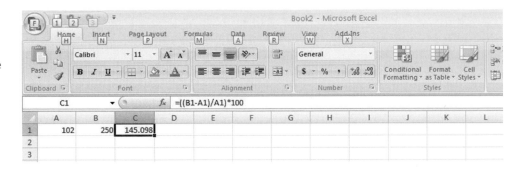

An important point here is to position the brackets in exactly the right places so that Excel can perform the calculations automatically in the correct order. Thus we enter the formula = ((B1 - A1)/A1)*100 after clicking in cell C1 and Excel tells us the percentage increase was 145 percent.

As noted previously, calculating percentage decrease involves a similar process. Say the population of Nowheresville falls from 250 to 94. As seen in Figure 11.12, we would ask Excel to calculate the actual decrease by subtracting the new population of 94 from the previous high of 250. To express that number, 156, as a percentage we divide it by the base population of 250, then multiply by 100. Thus we enter the formula = ((B1 - A1)/B1)*100 after clicking on C1. The result is a 62.4 percent decrease in population.

Incidence per 100,000

Excel is also a valuable tool for comparing occurrences and/or the prevalence of events in terms of population or other factors that can be measured by adjusting them so they are reflected as a proportion of 100,000. Such measures are particularly useful for comparing things like crime rates and the spread of diseases. Let's compare the rates of H5N1 Asian bird flu on the islands of Armageddon and Pestilence (see earlier example) by using a spreadsheet. We know that 192,000 people live on the island of Armageddon and there have been 12 cases of the virus in the

Figure 11.12

A formula for percentage decrease where B1 was the original number and A1 is the new number.

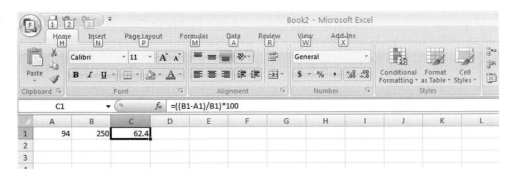

past month. We could open a new spreadsheet and enter the name of the island in cell A1, which we would widen so we can read the name properly, enter the population in cell A2, which we also need to widen or it will come up with an error reading consisting of hash signs (#), and then enter the number of flu cases in cell A3. As seen in Figure 11.13, row A tells us about Armageddon. We can then enter the relevant information for Pestilence in row B with the population of 90,000 listed in B2 and that island's nine cases of flu in the past month in B3. We then go to A4 and enter the formula = (C1/B1)*100000, which tells Excel to divide the 12 cases on Armageddon by the population (12 divided by 192,000) and to multiply the result by 100,000. This reveals that there are 6.25 cases of bird flu per 100,000 people on Armageddon. Thanks to another bit of Excel magic it is then simple to discover the virus' incidence on Pestilence. We can simply make Excel apply and adjust the formula we used in cell A4 by placing our cursor over the small square at the bottom right of the highlighted rectangular outline around that cell and, while still holding the right mouse button down, drawing the square down to cell B4. As if by magic, Excel automatically adjusts the formula for us so that it divides the 9 cases of flu on Pestilence by 90,000, then multiplies the result by 100,000, revealing an incidence of 10 cases per 100,000 on that island.

Sorting Lists

Excel is also a great tool for sorting and grouping lists and numbers. For example, it can be useful for taking random lists of numerals and listing them in rank order. Similarly, it can arrange long lists of names into alphabetical order.

Say you have the list of names on the next page and you want to quickly sort them by family name into alphabetical order. You can take the first steps toward doing that by copying the names as a group and pasting them into cell A1 in a new Excel spreadsheet and then widening the column so each name can be read properly.

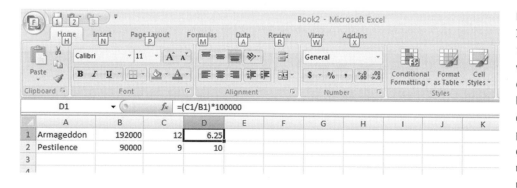

Figure 11.13
Incidence per 100,000 is a very useful way of comparing like with like in different sized populations, or for comparing occurrences against measures such as time, distance, temperature, etc.

John Howard
Tony Blair
Tony Abbot
George Bush
Paris Hilton
Helen Clark
Mel Gibson
Bill Clinton
Stephen Harper
Peter Beattie
Barnaby Joyce
Cyril Smythe
Ronald MacDonald
Bugul Noz
Harold Potter
Rowan Atkinson
Peter Foster
Bonnie Parker
Gisele Bundchen

At first the sheet would look like Figure 11.14.

To sort the names into alphabetical order by family name, we need to put them into two columns, one for the first name and one for the surname. But we must keep the first and second names of each individual correctly matched. How can we do that?

It is easy. First move the cursor to the top of the sheet and widen column B. Then click on the A at the top of column A to highlight all the names in column A. Now click on the Data tab in the toolbar at the top of the page, and then on Text to columns from the dropdown menu that appears. Accept the fact that Excel has decided the data is "delimited" and click Next. In the box headed Delimiters, ensure that the only box with a tick in it says "space." Click Next. In the next panel, click on the Text button. Then click Finish. Family names and first names are now matched in separate columns. This is important.

The names can now be sorted into alphabetical order by family name. To do that, highlight both columns at once. Click the Data tab and then Sort. In the sort box, click on the drop-down Sort by box and select Column B. Ensure Values is selected in the middle panel, that A to Z is selected under Order, and that the button at the top of the panel that says My data has headers is **not** selected. Then click OK. As seen in Figure 11.15, the names will then be sorted in alphabetical order by family name.

If we had wanted to sort alphabetically by first name, we would have told Excel to sort by Column A. If we wanted the names sorted in reverse order, we would click the Descending button. If the ages of each person were listed in Column C, we could sort by age simply by selecting Sort by Column C.

Conditional Formulas and Coding Data

One other powerful and useful tool in Excel is its ability to perform specific calculations if particular circumstances do, or do not, exist. In other words, we can tell Excel to do, or not do, certain things depending on a range of variables.

Figure 11.15
Delimiting data and controlling the sort order.

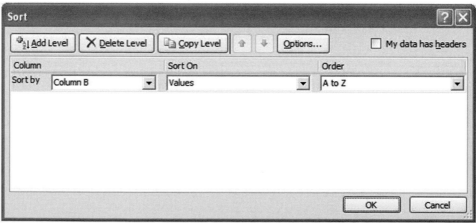

One of the most useful conditional formulas for journalists is the IF formula. It will tell if particular propositions put to Excel are TRUE or FALSE. The spreadsheet in Figure 11.16 is an example of the use of conditional formulas. It is also an example of how we can code information so that Excel can manipulate it. The spreadsheet is based on a hypothetical survey of how many people drive different makes of vehicle. You want to find out which brands are most popular with women and men and in different age groups. To calculate those things manually would be a big task that would take a long time. Excel can do it quickly.

Look at Column A in Figure 11.16. For the sake of the exercise, assume that we have collected our data from 20 people[1] and coded it. We code it to put text-based information into a mathematical, or statistical, format that Excel can work with.

As highlighted in the panel in Figure 11.16, the following code was used to represent brand names in Column A:

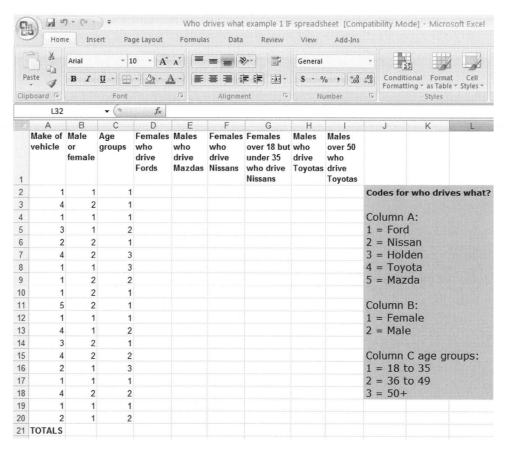

Figure 11.16
Coding variables by assigning them individual numerical values means complex data can be sorted easily by applying a formula.

---

[1] This would not be a large enough sample for a valid real-life survey of this kind.

1 = Ford
2 = Nissan
3 = Holden
4 = Toyota
5 = Mazda

In Column B, the following code is used to distinguish between male and female respondents to the survey:

1 = Female
2 = Male

Column C lists data about age groups. It is coded as follows:

1 = 18 to 35
2 = 36 to 49
3 = 50+

For our article, the first thing we want to know is how many females drive Fords. How do we do that? We use a conditional formula that says if Ford is listed in Column A and if female is listed in Column B, report TRUE in Column D but if that is not the case report that the proposition is FALSE. To do that, as seen in Figure 11.17, we click on cell D1 and in the formula bar enter = IF(A2 = 1,B2 = 1). Excel tells us our proposition is TRUE in this instance, which indicates that the person listed in row 2 is a female who drives a Ford.

The next step is to put the cursor on the small black square in the bottom right corner of the highlighted box surrounding cell D2, and holding down the left mouse button, extending the formula down the column to cell D20 so we can see how many times our proposition is true and how many times it is false. The result is displayed in Figure 11.18.

Although we can now see how many females drive Fords, the outcome displayed in Figure 11.18 is clumsy. To actually come up with a result and report how many females drive Fords, we would have to go through the column manually and count the number of times TRUE appeared. This would be a daunting task if the survey had involved hundreds or thousands of respondents.

A better approach is to assign a TRUE reply a numerical value that Excel can count and report as a total in cell D21. To do that we use the same formula but outside the final bracket we tell the formula to multiply each TRUE response by one. We do that because any number multiplied by one will equal that original number, unless the number is a zero, in which case the result will always be zero. Hence 1*1 = 1 or 0*1 = 0. All we have to do to make that happen is return to cell D2, clicking the cursor at that address, and add *1 to the formula. As seen in Figure 11.19,

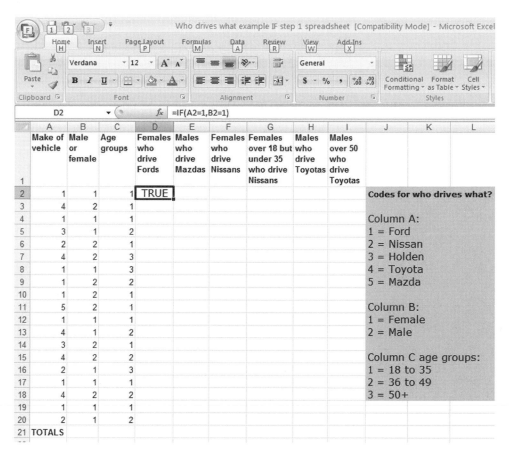

Figure 11.17 An IF formula will tell us if a proposition is true or false.

the new formula can now be extended down the column by again clicking on the small square at the bottom right of the highlighted box at D2 and drawing it down the column to D20.

As a final step in this phase of interviewing the data, we need to make Excel add all the ones in Column D. Figure 11.20 shows that can be done by clicking on cell D21 and entering the formula = SUM(D2:D20). This will reveal that six females in our survey drive Fords. Now that we have those two basic formulas we can adapt them for the next column so it can tell us how many males drive Mazdas. As seen in Figure 11.21, the answer is one.

But what if we want more information, such as a breakdown by age? That can be done by adding a new step to the formula. For example, to find out how many females between the ages of 18 and 35 drive Nissans we have to go back to our coding and ask Excel to tell us how many times there is a combination of a 2 (Nissan) in Column A, a 1 (female) in Column B and, a 1 (18 to 35) in Column C.

Figure 11.18

Applying a formula to a column is a simple as dragging the small square at the bottom right corner of a highlighted cell down, or up, that column (or across a row) as far as needed.

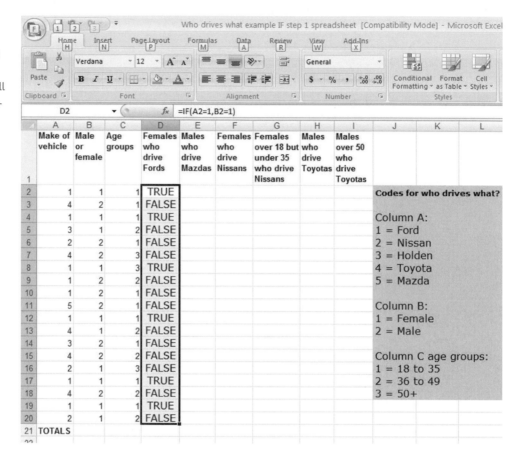

That is too much for Excel to work out in one chunk so we tell the software to solve part of the problem first, in this case how many females drive Nissans, by clicking on cell F2 and inserting the formula = IF(A2 = 2,B2 = 1)`1, and drawing it down the column. We then ask Excel to total the column. Then we must discover how many females who drive Nissans are in the correct age bracket. We go to column G in our spreadsheet, which just happens to be conveniently ready for us and is headed "Females over 18 but under 35 who drive Nissans." Click on cell G2 and apply the formula = IF(C2 = 1,F2 = 1)`1, which is extended down the column to G20 and then a total is added in G21. As indicated in Figure 11.22, the spreadsheet now reports that no women in the 18 to 35 age bracket drive a Nissan.

Say we now want to know how many males over the age of 50 drive a Toyota. Again we need to use two steps. To work out how many males drive Toyotas we apply the formula = IF(A2 = 4,B2 = 2)*1 in cell H2, which leads to the conclusion after we have drawn the formula down the column and added it, that four males

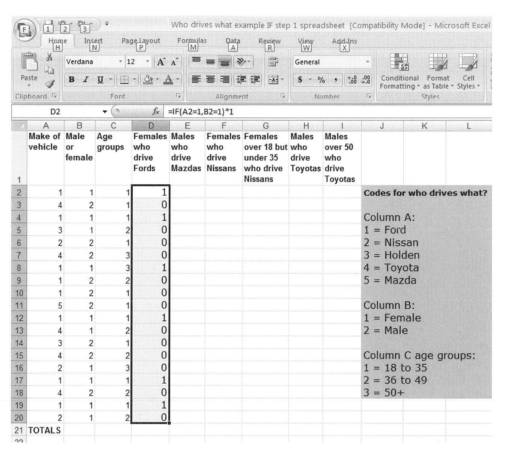

Figure 11.19
Coding TRUE to
equal 1 and FALSE
to return 0 makes
it simple to count
the number of
true responses.

drive Toyotas. Then, to make Excel calculate how many of that group are over 50, we go to cell I2 and enter the formula = IF(C2 = 3,H2 = 1)*1. The result, as shown in Figure 11.23, informs us that just one male over 50 drives a Toyota.

Obviously there is much more information we could extract from the simple survey example used here. Another very useful conditional IF formula tells Excel to do one thing if numbers in one column are greater than or less than numbers in another column. Briefly, that can be calculated because Excel recognizes the greater than (>) and less than (<) symbols. Thus conditional formulas can be used to do things such as tell Excel to list all the numbers in one column or row that are greater than some specific number we designate and to list them in a new column or row. The same can be done in reverse for numbers that are less than a specified number. Percentage differences can then be calculated between the greater and less than numbers and the original, or base, numbers. Calculations like that are excellent when comparing things such as crime rates and population change over time.

Figure 11.20
Adding the sum
of coded TRUE
responses.

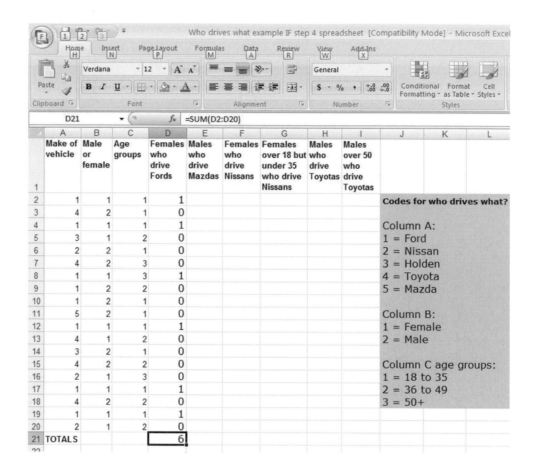

Information about how to use those formulas in Excel and a whole range of other relevant tips and advice can be found online at the Web sites listed in the section of this book's companion Web site http://ComputerAssistedReporting.com under the list of links headed "Using Excel."

Finding the Numbers to Crunch

Data files are available from a wide variety of sources. You can often request them from government officials, which is one reason why you should always carry a memory stick.

The easiest way to locate data files and statistics is via the Internet. A comprehensive list of statistics sources on the Web can be found on this book's companion Web site under the heading "Sources of Statistics." In a general sense, however, the best online sources of statistics include:

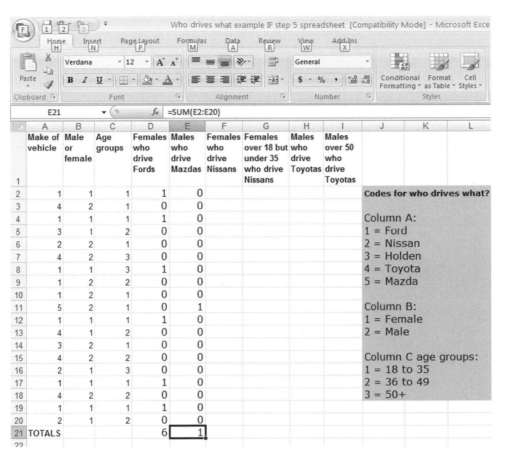

Figure 11.21
Adapting the formulas for different columns.

- Official government bureaus of statistics
- All levels of government departments
- Surveys and opinion polls, but be careful to check on survey methods
- Your own research
- Data from research organizations such as universities
- The research of reputable others

But beware of dubious sources of doubtful statistics. They are likely to include:

- Data gathered during vox pop interviews (they tell us nothing more than the opinions of a handful of people)
- Figures compiled by people and organizations with vested interests
- Many statistics used in advertising

Figure 11.22
Adding other
variables to the
formula.

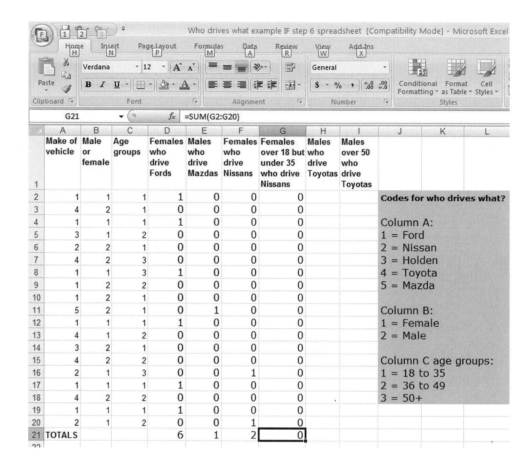

	Make of vehicle	Male or female	Age groups	Females who drive Fords	Males who drive Mazdas	Females who drive Nissans	Females over 18 but under 35 who drive Nissans	Males who drive Toyotas	Males over 50 who drive Toyotas		Codes for who drives what?
2	1	1	1	1	0	0	0				
3	4	2	1	0	0	0	0				
4	1	1	1	1	0	0	0				Column A:
5	3	1	2	0	0	0	0				1 = Ford
6	2	2	1	0	0	0	0				2 = Nissan
7	4	2	3	0	0	0	0				3 = Holden
8	1	1	3	1	0	0	0				4 = Toyota
9	1	2	2	0	0	0	0				5 = Mazda
10	1	2	1	0	0	0	0				
11	5	2	1	0	1	0	0				Column B:
12	1	1	1	1	0	0	0				1 = Female
13	4	1	2	0	0	0	0				2 = Male
14	3	2	1	0	0	0	0				
15	4	2	2	0	0	0	0				Column C age groups:
16	2	1	3	0	0	1	0				1 = 18 to 35
17	1	1	1	1	0	0	0				2 = 36 to 49
18	4	2	2	0	0	0	0				3 = 50+
19	1	1	1	1	0	0	0				
20	2	1	2	0	0	1	0				
21	TOTALS			6	1	2	0				

G21 — f_x =SUM(G2:G20)

- Statistics with no clearly identifiable source
- Statistics that have not been corrected for population change/difference
- Statistics used by political parties and interest groups to promote their own causes

Once you have found interesting statistics to work with, it is easy to download data files into a spreadsheet. To do so you need to know what the file extensions mean. Here is a list of the most common:

.txt,.csv,.prn,.asc text or ascii (American standard code for information inter-
  change)
.htm,.html hypertext mark-up language (Web pages)
.xls,.wk Excel, Lotus (spreadsheet files)

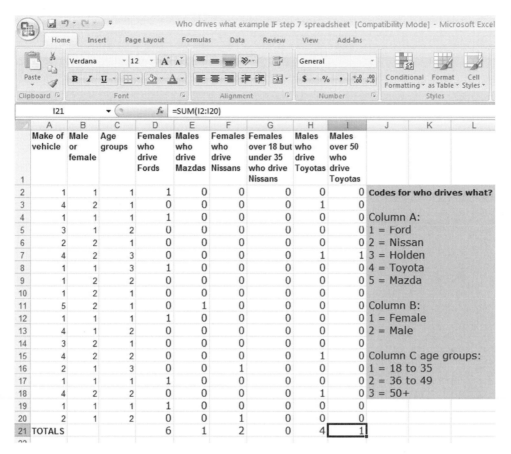

Figure 11.23
The approaches
and formulas used
to complete this
spreadsheet can
be readily adapted
to other, much
more complex,
research projects.

.mdb Access (database files)
.dbf database program, FoxPro
.doc Word or WordPad (word-processing file)
.wp WordPerfect (word-processing file)
.pdf Adobe Acrobat (portable document format)
.zip zip (compressed file)
.exe executable (a program file or a self-extracting zip file)

Downloading Data

There are several different ways to download statistical data to a computer. By a
happy coincidence, and because of the dominance of Microsoft, most data available online have been processed at some stage of its life as an Excel spreadsheet
of one type or another. That means in addition to finding files that can be directly
downloaded, it is often possible to copy and paste information in spreadsheets
directly from Web sites. Sometimes, depending on the formatting underlying a Web

page, you can also place the cursor anywhere inside a table, right-click, and use the Export to Microsoft Excel function. If this is going to work, it will only work when using Microsoft Internet Explorer.

Copying and Pasting from a Web Page

To copy and paste data from an online spreadsheet in a Web page, you should put your cursor at the top left of the working area of the spreadsheet, then hold the left mouse button down and drag the cursor diagonally across and down the sheet until you reach the bottom right corner at the end of the last line of data you wish to copy. Then right click your mouse and click Copy. Next, open a new sheet in Excel and click the cursor in cell A1. Click your right mouse button and select Paste. The table should now copy into your spreadsheet. Go to the top of the sheet and the File tab. Click Save As, then name and save the spreadsheet. Finally, in case of mistakes, save a copy of your downloaded sheet under a different name so that you can still go back to your base file later if there is a problem and you need to start again. To do that, click on File at the top of your page, then Save As. It is also possible to save text files and html files into spreadsheets. The authors offer a big thank you to Debbie Wolfe, technology training editor at the *St Petersburg Times*, for permission to reproduce these steps. She lists the instructions as a sequence to make the process easier to understand.

Downloading Text into Excel

1. Check the URL to make sure you are dealing with a text file (it will have a.txt extension).

2. Go to the File menu and select Save As. Save the file to your hard drive.

3. Minimize the browser window. Open Excel.

4. From the File menu, choose Open. Make sure the "Files of Type" box says Text Files. If it does not, click the down arrow and select Text Files. Select your saved file. Click Open.

5. The Import Wizard will launch. The Wizard will walk you through the import in three steps.

6. Determine if the file is "Delimited" or "Fixed Width." If there are commas or semicolons or spaces separating the columns, you probably have a *delimited* file. If your columns appear to be lined up, the data may be *fixed width*. Click Next.

7. If you selected Delimited, select the appropriate delimiter (comma, semicolon, space, etc.). Click Next.

8. If you selected "Fixed Width," insert the column lines where appropriate. Click Next.

9. In Step 3 of the Import Wizard, the column data format will default to *General*. You may want to change numbers like Zip Codes, addresses, and social security numbers to Text by selecting each column. Click Finish.

10. **Very Important!** Your file is still a text (.txt) file, you **must** save it as a spreadsheet (.xls). Select File from the menu, click on Save As. Name the file and from the "Save as Type" drop-down select Microsoft Excel (.xls).

Downloading html Files

To copy html data into Excel:

1. Check the URL and make sure that you are dealing with an "html" file (these have the .htm or .html extension).

If you're lucky:

2. Select the data that you want in the spreadsheet by highlighting that information. From the Edit menu, select Copy.

3. Open Excel. From the Edit menu, select Paste. Data should be in the appropriate cells. Save the file as a spreadsheet (.xls).

If you are not so lucky:

1. Select the data that you want to use. From the Edit menu, choose Copy.

2. Open Excel. Click in a cell and from the Edit menu, click Paste. The entire row of data will appear in one cell. You want all of that data to appear in individual cells.

3. From the Data menu, select Text to columns.

4. The Import Wizard will launch. The Wizard will walk you through the import in three steps.

5. Determine if the file is "Delimited" or "Fixed Width." Walk through the appropriate steps (see Steps 7-8 above). Click Finish. Save the file as a spreadsheet (.xls).

If that does not work:

1. Select the data that you want to use by highlighting the information. From the Edit menu, choose Copy. (**Note:** If you want the full page, save the page as a Text (.txt) file and jump to Step 4.)

2. Open Notepad. Paste the data into Notepad.

3. Save the file as a Text (.txt) file. Close Notepad.

4. Open Excel. From the File menu select Open. Open your file. (If you cannot find it, remember to change the "Files of Type" box to Text files.)

The Import Wizard will launch and you are home free (see text file importing above). Remember to save the file as a spreadsheet (.xls).

Downloading pdf Files

Information in pdf files can be tricky to download, but it can be done as follows:

1. To work with pdf files, you *must* be viewing the pdf file *independent* from the browser. To guarantee that you are not using Adobe as a "plug-in," RIGHT mouse click on the file that you want to work with. Select Save Target As and save the file to your desktop.

2. Open Adobe Acrobat. From the File menu select Open and open your file. You can now take advantage of all the tools that are in Adobe.

3. To select portions of the document, click on the Text Select Tool (this is the button that either says "abc" or has the capital "T" on it). Select the text that you want to copy. (**Note:** To clean the data effectively, you may need to select portions of the pdf file. See Step 4.)

4. If you want to select a *portion* of a table, rather than the entire table, click your CTRL key and *then* select the text you want.

5. Open Notepad. Paste the selected text into Notepad. Save the file as a text (.txt) file.

6. Open Excel. Find and open the text file. The Import Wizard will launch. Your data will probably be "delimited" and the delimiter is often a space. Follow the steps in the previous section. Remember to save the file as a spreadsheet (.xls).

Saving Files from a Browser to a Spreadsheet

Sometimes you can download files that are already online in a spreadsheet format. If your file has an extension like .xls, you can open the file directly into a spreadsheet. At times you may want to save the file (with a right mouse click) first and then open it from within Excel. If your file is an executable file (.exe), you will need to download the file and then open it. This process usually inflates the physical size of a file that has been compressed. The easiest way to find files already in Excel format is to do an advanced search in Google or another search tool. Select the Excel option (.xls) in the file format section of the advanced search menu.

Interpreting Statistics

Once you have your information in a spreadsheet, sorted it, and interviewed it, things like trends and variations from the norm should be apparent. While interpreting the results think in terms of news values and the types of information that news consumers would be interested in. Consider the following tips:

- Use measure of rate, or incidence; for example crimes per 100,000 people
- Avoid over-generalizing and jumping to conclusions
- Compare like with like
- Look at sample size: Is it big enough to be representative?
- Never make assumptions—stick with the facts
- As a general rule median is a more accurate reflection than average
- Always report statistics in context
- Think about who you can find—preferably a relevant expert, or experts—to comment on and be interviewed about your findings.

It is essential that you only report what the data can tell you. Be aware of what the numbers cannot explain and do not be afraid to pass along these caveats to your listeners, readers, and viewers.

There are some excellent Web sites that will help you interpret statistics. Among them are Robert Niles' page Statistics Every Writer Should Know at http://www.robertniles.com/stats/ and a good BBC site called How to Understand Statistics at http://www.bbc.co.uk/dna/h2g2/A1091350. Those and other pages are listed at this book's companion Web site.

If the techniques discussed in this chapter have whetted your appetite and you would like to try even more advanced approaches to CAR, it would be worthwhile learning how to use Excel at a higher level, and also how to get the best from

Access, SQL, mapping, social network analysis, etc. You could also enroll in one of the excellent CAR courses offered by the National Institute for Computer-Assisted Reporting (NICAR), which is an offshoot of Investigative Reporters and Editors, Inc. and the Missouri School of Journalism. Details of what NICAR has to offer can be found at http://www.nicar.org.

Suggested Reading

Conley, David and Lamble, Stephen (2006). *The Daily Miracle: An Introduction to Journalism*, 3rd edition, chapter 15. Oxford University Press: South Melbourne.

Fogg, Christine (2005). *Release the Hounds*, Chapter 8 "Scratching up the Numbers and Crunching Them." Crows Nest. NSW: Allen and Unwin.

Garrison, Bruce (1998). *Computer-Assisted Reporting*, 2nd edition, "Part IV: Advanced Database Reporting Strategies." Mahwah, NJ and London: Lawrence Erlbaum Associates, Publishers.

Houston, Brant (2004). *Computer-Assisted Reporting: A Practical Guide*, 3rd edition. New York: Bedford/St. Martin's Press.

Houston, Brant, Bruzzese, Len, and Weinberg, Steve (2002). *The Investigative Reporter's Handbook: A Guide to Documents, Databases and Techniques*. New York: Bedford-St. Martin's Press.

Online Reading

Analytical journalism site
http://www.analyticjournalism.com/

CAR in Canada
http://www.carincanada.ca/

CAR in south east European countries
http://www.netnovinar.org/

Global investigative journalism site
http://www.globalinvestigativejournalism.org/

International directory of investigative journalists
http://bolles.ire.org/dij/

Investigative Reporters and Editors
http://www.ire.org/

IRE's Educators' Center
http://www.ire.org/education/

IRE's training opportunities and tutorials
http://www.ire.org/training/

Math competency test
http://www.unc.edu/~pmeyer/carstat/mathtestquestions.html/

NICAR
http://www.nicar.org/

Statistics every journalist should know
http://www.robertniles.com/stats/

The numbers guy, a weekly list of Wall Street Journal stories involving numbers. It is quite fascinating,
http://online.wsj.com/public/page/2_1125.html/

Training videos at PC Show and Tell
http://www.pcshowandtell.com/

University of Texas training site
http://www.utexas.edu/cc/training/handouts/

References

Cohn, Victor (2003). *News and Numbers: A Guide to Reporting Statistical Claims and Contro-versies in Health and Other Fields,* second edition. Ames: Iowa State University Press.

Conley, David and Lamble, Stephen (2006). *The Daily Miracle: An Introduction to Journalism*, 3rd edition. South Melbourne: Oxford University Press.

Dedman, Bill (2007). Personal communication, March.

Fogg, Christine (2005). *Release the Hounds*. Crows Nest NSW: Allen and Unwin.

Houston, Brant (1999). *Computer-Assisted Reporting: A Practical Guide,* 2nd edition. Boston, MA: Bedford/St. Martin's Press.

Houston, Brant, Bruzzese, Len, and Weinberg, Steve (2002). *The Investigative Reporter's Handbook*, 4th edition. New York: St. Martin's Press.

Koch, Tom (1991). *Journalism for the 21st Century: Online Information, Electronic Databases, and the News*. Twickenham, England: Adamantine Press.

Lamble, Stephen (2004). "Media Use of FoI Surveyed: New Zealand Puts Australia and Canada to Shame" in *Freedom of Information Review*, no. 109, February 2004, Clayton: Legal Service Bulletin Co-operative Ltd., Law Faculty, Monash University, Victoria: 5–9.

Index